Practical Criminal Investigations

in

CORRECTIONAL FACILITIES

William R. Bell

Practical Criminal Investigations

in

CORRECTIONAL FACILITIES

CRC PRESS

Boca Raton   London   New York   Washington, D.C.

Library of Congress Cataloging-in-Publication Data

Bell, William R., 1943-
    Practical criminal investigations in correctional facilities/William R. Bell.
        p. cm. — (CRC series in practical aspects of criminal and forensic investigations)
    Includes bibliographical references and index.
    ISBN 0-8493-1194-2 (alk. paper)
        1. Forensic sciences. 2. Forensic sciences--Statistical methods. 3. Criminal investigation.
    I. Title. II. Series.

    HV8073 .B427 2001
    363.25—dc21   2001043663

Visit the CRC Press Web site at www.crcpress.com

© 2002 by CRC Press LLC

No claim to original U.S. Government works
International Standard Book Number 0-8493-1194-2
Library of Congress Card Number 2001043663
Printed in the United States of America 1 2 3 4 5 6 7 8 9 0
Printed on acid-free paper

Dedication

I dedicate this book to my magnificent and beautiful wife, Sherry, who has stood by me during the good times and the bad times. What a great opportunity for me to tell the world that I love her with all my heart and remain totally crazy about her.

Preface

This book is an inside look into the art of criminal investigation as it relates to crimes committed within prisons. The target audience are detectives in prison towns and criminal investigators working within the prison system. People who currently work in prison systems, not necessarily as investigators but who are the first responders to crimes committed inside the prison walls, will also benefit from reading this book.

This is not a traditional text. It contains many actual case histories told from the investigator's point of view. The intent is to prepare officers and investigators to investigate felony crimes within prisons. This nontraditional approach is geared to enhance the interest of the reader. In these case histories the names of the victims and perpetrators have been changed, not to protect the guilty, but to keep the families of the victims and perpetrators from dredging up old nightmares. All of these criminals have been prosecuted to the fullest extent of the law and remain behind bars.

Many people are responsible for the knowledge contained in this book, and I have tried to recognize all of them. Unfortunately, I cannot recall every school, seminar, or salty old street cop that has provided me with knowledge over the past 34 years.

Not all crimes committed in prisons are discussed in this book. What the reader will find, though, is that crime does not stop at the prison walls. This book attempts to visualize the difference between investigating a prison crime and a street crime. These differences are sometimes subtle, but greatly affect the outcome of an investigation.

Prison investigators are at a minimum and do not have the freedom to specialize in certain areas of law enforcement. They must be able to respond effectively to every crime imaginable, from a grizzly homicide to a complex fraud case. Prison crimes become very complex when the crimes involve many different players. These players range from the convict, the officers, and a variety of family to other civilian, soon-to-be convicts. Because of these complexities, I have added chapters on intelligence gathering, undercover operations, and the use of confidential informants.

Because the prison investigator will take a case from the beginning through prosecution and many times is the advisory witness for the prosecution, I have added a chapter on court preparation and testimony. With help from district attorneys from the 11th Judicial District, we have put together an in-depth look at what a prosecuting attorney wants and needs for a successful prison prosecution.

Sit back and enjoy your trip into the world of prison investigations with the practical applications of investigating the most violent subculture in the world—the convict.

Because of my experience with the Colorado correctional system, many of the statistics, methods, and cases reflect that jurisdiction. However, most of the methods can be generally applied, and the appendix addresses key differences in other states.

Acknowledgments

I would like to recognize former Denver police Lt. Tom Haney for being my mentor. Tom gave me the inspiration to continue on with this work and was largely responsible for me sticking to my guns. Tom is a true friend and a true cop. Tom is currently an investigator for the Denver District Attorney's office and continues to serve and protect.

Whatever I say about Vernon Geberth can never be enough. If it were not for him, CRC Press would not have seen my book. Vernon, the master of real live murder mysteries, has accepted me into his practical investigations series, and I am profoundly privileged.

Norm Cooling, the assistant district attorney for the 11th Judicial District, not only supported this book, but lent his expertise in writing a chapter on what the district attorney expects from prison investigators. Norm has been handling prison prosecutions for many years and is considered an expert in that area.

Marty Barta, an 11th Judicial District assistant district attorney, assisted in the preparation of the chapter on court appearances. Marty also was responsible for handling prison prosecution.

Don Tremmel, a Las Vegas metro homicide detective, has been a lifelong friend and was responsible for introducing me to Vernon Geberth.

At the Colorado Department of Corrections (CDOC), I would like to thank John Suthers, the Executive Director, and Mike Rulo, the Inspector General, for their support during the writing of this book; my immediate boss, Chief Alex Wold of the Criminal Investigation Division II, for his support and assistance; John Lutenberg for his donation of K-9 photographs; Wally Gunnels Parmenter for her guidance in my career planning; Sgt. Ricky Conway and Officer Kelly Black for allowing the use of their names to case histories; and former correctional investigator and partner Pat Crouch for his knowledge, expertise, and extremely proficient backup during operations. Special thanks go to Warden "Bobby" Johnson whose urging, support, and friendship during the writing of this book was invaluable.

Michigan Department of Corrections Warden John Prelznik is also a friend and a mentor. John, who is noted as a profiler of serial killers, has lent his support and knowledge in learning to understand the criminal mind.

Thanks to all the officers from the many police departments that have kept me alive through my years, especially the ones who gave me knowledge and provided backup during many undercover operations. If I have forgotten any of you in this list, forgive me as I am considered by some as "older than dirt":

Dearborn Police Department, Dearborn Michigan/Detroit Police Department, Detroit Michigan (especially 16th precinct narcs and the old stress unit)/Wayne County Sheriffs Department, Wayne County Michigan/ Michigan State Police/Colorado Department of Corrections Investigators and SORT team/Canon City Police Department, Canon City Colorado/Fremont County Sheriffs Department, Colorado/Colorado Bureau of Investigations, Colorado (Pueblo, Denver, and Montrose offices)/Adams County Sheriffs Department, Colorado/Colorado Springs Police Department, Colorado Springs Colorado/Drug Enforcement Agency, Colorado Springs Colorado/Alcohol Tax and Firearms, Colorado Springs Colorado/Westminister Police Department, Westminister Colorado/Aurora Police Department, Aurora Colorado/ Denver Police Department, Denver Colorado/Delta Police Department, Delta Colorado/Montrose County Sheriffs Office, Colorado/El Paso County Sheriffs Department, Colorado/Pueblo Police Department, Pueblo Colorado/Pueblo County Sheriffs Department, Pueblo Colorado.

I would like to thank Detective Sergeant Eric Cullum of the Dearborn Police Department, Sergeant James Rockey of the Dearborn Police Department, retired, and his wife Cindie Rockey for being there when I needed them. Only we know all they have done and I love them.

Special thanks to Becky McEldowney, Naomi Rogosin and Joette Lynch of CRC Press LLC for helping me through the red tape of the publishing world.

About the Author

Coming from a family whose involvement with law enforcement dates back to the Civil War, William Bell's own education and career spans more than 30 years. Greatly influenced by his father, a retired police inspector, he began with the Dearborn, MI, Police Department where his responsibilities included work in road patrol, SWAT, undercover narcotics, and pattern crime.

For nearly 20 years, the author has been employed by the Colorado Department of Corrections where he ultimately gained his expertise with the Criminal Investigation Division. He is noted for taking the investigation of prison crime into the streets.

Table of Contents

Introduction to Prison Investigations

1

Crime Does Not Stop at the Prison Doors

Have you ever heard the expression, "Lock them up and throw the key away?" Many people think this when they consider the fate of the convicted felon. In truth, current statutes ensure that convicted felons spend more time in prison than in past years.

In past years convicted felons served only a small portion of their sentences in prison. Violent crime increased and the public demanded that these violent offenders be put away for a longer period of time. Legislators, answering this call, enacted laws that kept violent offenders in prison longer. Of course, with this added time served, the inmate population increased. This increase in inmates demands more prisons and more prison employees.

The layman may think that once the offender is locked up the community at large no longer has to worry about them. These laymen may feel that the convict is the problem of the prison and they have nothing to worry about. This is not the case. Crime does not stop at the door of the prison. Criminals do not cease their criminal activity because they are imprisoned. The crimes they commit while incarcerated are not always confined within the prison walls. Criminal activity may even increase upon incarceration. Today's convict is more violent, more sophisticated, and more dedicated to crime than ever. Prisons are hotbeds of criminal activity and training grounds for the criminals. Inmates test, daily, their criminal skills against the department of corrections and the community.

Need for Prison Investigators

More departments of corrections are employing the use of criminal investigators within their systems, while many still use outside law enforcement agencies to investigate their crimes.

This book illustrates the need for all departments of corrections to create their own investigative units with full police powers to attack this criminal element at its core and to create an element of deterrence.

One might ask why police agencies cannot investigate prison crime. Police officers know how to investigate crimes, build cases, file affidavits, prepare warrants, present cases in court, and follow cases through to conviction. They are professionals who have all the qualifications and experience necessary to investigate any crime. Although cooperation with outside police agencies is the ideal, it would be very difficult for outside agencies to accept sole responsibility for investigating prison crime. Two of the main reasons are 1. manpower and 2. knowledge of the peculiarities of life within the prison system.

Manpower

An average police department and other local law enforcement agency employs, traditionally, about 1 officer for every 1000 citizens. Of these 1000 citizens, only a small portion will come in contact with law enforcement and very few ever commit or are investigated for a felony crime.

Prison populations, on the other hand, run into the thousands of inmates. Of these thousands of inmates, 100% of them are convicted felons. The number of criminal cases generated within the walls of the prisons are staggering. Should a local police agency be required to investigate all the criminal activity within the prison, they would be unable to handle the work load and as a result many of the crimes would go unprosecuted. Local and state law enforcement do not have the manpower to investigate these crimes.

Correctional Knowledge

Any officer assigned to a specific beat within his city knows the lay of the land. He knows what types of crimes are committed on his beat, knows the criminals who live or work in his area, and pretty much knows what to expect in his area. He knows the business locations, the business hours, and what the building should look like after hours. He knows who belongs in his assigned area and where to go for information. He knows what resources are available to him and has his own network of information and assistance. He knows many of the citizens as well as what vehicles belong on his beat. If you were to take an officer from another jurisdiction and put him on this beat, he would be lost until he learned everything the former beat officer knew. During this time he would be unable to effectively police the area.

It is the same with prisons. If you were to take a street officer and put him into the prison setting to investigate a crime, he would not know how to effectively pursue the investigation. It is like taking an officer from Earth and telling him to police Mars. He certainly would not know the lay of the land or who he needed to contact for assistance. He would not be prepared to deal with the sub-culture that exists within the prisons. It is a different world inside a prison. Even the most qualified investigator is not equipped to investigate a prison crime.

Inmates have a code that includes not talking to officials. The code basically is that no one rats on anyone else. This boils down to victims refusing to talk, witnesses refusing to talk, and suspects refusing to talk. The penalty for being a "snitch" is sometimes death. Not understanding the inmate mentality makes it difficult for an outsider to come in and investigate any crime. At best, an outside investigator would experience somewhat of a culture shock.

Summary

Subsequent chapters will discuss similar, yet unique, ways correctional investigators conduct prison investigations. The book will be laced with actual case histories to better illustrate the methods utilized. You will be exposed to drug investigations, homicides, thefts, sex crimes, fraud, solicitation, bribery, undercover investigations, the use of confidential informants, internal affairs investigations, and many other aspects of prison investigations. Reading this book will prepare the criminal investigator for the job and prepare the outside agency investigator to better assist.

Further Sources

Statistics from the Colorado Department of Corrections web site at
    http://www. state.co.us, the Colorado Department of Corrections Annual Report, and the Colorado Department of Corrections Criminal Investigation Division Reports.

Figure 1.1a Tower officer overlooking the yard at the Colorado Territorial Correctional Facility (CTCF).

Figure 1.1b Tower officer lowering keys to an investigator to enter the tower at the CTCF.

Figure 1.1c Tower in newer administrative offices of the CTCF.

Figure 1.1d Entry into living units of the CTCF.

Figure 1.2a Fence line and tower at the Fremont Correctional Facility.

Figure 1.2b Typical living unit at the Fremont Correctional Facility.

All photos courtesy of the Colorado Department of Corrections.

Drug Investigations

2

Overview

Drug investigations in prison can be the most rewarding and the worst experience for the criminal investigator. In prison investigator's cases, 70 to 80% are related to drugs. Homicides and assaults most often are drug related. Subsequent chapters will talk about the convicts' mentality and how they need power; drugs are money and money is power.

Illegal drugs eat away at the very fiber of a moral society. The best minds in the United States and the world have not been able to find an answer to this dilemma. Until an answer is found, this enigma will torment our society. This nation has not been idle in dealing with this problem and has attacked it at every angle imaginable. Law enforcement personnel must continue to vigorously attack all crime associated with the drug trade.

When investigating drug activity, keep in mind that some toes might be stepped on. Obviously, a warden would not be pleased to find out that a drug problem exists in his facility, and he would not want the bad publicity or finger pointing that might accompany such a discovery. However, many wardens are aware that the best resolution to the problem is an investigation. Often, the investigator will have to utilize the prison's correctional or administrative staff or call on offender services to move inmates around. Sometimes, medical staff must be used to retrieve evidence. Any of these things happening tend to create a storm of controversy. This causes a lot of heart burn. Try to remove yourself from the infighting that will take place as a result of your investigation. Other pitfalls and problems which occur during criminal investigations will be identified in other chapters. Just be aware of the potential danger.

This chapter presents different methods inmates use to introduce illegal drugs. The differences between street and prison operations will be discussed; the use of confidential informants, including their value and the problems associated with using them; the different methods of conducting a drug investigation; how the prison drug dealers use other inmates, their family, and friends and use the prison staff to accomplish their goals; and the prosecution of these inmates and the aftermath of a good drug investigation.

Case histories will demonstrate good investigations, bad investigations, and good investigations that have turned into bad investigations.

Methods of Drug Introduction in Prisons

Inmates are very creative and manipulative. A short list of methods utilized by inmates to introduce drugs into facilities has been compiled, but as soon as each is identified, the inmates create new ones.

Mail

Several methods are used to introduce illegal drugs and other contraband into correctional facilities. The investigators have learned from experience that with every safeguard instituted, the inmate creates another method.

- Soft pack envelopes have been used by inserting the drugs into the soft interior of the envelope. Currently, most facilities do not allow the inmate to have the soft pack envelope upon receipt of mail. The soft pack is first examined by the mail room staff. Of course this does not take into consideration the fact that inmates do not always have the drugs mailed directly to them. For example, an inmate will get a job in the library and will have a friend utilize the return address of a known vendor of books or other items. His supplier will purchase this item, put it into the packing, and mail the item to the library. Unfortunately, a lot of these packages are opened not by the staff person, but by the inmate. The drugs will be retrieved by the inmate and introduced into the facility. The department of corrections is currently researching more effective methods of handling mail.
- Recently, inmates have used holiday and birthday cards to introduce illegal drugs. One method was to put lysergic acid diethylamide (LSD) on a portion of the card. This is not easily detected. A black light will bring out the LSD, but it is not cost effective to black light every piece of mail, including the contents. Occasionally a two-ply card would be sent to the inmate. The plies would be pulled apart and black tar heroin, melted down, would be placed between the plies and used for the glue to bond it back together.

- Inmates will go to great lengths to get their drugs. Remember, drugs are money and money is power. The inmate wants power. Along the same lines of introduction, inmates will again get a job where supplies are introduced into the facility. They will have a co-conspirator get a job at one of the vendors. The person working at the vendor will plant drugs inside the item, i.e., paint, and mark the container in a manner recognizable by the inmate. During the inmate's course of duties, he will be able to identify the container, retrieve the drugs, and introduce the drugs into the facility.
- Drugs have been found under stamps, inside the walls of cardboard boxes, and in items with false bottoms. Drugs have been placed inside Polaroid photographs by slitting the bottom of the photo, placing the drugs inside, and gluing the photograph back together. All of these methods are very hard to detect because individuals go to great lengths to insure that the package looks original.
- Inmates used to be able to receive many items from their families. Drugs have been found inside radios, cassette players, televisions, coffee pots, and any other item you can think of. Many prisons changed procedures so that all items mailed in have to come from an authorized, verified retail outlet. This seemed to work until the inmates would have their supplier gain employment at the retail outlet and the drugs would continue. The prisons now have better control over all incoming items, including foodstuffs from their own canteens. This has helped. However, suppliers have gained employment with the vendors and drugs continue to come into the canteen. Inmates work at the canteen and the saga continues.

Some prisons are working on yet another method of interdiction. They are exploring the possibility of having a central warehouse where all incoming supplies are first scanned and searched before delivery. This will be a very expensive operation, but it is believed that it will help deter the introduction of contraband to some extent. The problem, of course, is that inmates will be employed at the warehouse and so it goes again.

These are a few of the methods used to introduce contraband through the mail. Mail is just one of many methods used by drug dealers inside the prison.

Visiting

Departments of corrections are mandated to allow contact visits to all inmates that meet certain criteria. These visits offer the inmate another opportunity to introduce drugs. The majority of illegal drugs introduced during visiting are done in body cavities. This, of course, makes it very difficult to detect.

Ways to capture these drugs will be discussed later in this chapter. Inmates are very creative and will not hesitate to utilize any method available to them. A few of the many methods used by inmates to introduce drugs through the visiting system are listed here:

- Inmate visitors package illegal drugs in balloons. These balloons are easily hidden in body cavities or swallowed. One method used not too many years ago was to have the visitor purchase M&M's* candy from a machine provided by the prison facility. The visitor would place a drug-filled balloon about the size of an M&M into the package of candy. The inmate would eat the candy, swallow the balloon and later retrieve it through regurgitation or a bowel movement. Since that time, however, M&M's were removed from the candy machines.
- A female visitor will package the drugs in balloons and place them into her vagina. Sometime during the visit she will go to the bathroom and retrieve the drugs. She will place them into her mouth and kiss the inmate on return. The inmate will swallow the balloon and retrieve it later as described above.
- A visitor will bring in drugs either in a body cavity or hidden in his clothing. During the visit he will go to the bathroom and hide the drugs in a predetermined location. Later, a "mule" will retrieve the drugs during routine cleaning of the bathroom. Many places are available to hide these drugs, and they are often not found by staff searching the area.
- A visitor will place the drugs into a used food package or other trash and merely place the drugs into the trash can. This trash is most often picked up by another inmate mule during routine cleaning.
- Visitors in maximum security or other noncontact visiting areas will often bring in drugs hidden in a body cavity. Sometime during the visit, they will remove the drugs and tape them under the table provided in the room. An inmate mule will pick up the drugs during routine cleaning. They will also discard the drugs into the trash and another inmate mule will pick them up.
- Visitors have concealed drugs in the diapers of their infant children and passed them during the visit. They have even hidden drugs in the body cavity of their infant child.
- At remote rural facilities, the visitors will leave their drugs alongside the road, in the parking lot, in the entryway trash, and in many other areas for later pickup.

---

* M&M's is a trademark of Mars, Inc., Hackettstown, NJ.

- Visitors may actually deliver drugs to an inmate they are not visiting while at the microwave or vending machines.

All inmates are strip searched prior to and after each visit. Unless the drugs are dropped for later pickup, they are always swallowed or placed in the rectum for introduction into the facility.

Inmates will use their friends, mothers, fathers, brothers, sisters, children, and anyone that they can either con or scare into bringing drugs into the facility. Drugs are the number one business of the inmate. Drug trafficking commands respect and power within the prison. Most assaults and homicides are in some way connected to drug trafficking in the facilities.

One might think that it would be easy to detect the passing of drugs, but it is very difficult. Even with the use of cameras and staff observations, if you do not have prior intelligence about a drug drop it is highly unlikely you will observe the pass. Hundreds of inmates and visitors are in these visiting rooms and a great number of inmates know when a load of drugs are coming in. They will create a multitude of diversions to keep the staff from recognizing the transfer of these drugs.

Drug Drops

Inmates are very innovative in the methods they utilize to get drugs into the prison. Whenever a bust is made and a method is known by the good guys, the inmates will find yet another way to introduce their goods. A few of the methods used to introduce drugs into a correctional facility are discussed here:

- For about 2 years inmates at a prison were orchestrating drug drops for the outside crews to pick up. Surveillance after surveillance was run and yet the drop or the pickup were not seen. The inmate would order up his drugs and have them prepaid. He would then contact his mule either by letter, telephone, or during a visit. A specific drop point would be picked out and the mule would drop the drugs. This particular drop point was just outside the fence of the prison. An inmate assigned to the outside cleanup crew would make his daily rounds and pick up the drugs. The drugs would usually be in balloons that were concealed in a McDonald's bag, a soda pop can, or some other trash that would be left off the highway near the prison fence. The inmate would pick up the trash and put it into his container. When he was out of sight of his supervisor or the tower guard, the inmate would then place the balloons in his rectum or swallow the balloons. This would depend on the size of the drug cache. On occasion, when the load was large, the inmate would bring the drugs into the prison still in the container described. He would then place the drugs into a trash dumpster and another inmate would come out and pick up the drugs for delivery.

- Most drug drops were handled in the same manner for outside crews. Inmates would often change their drop locations. Inmates assigned to outside crews worked in many areas doing grounds maintenance, trash removal, and other work. One such operation was done at a collection point for a nonprofit organization. The drugs would be dropped during the night at the work location and later picked up by the prison crew.
- One drug operation included a drop inside the prison walls. The mule would purchase a tennis ball and cut it open. He or she would insert the drugs into the ball. The ball would be sealed up again and then thrown over the fence into the recreation yard for later pickup by the inmate assigned to pick up trash in the yard. A load of drugs was thrown over the fences at several different prisons. This even included the prison located within a prison compound housing several prisons. Fewer incidents have occurred since the office of special services (OSS) was established. The OSS combined the escape team, the special operations response team, and external security. They added staff, increased perimeter patrols, and purchased additional tracking dogs. Now more frequent patrols and better trained personnel do the patrols.
- Some facilities have trash cans outside the walls of the prison that are emptied daily by the inmates. This is always a good place to drop drugs.
- One correctional facility had a vehicle maintenance program where state vehicles were serviced. Because it was a correctional industries program, the staff was allowed to have their cars serviced there. The inmates had access to the schedule. Inmates at the service station would find out who was going to have their vehicles serviced on a given day. They would notify their mule by letter, phone, or during a visit. The mule would go to the staff person's home and tape the drugs under the vehicle. The drugs would later be picked up by inmates at the service station.
- Inmates are sometimes assigned to pick up trash along the highways. This offers yet another opportunity to drop drugs along the highway. As always, they would be in balloons and concealed inside some sort of trash item.
- A few prisons, usually minimum security, are located within the city limits of larger cities. These places offer more locations and better access by the inmates. Staffing is such that it becomes difficult to have an effective interdiction program. These facilities are so small that a full-time investigator is not on site.

Work Programs

Correctional departments have many work programs based inside and outside the prison walls. These programs offer opportunities for the inmate drug dealer to introduce drugs and other contraband.

- Because many of these programs include the assistance of civilian workers, the inmate may easily manipulate someone into supplying him with contraband. These hand-to-hand deliveries are very hard to detect.
- As previously stated, these work sites often receive materials from many different vendors. Inmates have suppliers obtain jobs with the vendors and have the drugs secreted in these deliveries. With prior contact through mail, visits, or telephone, the inmate will know which package contains the drugs.
- Many of these work programs include volunteer workers with the expertise to teach the inmate a trade. These civilian volunteers do not normally attend a full basic academy and sometimes are easily manipulated.

Staff

Unfortunately, staff become involved in illegal drug trafficking for many reasons. This is the most difficult method of introduction to detect. There is an inclination to trust fellow employees and co-workers. It is human nature to trust people. On the surface, most of the staff give the appearance of being professional and trustworthy. The staff person involved in drug trafficking will give an even more trustworthy and professional appearance because they want to look good to their peers and supervisors. Although some staff members have hired into corrections for the sole purpose of committing crimes, the vast majority are manipulated by inmates into committing crimes. Chapter 8 talks about the book *Games Criminals Play* and discusses the great lengths inmates will go to get what they want. The way to combat this is to provide the very best training academy possible, along with constant reaffirmation and follow-up training. A substantial deterrent to committing crimes must also be provided. This is where the criminal investigators come in. Criminal investigators must assist in providing training in areas that will aid in deterring staff from crime.

Staff involvement in crimes usually starts with simple violations of the departmental regulations. Similar to criminals on the streets, it becomes easier to continue the violations as time goes on, and they do not get caught. It is imperative that mid-level management maintain control and insure that all of their staff follow regulations.

The most common staff violations come from a "too close" relationship between an inmate and the correctional officer. Case history #1 and other examples that follow illustrate how some staff become involved in drug trafficking.

Sex

Whenever you put males and females together, there is always the chance for romance. This may be why male and female inmates are not housed together. The same is true when you have inmates being supervised by both male and female staff. On occasion, when a romance develops between a staff member and an inmate, it becomes easy for the inmate to manipulate the staff member into muling drugs into the facility.

Case History #1

A male correctional officer working in a woman's facility let his hormones do the talking. He became so involved, in illegal sexual activity with several of his wards, that he gained the moniker "Bunkbed Man." The inmates asked the officer to bring in some contraband that included hamburgers, makeup, and other sundries. The plan, from the beginning, was to use this officer as a mule to bring in drugs

Initially the officer refused, but soon realized two things. First, if he did not bring in the drugs, he would lose his job for having sex with the inmates. Second, through his close relationship with the inmates, they knew that he was in financial trouble. When he figured out he could make a lot of tax-free money and keep from losing his job, he agreed. It started with small amounts of marijuana and quickly progressed to gram weights of heroin. Black tar heroin was the drug of choice for this particular group. The officer was soon supplying most of the tar heroin for all of the inmates. He received all the sex he wanted and anywhere from $200 to $400 for each delivery.

This went on for several months until one of the inmates made a mistake. The inmate who originally orchestrated the operation thought she might use another method of introduction and save the delivery money paid to Bunkbed Man. She had her main squeeze inmate (Main Mama") get a job in the prison library. Library books were often mailed into the facility and went directly to the library. Main Mama contacted a parolee ("Outside Mama") to deliver the drugs. Main Mama invited Outside Mama into the operation. Outside Mama was instructed to purchase a book and place it into a padded envelope. The envelope was carefully cut and filled with illegal drugs. Outside Mama sealed it, put a return address of another library on it, and mailed it to the facility. Main Mama even provided a label for the return address. The plan called for Main Mama to wait for the staff member in the library to open the package, take the book out, and discard the envelope. She would then retrieve the envelope and get the drugs out for delivery. Well, the plan was formalized. Outside Mama got the package together and went to the post office, mailed it priority and sent it to the facility. It was loaded with cocaine, heroin, and marijuana. It would have been a great haul and would have avoided paying Bunkbed Man.

Thanks to a very alert mail room officer who was working that day, the plan failed. The mail room officer knew the job, had an excellent memory, and paid close attention to detail. The package arrived and the drug cache was not detectible. This package would have been opened and immediately sent to the library with no questions asked. But what no one counted on was Outside Mama's handwriting being recognized by the mail room officer. The officer immediately knew something was wrong and examined the package more closely. The stash of drugs was found and investigators were called.

This was the beginning of the end for Bunkbed Man. Outside Mama had already been identified. It was a simple matter of locating the post office she used. The post office was located and the postal employee who took the pacakge was identified. A photo lineup, which included Outside Mama, was put together. The postal worker made an instant and positive identification of Outside Mama. Also, fingerprints on the inside of the package sealed the deal. They were a match with several points of recognition.

The next step was to monitor telephone communication between Outside Mama and Main Mama. Outside Mama's telephone number was on Main Mama's Colorado inmate phone system (CIPS) list and monitoring began. Calls made prior to the delivery corroborated that they had conspired to mail these drugs. These calls detailed the whole deal between these two co-conspirators. They talked about the drugs being found and the fact that prison officials would not be able to put the connection together. What was not expected was for them to talk about how to get another load in.

When they began to discuss Bunkbed Man, prison officials were a little confused. It was obvious that it was a male and that he was a correctional officer. It was finally narrowed down to about four suspects. Investigators learned that the suspect had made many previous deliveries and that at least one other delivery was made during the investigation. Surveillance did little to better the case. Investigators did not want to file a case on these two females until the staff perp could be identified and a case started on him.

Phone monitoring was expanded to several other inmates and parolees. (These parolees were on the CIPS list of incarcerated inmates, which is against regulation.) The monitoring continued until there was a break. A gram of tar heroin was to be introduced through Bunkbed Man. This load was to be provided by a parolee. It was originally to be delivered to a drop zone near the prison and be picked up by Bunkbed Man. Investigators made a quick visit to the parolee who agreed to go undercover. Soon after, the parolee contacted Bunkbed Man to say that she would pay for the delivery, rather than Main Mama, and she would deliver it personally to Bunkbed Man and pay him at the same time.

The deal was set. All the calls were made. CID and Denver local narcotic officers were ready. Air support would be provided to maintain surveillance. The plan was to observe the delivery and payment, follow Bunkbed Man to work, and take him as he tried to enter the facility.

It was Halloween, snowing and cold, and the air support plane was grounded. Investigators believed the situation was still workable—plenty of ground support was available. The parolee and Bunkbed Man showed up on time. Everyone and everything was ready, then, Bunkbed Man pulled up and yelled at the undercover parolee to "follow me." They immediately drove about a mile to a location where surveillance could not be maintained. The delivery was made and Bunkbed Man took off in excess of 80 mi/h down a gravel two-lane road. Investigators found the undercover who gave her report.

The investigators had just lost their man, money and dope. Part of the team was at the prison to intercept Bunkbed Man. One of the narcotics officers (narcs) soon spotted Bunkbed Man. Surveillance continued and Bunkbed Man was busted trying to get into the prison. The dope and most of the money were recovered. Bunkbed Man was arrested and convicted. Because of this being a first offense, he did 2 years in the county jail. He lost his job and his credibility in this small community. When asked later why he had done it, he revealed that most of the investigators' suspicions were correct. He became too involved with the women inmates. Once they had him hooked, he did not have any recourse. He thought, as most criminals think, that he would not get caught. He revealed that he was having some financial problems, and it became easier as time went on.

Sex, of course, is a motive, not a method of introduction. This case history merely illustrates again how easy it is for staff to be manipulated as everyone else is by the motivated convict. Some of the methods that have been utilized by staff in introducing contraband for the inmate are the following:

- Staff will bring in amounts of illegal drugs secreted in body cavities. It makes it almost impossible to detect. A pat search or search of the staff member's property will not result in finding the drugs. Dogs cannot even detect drugs being introduced in body cavities.
- Staff will collect drugs from drop points inside and outside the facility.
- Staff will sometimes become the supplier, making their profit margin much higher.
- Staff may become involved by turning a blind eye to the movements of the inmates.
- Staff may provide valuable information concerning ongoing investigations.
- Staff have utilized many of the methods previously mentioned in this chapter.

- Staff working in the mail room have allowed contraband in that otherwise would have been detected.
- Staff have offered or allowed inmates to get a certain assignment that will allow them to carry on their business.

Summary

Hundreds of methods of introducing contraband into a correctional facility exist. To note them all would be impossible. For every method detected, new and innovative methods are created. More methods will be discussed later in this chapter. A quote pertaining to this situation is, "Anything man can think, man can do." Think about all of the things mankind has come up with in your lifetime. With every innovation, though, criminals come up with new crimes. Therefore, new ways to detect crime and apprehend criminals must be developed.

The introduction of contraband into prison is ongoing 24 hours a day, 7 days a week. These convicts are gathering intelligence on everything done by investigators. They have a communications network that will knock your socks off. They often know about new procedures before they are put into operation and have prepared ways to get around them.

Methods and Tools of the Prison Investigator

Street narcs will appreciate the difficulty prison investigators have in trying to make drug cases. Street narcs have their street informants and complaints from citizens about the local crack house. They gather intelligence, run their surveillance, and develop patterns to assist in warrants. They work undercover in known drug areas, make a bust, and turn a perpetrator (perp). Prison investigators do much the same inside and outside the prison. However, street narcs would be amazed at how things work inside.

Prison investigators work in a community made up of 100% offenders. In prison no local citizens complain about drug activity in their neighborhood. An officer cannot be put undercover in a known drug area inside the prison. All witnesses, victims, buyers, sellers, and users are convicted felons. Inmates that come forward with information are not the norm. They are, at best, very hard to work with for all the obvious reasons (see Chapter 7, "Confidential informants").

What the investigators lose by dealing with 100% convicted felons, they gain in resources because these individuals are convicted felons. Intelligence gathering is essential in any drug-related work. Prison investigators and street narcs gather information in much the same way. They depend on their line officers, confidential informants, and other sources. Illustrated below are some of the tools and how they are used.

Officers

Officers are working on a daily basis in close proximity to the inmate offender. They are constantly watching for any criminal activity. Tower officers watch the yard for any illegal activity and control center officers watch security cameras. The inmates are aware of these officers and will try to avoid dealing in front of an officer or a camera.

Confidential Informants

Even though the prison code does not allow for "snitching," investigators frequently receive information from an inmate wanting some favor for the information. An investigator might consider the words of an old correctional officer, "If the inmates lips are moving he is probably lying." Do not ever accept any information from an inmate as fact unless it can be corroborated. Chapter 7 on confidential informants further explains their uses. Prison investigators have successfully utilized confidential informants inside and outside the prisons for many years.

Phones

The CIPS is the very best tool offered to reduce crime in prisons. It has been instrumental in solving a high percentage of the caseloads and is like having a wire tap on every criminal in the city. Most prisons use this type of phone system. Inmate drug dealers use the phone on a daily basis to conduct their drug business. They are all aware that all phone calls are tapped and that live monitoring is done on a daily basis. They also realize that there are too many inmates in the system to monitor all of them and that inmate populations are increasing daily. They know that there is no way that all calls will be screened for criminal activity. Still, these inmate dealers talk in coded messages to avoid detection. Unfortunately for them, these codes are easily broken when the inmate dealers become targeted. It is important to train investigators and other staff to recognize these codes.

Mail

All mail, incoming and outgoing, can be scanned by the mail room. This does not include legal mail. During normal operations of the mail room, outgoing mail is not usually scanned. All inmate-to-inmate mail is read on a regular basis. If there is an active case on an inmate, all his outgoing mail will be opened and read. This is an acceptable practice and legally authorized. It is usually done because probable cause has already been established. It boils down to an issue of time and staffing.

Written Codes

Since during normal operations outgoing mail is not routinely opened, the inmates will utilize coded messages in their correspondence. These codes are not always easily broken. Inmate codes have been used by inmates for a long time. The Federal Bureau of Prisons has broken many of these codes and gives seminars to departments of corrections. Street gang members are coming to prisons in very large numbers. The street cops are making it difficult for these gangs to survive, but the problem has reached an epidemic proportion inside. When entering prison, these gangs continue and actively recruit new members. The Colorado Department of Corrections (CDOC) has proactively addressed this gang problem. One of the actions taken by CDOC has been to make it difficult to recruit, and any recruiting or gang activity is forbidden. There are severe sanctions for gang activity. The inmates have gone underground with their gang activity and have utilized several different codes to pass messages to other gang members.

As an investigator, it is necessary to know how to identify inmate codes and how to break them. This is something which will have to be researched. This research will enable the investigator to identify coded communication about criminal activity. Some basic knowledge on inmate codes will help the investigator.

Some of the ciphers developed by gang members include the crosshatch, pig pen, clock, squares, telephone dial, and vowel change ciphers. There are literally hundreds of codes that have been broken over the years.

It would not be appropriate to give examples of these codes in this book. The codes are confidential material. When an investigator runs into coded messages in inmate correspondence, he should try to break it himself. If that fails, contact one of the resource agencies for assistance.

Not every action taken will result in positive results. Regardless, you must be innovative in your approach. Inmates will take every chance and do anything to get the drugs they need for their power and control (not to mention their drug habit). Read Case History #2 for background.

Case History #2

A few years ago, one of the facility intelligence officers was working a drug case within the facility. An intelligence officer works a case and gathers information to a point when he thinks the CID should get involved. In this case he lost control of the investigation and locked the inmate down for unrelated administrative charges. He contacted the CID and reported what information he had.

The inmate, although locked in segregation, was allowed to write letters. He wrote to his supplier/mule on several occasions using code. It is against regulation to write coded letters and they can be confiscated. In this case it was an easy code to break. The letters were copied and allowed to go out.

In one of the letters it appeared that inmate's female friend still had the drugs. In the coded messages, he wanted her to send money to a couple of inmates' accounts. This in itself is a violation; no inmate's family can send money to another inmate's family. The facility intelligence officers directed the mail room to send all outgoing mail addressed to this woman to their office.

In the next letter the inmate wrote a coded message about sending more money to other inmates. It seemed he was paying them back for the drugs they ordered up and which would not now be coming in. Because the code was in straight horizontal and vertical lines, the ink he used was matched as closely as possible and the facility intelligence officer added another coded message to the inmate's hand written letter. In this message she was told that a friend of his was going to call her and let her know what was going on with him. She was also told that she could give the dope to his friend and he would see that it came into the prison through another inmate's visitor.

After a few days to ensure delivery, the inmate's female friend was called at her home, using an inmate telephone. The undercover officer told her what had been happening to her inmate friend. During the conversation she was told that her friend wanted her to give up the dope to a friend of his so it could be delivered into the facility. She said she knew that because her inmate friend had told her in a letter. She said that it was unfortunate but she had already sold the drugs. She was asked if she could purchase another load that could be brought into the prison. The undercover officer offered to front the money. She said she needed to get the okay from her man.

In the next letter from the inmate (actually from the undercover officer) she was given the okay to deal with him and told everything was cool. The inmate's phone privileges were stopped, but prison communications was contacted to make sure and his access to the phones was turned off. Then a block was put on her phone number so that no other inmate could call.

Everything went downhill from this point. The inmate's cell was close to one of the inmate telephones. He gave the number of his girl to another inmate. The other inmate made a three-way call and connected up with her. He passed messages back and forth to the celled inmate. The conversation proceeded with him screaming from his cell to the phone, "I don't know that m- – f-. Don't deal with him," etc.

Just because it did not work out it does not mean it was not worth trying. You can learn from the experience.

Visiting

Most visiting rooms are equipped with security cameras. An officer monitors the video display and tapes the visits of targeted inmates believed to be involved in drug trafficking.

Intelligence Unit

An intelligence unit tracks all reports concerning inmates, gang activities, and urinalysis (UA) results. All inmates found to have hot UAs are reported to the CID. These reports are valuable in determining not only who is using drugs, but also which facilities have a higher rate of drug usage.

Staff Assistance

Each facility has a gang coordinator/intelligence (intel) officer assigned. These officers track all gang activity and work directly with the intelligence unit. They are extremely useful in working a drug case and are qualified to use the inmate phone system.

   When time is available, the CID unit will gather intelligence in a proactive manner. All inmates that have serious drug charges against them are tracked, establishing a list of telephone numbers they call, who they write, and who visits them and gathering intelligence on the inmates they associate with in the prison. This information is run through the DEA computer to see if there are any heavy hitters. Once a viable target is established, the intel officer will begin to actively work these inmates until it is determined whether or not this inmate is active in the drug trade.

   One of the first things learned when starting to work prison drug cases is that usually very small amounts of drugs are being introduced. (This has changed recently to larger amounts.) It did not appear that inmate dealers could be making much money. Once these cases were actively worked, it became apparent that the value of drugs inside the prison is at least ten times the value of street drugs (see the chart on drug prices later in this chapter in the section on prison drug prices).

   For example, the cost of 1 g of tar heroin was $250 on the streets. Now it costs less than $150. In prisons, this gram is broken into a minimum of 50 pieces (50 hits). These pieces are called papers because they are bundled into a piece of paper. Each of these papers is purchased by the user for $50. That is $2500—quite a profit margin.

   The size of the drug shipments has drastically increased with the inmates' ability to manipulate the system and personnel. They have devised many schemes to introduce large amounts of drugs. Prior to this, the normal amount of drugs introduced at one time was small. The following case history describes more about drugs in prisons.

Case History #3

CID had intelligence about an operation where $\frac{1}{2}$-lb loads were introduced through a work program at least bimonthly. More often it was suspected that these $\frac{1}{2}$- to $\frac{3}{4}$-lb deliveries were actually biweekly. Based on the pricing schedules in the section on prison drug prices, this was "one big operation." Intelligence was limited as only a few disgruntled dopers were telling CID tidbits of information.

The main inmate involved was identified, and drug deals were being made by telephone. The inmate's phones were monitored daily, but drugs, either coded or noncoded were not discussed. The confidential informant (CI) insisted that the drugs were continuing to be introduced. The number of hot urinalyses had increased in the whole prison complex.

Further informant details indicated that these introductions were all marijuana, that one inmate was operating the entire operation, and that prison staff may be involved. CID was also advised that the drugs could be coming into the prison worksite via vendors. Actually, six or seven different scenarios were brought to CIDs attention, none of which could be corroborated. This information did have one common thread: an inmate named "Red" was running the operation. Red was assigned to the computer services building where computers were built and repaired for the department of corrections. Further investigation revealed that Red was running the operation and his supplier was a female friend. Inmates have an inmate account and know that banking within the prison facility is monitored. If money is being sent to other inmates or to a suspected drug dealer, CID will know. To avoid detection, inmates will normally have money for drugs sent from someone on the street to the dealer on the street, prepaying for the drugs.) In this case, money was being sent to a mail drop. CID estimated a possibility of four people involved in the actual purchasing and delivering of the drugs and an indefinite number of inmate purchasers. This was a big operation.

Then, CID got a break. An anonymous note revealed the name and address of the person receiving money to pay for the drugs. The U.S. Postal Service provided the name and address of the box owner. The box owner was Red's female friend who was his supplier. She was on his phone and visiting lists. CIPS still revealed no telephone conversations between Red and this female known as the western slope supplier (WSS).

Visiting records revealed no visits between Red and WSS. CID still had not been able to develop an effective investigative plan. Investigators stuck with the basics and continued to gather intelligence. CID still had the information that staff members may be involved and began to look in that direction. The drugs were still coming in, according to informant sources, and hot urinalyses were on the rise.

A second break in the case came in the form of a letter from an inmate's mother. She reported that she had been sending money for her son to a post office box. The mother said that she recently found out that she had been duped into sending money for drugs. She said that she had questioned her son and was told that they money was for drugs, $\frac{1}{2}$-lb loads of marijuana. The mother reported that someone named Red was the kingpin and he used a lady friend as his supplier. She said that the drugs were being delivered by the United Parcel Service (UPS) or FedEx to a staff supervisor in the computer shop. The mother also reported that she had just sent additional money to the post office box and the delivery was to be made very soon via FedEx.

FedEx was notified and given a description of WSS from her driver's license information. All main areas of operation for FedEx were contacted and were given the address where the package was to be delivered and the name of the suspected supervisor it would be addressed to. Then, CID waited.

A third break came when CID talked with their confidential source. Red had been busted at his job for using the staff telephone to make personal phone calls. He had called a halfway house to try and lay the groundwork for his appointment to the halfway house. The staff member at the halfway house reported the phone call and Red got busted. He was only away from his job for a few days when his supervisor stood up for him and reported that he gave permission for Red to make the call. Red returned to work.

This was a break because Red had to use his own telephone to call WSS. He made several calls that were coded to set up the delivery. He knew he was going to be helped by his supervisor so he told WSS to go ahead and set up delivery. During these calls WSS let Red know that she was going to send the marijuana via FedEx, the same way she did it before.

Finally, FedEx notified CID that a female matching the description given had just mailed a package to Red at the prison computer shop. A photo lineup was set up by local law enforcement. When shown WSS's picture, the FedEx worker made a positive identification of WSS.

The next day the package was delivered to CID. The package contained some computer parts and more than $\frac{1}{2}$-lb of marijuana. CID knew the package was to be delivered overnight, but time did not allow for the package to be delivered the same day. There were too many things to coordinate and an investigative plan had to be developed.

First on the plan, the drugs were to be removed from the original packaging and the original packages would be held for latent prints. The new packaging would be sprayed with a substance that could only be seen under ultraviolet light. The drugs would be reintroduced to the original package and a controlled delivery would be made at the computer shop by FedEx. Time would be allowed for the drugs to be dispersed to different mules before the bust signal was given. CID had information that these drugs supplied the entire complex which was composed of seven separate prisons. CID assumed that the drugs would be split and given to different mules to go to the different prisons. CID did not know who these mules were or if they were staff. CID also had information that the supervisor may be involved and did not know how he got paid for his services—drugs or money.

The Colorado Bureau of Investigations (CBI) provided state-of-the-art surveillance equipment. That evening CID investigators set up cameras in the computer shop. CID had a choice of putting the equipment in the office area or in the shop area. The drugs would be delivered to the upstairs office, but CID did not know where the drugs would go from there. The shop area was chosen because CID could better observe anyone leaving the building. A location was chosen for the camera that offered a view of the stairs leading to the office and yet gave a partial view of the entryway, some work stations, and the hall leading to the rear door. CBI had the capability of live monitoring as well as recording the cameras. The cameras were hard wired to ensure no battery failure. At about 10 p.m. everything was set up and CID left the area. This was a covert operation and, with the exception of the intelligence officer from Red's prison, no one knew about the operation.

CID had already assembled a team composed of CID investigators, CBI agents, and emergency response team members (ERT is the nonlethal response team). CID had elected not to use weapons on the entry team and to use limited armed backup in case of emergency. The team would most certainly be outnumbered inside the computer shop and did not want to be disarmed by inmates. The CID, CBI, and intelligence officer were the only people who knew the target. FedEx agreed to do the controlled delivery.

The next morning the team assembled at the prison visiting center and copies of the operational plan were given to each member. The team was briefed on the plan and given assignments. The drugs were to be monitored with the cameras and the team would wait until the drugs were dispersed to capture as many inmates as possible. The team was advised that when the bust signal was given, speed, violence of action and officer safety were essential. (Violence of action means that the team does not come in with guns blazing. It means that an immediate show of force will deter any violence on the part of the inmates. It is common terminology in any tactical maneuver. This type of action serves as a diversion as well as a deterrent.) The team did not want to lose the drugs. Bathrooms or other areas where drugs could be disposed of were first responders. Surveillance teams were dispatched and CBI checked their camera equipment. The team was ready.

The FedEx driver arrived on time and was briefed. He was given the package containing the drugs. He rolled his truck toward the computer shop. With the live monitoring of the camera by CBI agents, the team was advised on the location of the drugs. The FedEx driver arrived and entered the door. The cameras caught him coming in the door and heading for the stairs. Red and another inmate made an attempt to grab the delivery, but the FedEx driver pulled away and started up the stairs. The FedEx driver returned down the stairs and before he could exit the building, Red and the other inmate came running down the stairs with the box. They entered a workstation and began to open the box. The camera was at the perfect location. They were quickly throwing the bags of drugs into a trash can. CBI said that Red was running with the drugs in the direction of the rear door. Something was not right. Things were happening too fast and the team could not wait for dispersion of the drugs. The bust signal was given immediately and the team charged to their assignments.

The team's fast execution paid off. Red was found in the bathroom getting ready to flush the first baggie of drugs, but he did not get it done. Everyone executed their assignments perfectly and the operation was a success.

CID found out later that Red was "hinked up" (worried) because he had not received the drugs overnight. What CID did not know, because they installed the cameras at night, was that the visiting center and the check point were visible from the office window. Red was watching the whole thing. He knew something was up, so he elected to try and flush the drugs before anyone came. He apparently had not seen surveillance or the team in position to enter. Any number of bad things could have happened.

What happened after that was an exercise in good interviews and luck. During CIDs first interview with Red, he opted to waive his rights and talk. He took responsibility for the entire drug operation, but refused to involve anyone else. What he did not know at that time was that CID was getting ready to execute a search warrant at WSS's home, that CID had a final phone call between WSS and him where she thanked him for the stolen computers; that he qualified for habitual criminal; and all of the $\frac{1}{2}$-lb plus of marijuana was allowed into the computer shop, constituting a more serious offense. The deck was stacked against Red. He was advised that CID was going to initiate several charges against him and that habitual criminal charges would be sought. This would give him something to think about. CID executed a warrant at WSS's home. A stolen computer and another $\frac{1}{2}$-lb of marijuana were recovered. CID elected not to shut down Red's phone privileges and were rewarded for the effort. Red found out that WSS had been busted and a search warrant was executed.

Because of the heavy charges and the arrest of WSS, Red requested another interview. As a result of that interview a major theft ring that involved many inmates and staff was uncovered. CID identified $200,000 in thefts and recovered over $50,000 in stolen property. Five staff members, three civilians, and a handful of inmates were arrested.

Typical Prison Drug Investigative Tactics

A criminal investigator within the prison must possess great attention to detail. Since the normal resources and methods are not readily available, the investigators need to rely on themselves for creating the ability to seek out and prosecute prison offenders. The investigator must be tenacious, be flexible, and use creative methods to bring the investigation to a logical conclusion. This may indeed precipitate the use of deception. In prison investigations it becomes necessary to use tactics that have not been used in the streets. Remember your SWAT training, "Good tactics are tactics that work." Be fair; be honest; and do not violate the law, moral standards, or your own integrity.

A criminal investigator studies law enforcement and receives a bachelor of science degree. Police work has always been considered a science. Sometimes an exact science, and sometimes a not-so-exact science. When investigating some crimes, especially in drug enforcement, police work also becomes an art. No two drug investigations are alike. The investigator will have to adapt to many changes as the investigation continues. He will have to be innovative and resort to trickery and deceit to get his bandit. When conducting undercover operations, the investigator will have to play many different roles and become artistic in his approach to drug enforcement.

The following is an analysis and outline of a typical prison drug investigation:

Information is received that an inmate is causing illegal drugs to be brought into a prison. Assume the information came from an inmate confidential informant (CI).

1. The first step would be to determine if the inmate CI is giving good information and then determine what his or her motive is for giving the information. Corroborate *all* information received from an inmate.
   - Utilize the inmate phone system.
   - Utilize the mail room.
   - Utilize staff observations.
   - Utilize the intelligence group.
   - Utilize the facility intelligence officer.
2. Once it has been established that the information is valid, the work begins. Each case is different and an investigative plan will have to be developed to accommodate each case. The only thing that remains the same is the elements of the crime and the probable cause that will need to be prosecuted.
3. Begin to actively monitor phone calls to identify the bandit on the outside.
4. Track the money. This is very difficult, as most of the money used in prison drug deals is sent from the streets to the streets. You will need to identify some of the users in this particular case to monitor the mail and phones of the user. This will usually lead to the money collector on the streets. This may or may not be your supplier.
5. Mail watches need to be put into place.
6. Connect with the facility intelligence officer and request his or her assistance. The intelligence officer can also track the movement of the suspect.

7. Establish whether there is a need to set up any surveillance and determine the most effective location. Do not leave the location to chance.

These steps only give a reasonable suspicion that the investigation needs to continue. By now, the investigator may have established who is selling, supplying, using, and delivering the drugs. Many other steps to take must be decided during this initial investigation. The investigator now has a starting point and this is when the work begins. Corrections is a very complex operation and every division within the department is equally important and dependent upon the other. No one case is exactly the same as another.

Because of the differences in each case, devise an investigative plan designed to work in this particular instance. Investigators with SWAT experience or training will remember to improvise, adapt, and overcome (IAO). Be creative and cunning when tracking the suspect and use all the resources available.

Once an investigative plan has been developed, decide how much to use the CI. Notify the affected warden and touch base with offender services. The investigator may have to quickly move inmates to insure the safety of the CI and the security of the facility. Identify what personnel are going to be utilized and if any outside agencies need to be involved and make any equipment or funding requests to your chief and inspector general. The following case history describes the steps in planning an investigation.

Case History #4

CID was monitoring the calls of a suspected inmate drug dealer. During the first few calls, CID determined that the inmate had a load of drugs delivered to a female mule whom he had used before. This mule had decided she was not going to deliver drugs anymore. The inmate had begun to feel the heat himself and told her that this may be one of his last drug deals for a while.

The inmate's problem was that he did not have a new mule readily available to introduce these drugs into the prison. He made several calls to male and female associates. A female friend said that she would pick up the drugs, but she would not introduce them into the prison. It became obvious through these calls that the female holding the drugs did not know these other people that the dealer was talking to. After several days and several telephone calls, the inmate dealer connected with a parolee. The parolee said that he would pick up the drugs from the female holding them. The parolee did not have his driver's license and he would have to wait a few days to pick up the drugs. CID was presented with a problem: they did not know much about this suspect (parolee) and did not know how, or if, he planned on introducing the drugs into the prison. CID had to improvise a fast-acting plan to gather enough evidence to pursue this investigation.

An appropriate plan was developed for the circumstances. First, the inmate dealer (bandit) was locked down where he would have no outside contact. His phones were shut off and a block was put on the phones of the other two suspects. A CID investigator, working undercover as the parolee, contacted the female who was holding the drugs. The investigstor told her that he was a friend of the bandit and that the bandit wanted him to take the drugs. He told her that he was in the area and could pick up the package. She gave him directions to her home and gave him the package. The package contained 1 oz of marijuana.

Upon returning to the office, the investigator phoned the suspect (parolee) who was to pick up the drugs. While engaging him in conversation, it became obvious that he had agreed with the inmate dealer to introduce the drugs into the facility. The suspect agreed to pick up the drugs from the undercover investigator, but did not seem interested in coming from another city to pick up the drugs. In addition, he did not seem like he wanted to give the investigator his address or even meet anytime soon. He did seem like he was a little hinked up (worried).

In an effort to gain the interest of the suspect, during general conversation, the undercover investigator told a story to the suspect. He said that when he was on his way to pick up the dope from the female holding it, he had to stop at a rest area. When he was returning to his car he saw a vehicle come through the rest stop at about 100 mi/h. He said the occupant of the car threw an object out of the car. Two or three police cars were chasing the vehicle. After they blew through the rest area, the investigator picked up the object thrown from the car. He said that the object was about 100 g of tar heroin wrapped in duct tape. He told the suspect that he knows it is worth some money, but he did not use heroin and did not know where to unload it.

The suspect was immediately interested. He offered to sell the dope for the undercover investigator. The investigator agreed and told the suspect that he would give him 10 g of dope to sell. If they split the money and did okay, the undercover investigator said he would then front the suspect the rest of the heroin to sell. The suspect jumped at the idea. Now he wanted to make the trip from out of town immediately. The suspect offered to meet with the undercover investigator at a local restaurant. Within an hour, CID was set up at the restaurant and waiting.

Because of being able to improvise and use the tools available, CID arrested this bandit on charges of conspiracy to introduce contraband into a state correctional facility and possession of a Schedule I illegal substance. CID obtained warrants for the female on the street and the inmate in the prison. All three were convicted or pled to reduced charges.

Rules of Engagement

Every police and military operation has rules of engagement. Every police operation has many statutory requirements, but some very significant rules apply to corrections. These rules of engagement were developed as simple guidelines to insure the safety of the investigator, correctional staff, inmates, civilians, and innocents. The rationale for these guidelines is based on common sense. These guidelines (short list) are:

- Never intentionally allow illegal drugs to enter a correctional facility.
- When leaving drugs at a drop site, make every attempt to reduce the amount of drugs left for the mule to pick up. Sometimes emergency situations exist where the entire load of drugs is left at the scene. The need for real drugs to be left for pick up is obvious—no drugs, no case.
- Never put an officer undercover in a prison.
- Always attempt to make the arrest of the mule before he or she can ingest the drugs.

Case History #5

During a recent case, a load of 3 g of tar heroin was to be left under a trash dumpster in a soda pop can for a mule to pick up. CID changed the load to include a balloon filled with $\frac{1}{2}$ g of heroin and two other balloons filled with placebo drugs. Surveillance of the area was established and six young, quick CID officers were staged in a building very close to the drop site. The inmate was observed leaving his worksite and walking directly to the dumpster for pickup. The bust signal was given immediately and the six officers ran to the site. However before the officers could make contact, the inmate mule picked up the can, ripped it apart, and swallowed the balloons. The suspect was arrested and placed in a dry cell for possible retrieval of the drugs. The drugs were later retrieved from the dry cell and warrants were issued for all of the bandits.

Unfortunately, that was not the end of the case. The criminal investigation unit needs to communicate with and train the prison administrative staff in the methods and reasons why investigations are conducted in a certain way. Due to some miscommunication and a lack of knowledge, a tempest was created. Administrative staff questioned, "How could you use real drugs?" and "Why did you let the inmate swallow the drugs?"; they said, "The inmate is going to die now because of you" and "We are going to be sued for our efforts."

Most prison administrators have little if any experience or knowledge of police work. A criminal investigation unit in any prison is responsible for insuring that the administration is schooled in the art of police work. Be sure that the investigation unit establishes a very good line of communication with prison administrators. With better communication, the following would have been known by all and the problem would not have been created.

- Real drugs were being used.
- Inmates almost always ingest the ballooned drugs for entry into the facility without detection.
- Utilizing an effective dry cell will usually retrieve the drugs.
- Since the inmate was under constant supervision by medical personnel, he would not have been in any danger of dying. This would not have been the case if the inmate had ingested the drugs without our knowledge.
- When doing reversals, utilize lesser amounts of drugs than you are selling. Insure that you never let drugs walk. You can walk money in an attempt to purchase larger amounts, but you cannot walk drugs.
- During controlled deliveries, it may sometimes be wise to lessen the amount, but not always.

Planning the Operation

Putting the plan together, calling on resources, making notifications, and gathering intelligence are only the first steps in an investigation. You must have the evidence to make the case. The investigator now has all the information needed and must prepare for the operation to "catch the bad guys." Many different methods are available to make the bust. These methods will be discussed shortly. Remember that each case is different and will require its own methods. Before discussing the techniques utilized, the operational plan (OP) should be introduced. An operational plan is a detailed plan for a drug operation which includes but is not limited to a general scenario of the operation, officers, and assignments; contingency plans; and everything needed to bring the operation to a successful and safe conclusion.

A typical operational plan outline is as follows:

1. Scenario—Give the type of operation, who is involved, what the plan involves and how the plan will be executed.
2. Date, time, and location of the operation.
3. Officers involved.
4. Assignments of officers—Be sure to show locations, vehicles used, and what their assignment is (i.e., surveillance, bust team, etc.).
5. Equipment—Communications, weapons, door rams, surveillance, etc.

6. Surveillance—Be sure to include presurveillance of the operational area. This presurveillance can often locate any countersurveillance set up by the bandit. Be sure to include surveillance during the operation. Include an assigned countersurveillance team. The bad guys will sometimes have their own surveillance going, and they have to be located and watched. If you do not recognize the need for countersurveillance, major turmoil can arise and you will fail.

7. Undercover—If you are using an undercover officer, be sure to include a bust signal, an audio and visual trouble signal, and an abort signal. The undercover officer should be the one to identify signals that he or she is comfortable with. Everyone needs to know if the undercover officer is armed. This is a choice of the undercover officer, unless he or she is not a peace officer. If that is the case, then no weapon should be allowed.

8. Medical—If no ambulance is on standby, then know the phone numbers and location of an ambulance service and a hospital. If the operation is on prison ground, either notify medical staff or have communications with them.

9. Maintenance—Occasionally, a door will be broken and some damage will be caused. Have someone available to make at least temporary repairs to secure the crime scene.

10. Transportation—Make arrangements for the suspects to be transported to jail after the bust. This is usually done by uniformed officers.

11. Advisements and assistance—Criminal investigators often work in different jurisdictions. It is policy to notify local law enforcement of every operation in their city or county, along with a request for their assistance. This assistance normally comes in the form of a uniformed, marked police vehicle for transporting the suspects when the bust goes down. These jurisdictions will normally offer assistance from their narc unit.

The operational plan is always written up prior to the operation. There should be a briefing that includes maps and diagrams of the operational area. During this briefing, all phases of the action are laid out to all officers, including the making of assignments. At this point, all questions will be addressed to insure that everyone is on the same page. This will also identify everyone involved to each other. The undercover officer will give his signals and his plan. Everyone knows everyone so there should not be any mistaken identities.

Different types of drug operations exist. The difference between a drug investigation and a drug operation is obvious. Although the entire process would be considered the investigation, it is categorized into two phases. The first phase of the investigation is the initial information, the gathering of intelligence and evidence, putting it together, and finalizing your plan. The second phase is putting an operational plan together for the arrests and interviewing the suspects. A third phase, however, details the handling and analyzing of the evidence. This third phase is merely a continuation of the investigative phase of the operation. Be aware that in each of these types of operations there can be many variations. These variations depend on the investigator's imagination and ability. His ability quite often depends on the resources available to him and his unit.

Buy–Bust Operations

In this operation the investigator meets with a drug supplier and purchases the drugs. Once the drugs are purchased, the bust signal is given and the subject is arrested. There are a few things to consider when making a buy–bust. The investigator will need to have prior conversations with the dealer, indicating what product is being purchased, how much product, and the price of the product. When meeting with the suspect, if possible, engage the suspect in conversation about the quantity, quality, and price. Since these investigations will always be connected with the prison, insure that other bases are covered. The investigator should already have recorded conversations or written communication between the supplier and the bandit inmate inside the prison. What needs to be done during these conversations with the supplier is verification of the drugs being bought for introduction into the prison. This is important because the investigator will need to show the conspiracy to introduce these drugs into the facility. Failing to show this in the investigation could result in no charges being filed against the inmate. This is the investigator's job and what the CID unit is all about. Investigators try to insure that inmates do not continue committing crimes while they are incarcerated. In most cases involving buy–bust, the initial investigation has been completed and arrests need to be made to bring the case to a conclusion. Sometimes the buy–bust has to be done before planned because of problems the CI may have inside the prison.

Once the drugs are identified, the bust can go down, but investigators usually like the money transaction to take place before the bust signal is given. This will sew the case up nicely and the suspect cannot testify that he was merely giving an individual drugs and was not a dealer. This operation can be very dangerous to the undercover officer and everyone else because the suspect may be armed and the undercover officer may not feel comfortable being armed. There may be countersurveillance that has not been detected and problems can occur. This is why a complete operational plan must be put together. The investigator needs all the backup and contingency plans. The undercover officer needs to know what to do when he gives the danger signal and all the backup officers need to know what they are supposed to do.

Buy–busts are actually a frequent operation. These operations are the result of using a CI inside the prison. An undercover officer is introduced through a letter or phone conversation. The CI reports that he has a mule lined up and wants to buy some drugs to introduce into the prison. The bandit may have a supplier, but does not have a mule. Quite often in these cases the mule or method the bandit was using has been busted. The CI will be paying for the drugs and offering a cut of the product to the bandit for setting up the mule. The supplier gets his money at the transaction and everyone is happy (until CID makes the buy–bust). In some of the multijurisdictional cases, the investigator will offer the street supplier to the agency that assisted in the operation and will take the inmate bandit.

In cases where the conspiracy is started at the prison and adjusts outside to another city or county, the case can be prosecuted in either jurisdiction. This comes in handy when an outside agency wants to be a part of the prosecution. In many cases, the outside agency will turn the supplier and use him to net bigger fish. It is easy to see that drug cases are like a spiderweb in that they finger out in every direction and become very complex at times but offer a rewarding challenge.

Note that whenever a case dictates a buy–bust, the investigator has to be ready to execute all his facility moves. Prior to the bust, shut down the phones on all suspects in the case. This is a good option, but not foolproof. Remember that the inmate communication system is very advanced and their pipeline of information cannot be stopped. These inmates are a whole lot sharper than officers might think. Even though the phones of the bad guys are shut off, the rest of the prison phones are not. Although three-way calling is not authorized, inmates still do it. Any inmate can call someone on his CIPS list and do a three-way call to the other inmate's people. All of these people know each other. When the bust goes down, the phones are ringing. Another inmate's family will talk to their incarcerated relative and the information comes into the prison.

Case History #6

A couple of years ago, CID was working one of the many cases involving a buy–bust. CID had hooked up with another agency to make the bust.

When CID presented the request for assistance and named the bandit, the agency became very interested. They had been working this female bandit for a while and were particularly interested in her son. The son had escaped this agency before during other drug operations. CID did not have any information on the bandit's son. CID had not heard his name and had not talked to him on the phone during the initial investigation.

An operational plan was put together utilizing CID and the agency forces. The undercover officer was to phone the bandit on arrival at a location close to her apartment. She was to provide three eightballs of cocaine (that is three $\frac{1}{8}$-oz packages of cocaine).

The call was made and the bandit said that she needed to wait for her delivery man to bring her the dope. CID had her apartment under surveillance and had done a presurveillance operation. While the surveillance team was waiting to escort the bandit to the undercover officer's location, the countersurveillance team observed a vehicle with two male occupants cruising the lot. At first it looked like they were going to boost a car in the lot, but they kept changing their location. They paid only momentary notice to the undercover officer, but soon left the lot. A team broke off and followed the vehicle. The vehicle went to the bandit's apartment (or near it). One of the vehicle's occupants exited the car and went to another vehicle. He opened the gas tank compartment of one vehicle, took out a package described as a plastic baggie, and placed it into the gas tank compartment of the other vehicle. He walked in between the apartment buildings and was out of sight for a while. Soon he came into sight again and was with the bandit. One of the local law officers identified the male suspect. It was the son of the bandit that the assisting agency wanted so badly. The bandit got into her car and left to meet the undercover officer. One team stayed with the son and one team followed the bandit to the undercover's location. Once the bandit arrived and made contact with the undercover officer, the other team took down the son. The bandit would not get into the undercover officer's vehicle, but asked the undercover officer to get into hers. Once in the vehicle the undercover officer engaged the bandit in conversation about the fact the drugs were going into the prison. Price was again discussed and the undercover officer asked to see the product. The money was counted out in front of her while the bust signal was given.

This case cemented the relationship between CID and the assisting agency. The agency got their guy, CID gave them the female bandit, and CID got the convict. As it turned out the bandit and her son wanted to work with the agency to clear up some larger cases. The inmate was convicted.

Notice the mention of the fact the bandit would not get into the undercover vehicle. It is policy to maintain control of all operations, but sometimes this is not possible. Always try to get the bandit out of their vehicle or into the undercover vehicle. If a crisis happens, the bandit has a 3000-lb weapon. So many things can happen and none of them are good. The safety of the public comes into harm's way when the bandit has control of a motor vehicle during any operation (especially when a bust is planned). Always make contingency plans for things such as this.

In the previous case history, why was there a need for further conversation about the drugs? It is always possible that the bandit may be trying to rip the undercover officer off. If the bandit presents a placebo in place of the drugs and it cannot be proven that the undercover officer was buying what was reported to be drugs, the investigator may not have a case. Always try to cover all the bases. Do not leave anything to chance.

Buy–Walk Operations

There is one reason why buy–walks are not common—no funding. Investigators usually do buy–walk cases when they are working with other state agencies or the DEA. These cases will usually net only the inmates inside, but they put a big dent into the street vendors. Although a few of these buy–walks had been done in the past, they seemed to become a larger issue in 1998. Investigators work with the DEA often and know the local agents pretty well. Because of the investigators' resources in tracking inmates and gang activity, they have been able to assist the DEA frequently. The DEA has no problem reciprocating assistance.

Case History #7

In a case that began in 1996 and continued through May 2001, a staff member ("Cookie") was suspected of introducing illegal drugs into a correctional facility. Cookie was a food service supervisor. Several investigators had worked cases against Cookie and each time the case fell apart. Cookie was very cagey and trusted only inmates. During at least two of the cases the confidential informant (CI) told Cookie he was being investigated. During three other cases, Cookie, for some reason, failed to meet an undercover officer, failed to make a call, or just decided not to continue the drug deal. Investigators were confounded by the seemingly infallible luck of Cookie. The facility administration never felt they had enough to take any administrative action and investigators had no probable cause to arrest him.

In March 2001, investigators decided to pull out all the stops. Investigators utilized all the resources available. Phone monitoring and mail watches were put on all inmates who worked with Cookie. A U.S. Mail trap was put on Cookie's address to look for mail from inmates and inmate families. All investigators talked to their CIs. Every inmate who was previously suspected of dealing drugs with Cookie was looked at as a possible CI.

In April 2001, investigators began two cases. Both these cases were initiated by inmates who had previously reported Cookie for drug introduction. The first case fizzled out immediately because the CI was giving false information, but the second case progressed quite well. The CI introduced a female undercover officer to an inmate ("Shredded Wheat") who was working with Cookie. This undercover officer was to receive drugs from the wife of Shredded Wheat. The undercover officer was to then deliver the drugs, which consisted of marijuana and heroin, to Cookie and pay him $750 to introduce the drugs to Shredded Wheat inside the prison.

Everything was ready to go. Introductions were made and a meeting was about to take place with Shredded Wheat. Trouble appeared on the eve of the exchange. Shredded Wheat, a known gang banger, had a contract on his life and had been previously attacked with "shanks" (homemade knives). On this evening, Shredded Wheat was attacked by a rival gang member. It was lucky for Shredded Wheat that the attacker could not handle the job and was beaten severely, but it was unlucky for investigators when Shredded Wheat was put into segregation and Cookie would not continue with the deal.

Investigators had previous intelligence that a particular inmate ("Smokes") had dealt with Cookie from 1995 to 1996. Smokes had paid Cookie $300 a week to bring in 1 oz of marijuana. When Smokes was paroled in 1997, he was reportedly seen at Cookie's home on several occasions. Investigators decided to take a run at Smokes. CID checked to see if Smokes was still on parole and found that he had absconded from parole in 1998. A plan was hatched to make every effort to apprehend Smokes and make him an offer he could not refuse. It was likely that parole would take Smokes off paper (off parole) because he was a non-violent offender and, since he had not been arrested during the last 3 years, investigators wanted a shot at him first.

For 6 weeks investigators traced the movements of Smokes. He was tracked to three different states. Investigators utilized U.S. postal inspectors and the department of labor resources during this search. In late April of 2001, a break was made in the case. Smokes' mother filed for unemployment compensation from Colorado and wanted her checks mailed to a different state. While Smokes was not immediately found, his mother was. The local state police and sheriff's office were sent photographs of Smokes. A deputy that frequently rented movies for his family recognized Smokes as the clerk at the local video store. Smokes was immediately taken into custody and quickly extradited to Colorado. At the county jail, Smokes was visited by prison investigators. Smokes was told the short version of how he was captured, and it was impressed upon him the importance of what they were about to discuss. Smokes told of how he had started a new life and was living clean for 3 years. He was not interested in going back to prison for the rest of his 2-year sentence. He agreed to work the Cookie case.

Smokes confirmed that he had solicited Cookie to introduce 1 oz of marijuana into the facility every week for $300. Smokes said that Cookie and he had a close relationship in the past and that he had spent a lot of time at Cookie's house while on parole. Smokes agreed to work with investigators on this case. He was told to reestablish a relationship with Cookie and ultimately purchase illegal drugs from him. Smokes spent the better part of a month regaining the trust of Cookie. Smokes reported that Cookie was very careful in everything he did and frequently hugged him and touched him where a body mike could be placed. He was certain that Cookie was checking for a bug. Smokes finally reported that Cookie had agreed to sell him $\frac{1}{4}$ or $\frac{1}{2}$ oz of marijuana for about $40.

It was determined that investigators would do a "buy–walk." The money for this small amount of marijuana would be flushed and another deal for more product would be established. Surveillance was set up, a call from Smokes to Cookie was recorded, and the deal was set. Unfortunately, Cookie reported that his supplier had not shown up and he would have to put it off again. The next day surveillance was again set up, money with the serial numbers recorded was given to Smokes, and another call was placed to Cookie. Cookie still did not have the dope because the supplier had not shown up. After about 6 hours and 4 phone calls to Cookie, the deal was finally set into motion. Cookie said the supplier was on the way. Prison investigators and narcotics officers had surveillance on Cookie and other investigators were running surveillance on Smokes. As it turned out the supplier was observed going to Cookie's house, picking up money, returning to his house, and then going back to Cookie's house with the dope. Cookie immediately got in his car and went to pick up Smokes. The delivery went without a hitch and Cookie agreed to sell 1 lb of marijuana to Smokes.

Prison investigators were now aware of the supplier and had a case on Cookie with hopes of a larger case against him. Two days later it was determined that it would be in the best interest of the department of corrections if Cookie was taken into custody. Cookie posed a serious threat to the security of the prison he worked at and there was concern that he would continue to deliver drugs on a regular basis. In the first week of June 2001 Cookie was arrested and charges are pending against him.

What is a buy–walk? A buy–walk is when the CI or undercover officer purchases drugs and lets the money walk away with the bandit. Never let drugs walk away. The object of this method is to create trust between the dealer and the undercover officer. The undercover officer buys some small amounts of drugs. The dealer does not get busted and he tends to trust the undercover officer (at least a little). With this method, many things can be done: identify other players, identify suppliers, and set up bigger deals. Also gained from this type of operation is an established pattern of behavior on the part of the dealer. He cannot testify in court that this was a one-time deal or any other excuse.

These cases usually do not involve introduction into the facility; they usually involve a dealer inside a facility who does not deal inside. The dealer is continuing his street business. Investigators work these cases slowly and keep the CI as far removed as possible. These operations are usually conducted very covertly. Few, if any, correctional staff are involved in these cases.

Howevere, there are times when, because of logistics and safety issues, security people are involved.

These cases illustrate that even if the operational plan is adequate and all the support needed is obtained, things may not go well. Investigators have had presurveillance and counter-surveillance set up and still gotten beat. Dope deals never go exactly as planned, so be ready for anything. Dopers are very unreliable. In one case investigators waited hours for a deal to go that had been set up only hours before. The inmate CI was moved, the phones were cut off, and all the bases were covered. The dealer never showed. The CI had been moved for nothing and could not be brought back to finish the deal. The investigators ended up with nothing.

Sometimes when making a buy–walk the investigator will use a CI. A CI is rarely used for a buy–bust, but sometimes emergency situations cause the investigator to make a bust to save the CI.

When using a CI for a buy–walk the investigator must follow some simple guidelines. Understand that a CI is someone with uncorroborated motives. CIs have been known to set up their target by faking a buy. Some dealers will only sell to people they know. This will, of course, cause the CI to have to testify. Try to arrange an introduction of an undercover officer on a future buy. Here are some helpful hints in dealing with a CI during a buy–walk.

- Try to maintain visual surveillance during the entire operation. (This cannot always be done, but in a perfect world it is the way to go.)
- Thoroughly search the CI prior to letting him make the buy.
- If visually observing the deal, make sure the CI insures that the investigator can see the hand-off and observe which pocket he places the drugs in.
- Use a wire whenever possible to record the transaction.
- Remember that the investigator will need corroboration of the CI's testimony. Ever since the Rodney King and O.J. Simpson cases, jurors have talked about not believing the police. Law enforcement personnel no longer enjoy the White Knight image.

Controlled Deliveries

The controlled delivery, though seldom employed, is an effective way of closing an investigation. In Case History #3 presented earlier, drugs were delivered via FedEx. CID guidelines pretty much prohibit drugs going into the facilities, but in that case the computer shop was located outside the prison walls. It was still on state property, but outside the walls. Investigators would not have made the delivery inside the walls because they would have lost any control and put too many lives in danger. When using a controlled delivery, there are some steps to take in setting it up and insuring that the evidence is gathered.

- Establish that the package is received by the intended recipient.
- Wait for the recipient to open the package and take possession of the drugs.
- Determine that the sender and the receiver both have knowledge of the intended delivery. Receiving a package with drugs is not *prima fascia* evidence of guilt. (*Writers note*: We have had incidents where inmates have received drugs in the mail. We did not have probable cause to believe that the inmate knew he was receiving the dope. Always work the mail and phones to see if there is a connection. Inmates and civilians have been known to set up inmates. Remember, do not violate the law, do not violate procedure, do not violate your morals, and do not violate your own integrity. We do bust the bad guys, but we only make righteous busts.)
- Consider putting an ultraviolet substance on the drug packaging that will come off on the hands of the suspect and show up under ultraviolet light. There is always the possibility that the drugs will be flushed or otherwise disposed of before the investigators make their entry.
- Be sure to have adequate surveillance and control movement in the area where the package is received. Investigators really do not want to lose the dope.
- Do not use the mailman or the delivery driver, if it appears that there could be any danger to the delivery person. Use an undercover officer. (Investigator tip: If you do not have any evidence that the inmate has knowledge or is expecting a package, sometimes you might hold the package in the mail room and see if the inmate comes forward, looking for his package. At this point you will at least have code charges to file or a direction in which to start looking for further evidence.)

Safety Guidelines for Undercover Drug Operations

Notice that all of these rules of engagement are referred to as guidelines. The investigator must have rules to govern his operations, but since the drug business changes so rapidly he must have the flexibility to operate. Remember this when putting together any departmental procedures. Also, it is not wise to be saddled with regulations written by another division that directly affect an investigator's operation. There are enough statutes to insure that investigators do their job properly, they do not need to be reined in further by the policy of another division. Here are some safety guidelines for undercover drug operations:

- Do not trip (take drugs) with the bandit. If the investigator has to trip to make the case, try and insure that the undercover officer is driving. He can control the speed and make sure his cover is in place. If it looks like the investigator will be tripping in the bandit's car, make sure there are two undercover officers in the vehicle. The investigator puts himself in a dangerous situation when he makes the decision to trip with the bad guy. This decision can only be made by the undercover officer. Some good advice to undercover officers is do not trip with the bandit.
- Do not front the money. Do not expect to get the dope if a doper is given money to get the drugs. Also, the investigator will not be able to determine where the dope came from. Investigators should never front the money, but remember that the dope business changes with each operation.
- Do not walk the dope. The investigator can let money walk, but he cannot do a reversal and let the dope walk. Reversals are bottom line bust deals. It is illegal for an investigator to allow dope into the community.
- Never allow the dope to enter the facility. There is no occasion where it would be appropriate to allow drugs to enter a prison. The exception is when the drugs are going to a worksite or other area outside the prison walls.
- Know when to drop a case. Do not let the investigator's tenacity turn into a personal vendetta. Keep the information as intelligence for future execution. An investigator cannot make a case out of every bit of information gathered. Patience is the key to a successful investigation.

Drug Drops

Often, investigators will have information that drugs are going to be dropped at an inmate worksite. The information may be fresh enough for surveillance to be set up to watch the drop. At other times the investigator may find the drugs already in place. In either case, he will still want to get the probable cause (PC) needed to bust the inmate offender. Depending on the circumstances, the investigator must come up with a plan that will give him the best chance of arresting everyone involved. Busting a mule is great, but getting the buyers, sellers, and users is even better. Here are a few ideas for working the drug drops.

- If the investigator is lucky enough to get to the drop site before the drugs are dropped and can set up surveillance, then do so. If possible, film the area during the drop. The suspect dropping the dope will need to be identified. In order to do this, the investigator will need to get as much information as possible. The license number of the vehicle and a description of the occupants in the vehicle are very important. If time permits, have a marked police car in the area to do a pretext stop and identify the occupants. If that is not possible and adequate personnel is available, then follow the vehicle to its final destination.
- If time permits, get to the dope, test it, and replace a portion of the drugs with a placebo. Quite often time does not permit this. It may be that the drugs are dropped in an area that can be watched by the inmates. If that is the case, leave it alone and maintain surveillance.
- The one control an investigator will have in an operation is that he can insure the drugs will not get into the facility. This is good, but there are risks. The inmate can swallow, keister, or get rid of the drugs in many ways. Paying attention to detail is all important during surveillance. There are always concerns that if an inmate swallows the drugs he will be put in danger of an overdose. Although this is somewhat true, he is safer when the investigator knows that he has swallowed the drugs. Inmates swallow balloons of drugs every day on their own in order to introduce them into the facility. If that happens, the inmate will be put into a dry cell with medical personnel observing him. There are procedures that medical personnel can follow that will insure the inmate is not in danger. There is always the chance that the drugs will not be recovered. More than likely if they are not recovered, they will also *not* get to the buyers.

Use of an Unwitting Accomplice

An unwitting accomplice or co-conspirator is someone who is unknowingly involved in an investigation. He or she is used in developing a case, but more than likely will not be charged as part of the crime. Because of the complexity, unwitting accomplices are rarely used by law enforcement. Sometimes, however, it becomes necessary. Although the unwitting accomplice can be anyone involved in the drug trafficking, in most cases it was the wife or girlfriend of the CI. The CI is willing to give up the information, but does not want his wife or whoever the unwitting individual is to be involved or prosecuted. Be very careful to plan an operation where the unwitting accomplice is not an integral part of the investigation. If there is probable cause to make the arrest, the investigator sometimes will be compelled to make it. If he makes the arrest, he will inevitably lose his CI's cooperation.

Case History #8

CID received information that a staff member was bringing large amounts of marijuana and gram weights of tar heroin into a close custody facility. The information came from a CI who was trying to get out from under code charges. The staff bandit would usually pick up the drugs from the supplier. It was obvious that the CI had at least been involved in trafficking drugs, but there was no ongoing investigation. What CID suspected was that the CI may have been the supplier for a minicartel within the prison. For whatever reasons, besides trying to get out from under code charges, he had decided to go against this cartel. Of course, he was not burning an inmate. The mule was a staff member that had been manipulated into delivering drugs. The cartel must have had the staff member wired up very tight.

CID tried to get the CI to work out a controlled delivery, reversal, to the staff member. He would not go for it. CID tried to get him to deliver drugs to an undercover officer for another way to introduce the drugs. He would not do that as he did not want to lose his position or pay from the cartel. CID found out later that the staff member had a heavy marijuana habit and may have sold some of the drugs on the side for extra money. He was being paid 1 to 4 oz of marijuana for his deliveries.

The staff member would not vary in his method of introduction. He would pick up the prepaid drugs from the CI's wife. He would then deliver them to the prison. He would never let the inmates know exactly when he was bringing in the drugs. The CI insisted that his wife not become involved in the case. He would allow CID to use her, but CID could not contact her. She could not know that her husband was a CI because then she would not have cooperated (for unknown reasons).

CID continued to collect intelligence from the CI. The staff member had been laying low for a while, and just when it seemed like CID's plan would not work, a call was received from the CI. The next day, Saturday, the staff member was going to make a road trip up and pick up a load.

Not knowing when the staff member was leaving, an early morning surveillance of his residence was set up. At about 6 a.m. the staff bandit began to move. CID had him under surveillance. CID originally thought he would go straight to the freeway and head north, but he did not. He had his wife with him and began to run a circuit. He took his wife to breakfast. He seemed hinked up, but CID knew they had not been burned. Soon after breakfast, CID followed him as far as the freeway and then made a phone call to an investigator's friend. This friend agreed to pick up the surveillance as the staff bandit exited the freeway.

Surveillance continued as the staff member exited the freeway. He was followed to the home of the CI's wife, where they hooked up and went to the supplier's house. They made two stops and returned to her house. The staff bandit then hit the freeway and came back home. CID surveillance was waiting and observed him go into his house.

The CI told CID that the bandit had agreed to bring in the drugs from home the very next day. CID opted to wait for him at work, rather than follow him from home. CID wanted to keep it simple. Ever hear of the KISS system (Keep it simple, stupid)? CID figured that they did not want to overdo it. The CI told CID that the staff bandit had picked up 12 oz of marijuana and 3 g of tar heroin. He was going to keep 6 oz of marijuana and bring in the rest.

CID wrote up a warrant based on the probable cause and left a paragraph open in the event gold (or is it green) was struck. CID had intelligence that he was not very careful about how he brought the drugs in. It was suggested he had them in his briefcase.

The next morning CID waited at his place of work. He showed up about 20 minutes early and was immediately picked up and taken to the security manager's office. Six ounces of marijuana were recovered from his briefcase. CID did not find any heroin during the strip search but since his rectum was greased up it was easy to assume where the heroin was located. CID had not anticipated this and did not have a body cavity search warrant, which was needed to complete the search.

The staff member was arrested and transported to the county jail. CID requested a dry cell and a watch was put on the staff member him until the warrant could be obtained. However, he was placed in a wet cell and not watched. The toilet had flushed a few times before CID was notified. CID did not bother to get the warrant.

During questioning, he admitted to his wrongdoing and claimed he had a severe drug habit. He said he was doing it for his habit. He denied the heroin possession, but it was lost anyway.

The CI's wife was not made a part of this case. It was not because CID made a promise. CID was careful not to get enough probable cause to arrest her. CID used her as corroboration that the CI was telling the truth. CID saw no drugs on her, but did see the staff bandit come to his house. In short, CID had no case on the unwitting female accomplice. Be careful when doing these cases. There is always the possibility that you will burn yourself in a case of this type. Remember, do not violate the law, do not violate your regulations and procedures, do not violate your moral obligations, and *never* violate your own integrity. CID did what they set out to do. CID stopped a large supply of drugs to the facility and arrested a dirty cop. CID always hates it when one of their own is turned, but the staff member knew what he was getting into. The one thing CID did not get on this go round was the cartel.

Cigarettes as Contraband

Recently, the CDOC has begun a no smoking policy within the department of corrections. To start with it will be the inmates only, but soon it will directly affect staff. This could develop into an "us" against "them" problem. The bad news is that the us may become inmates and staff with a common problem. Whatever the reasons for this new policy, it is a development that will have to be dealt with, regardless of the individual's stance. It should be noted, however, that it seems to be working in some prisons, but not without some problems. Investigators will have to develop some methods of dealing with the introduction of tobacco as a crime.

The price of smoking has already gone up. The going price for one store-bought cigarette is approaching $5. A pack of cigarettes is $10, but is quickly rising. A carton of cigarettes for $100 is now cheap. A can of bugler tobacco with rolling papers was $75 a short time ago, but is now $100. As the supply dwindles, the price is going up. We have recorded telephone conversations where inmates are already planning methods of introducing tobacco products. They will use the same cunning and deception to deliver this new and valuable contraband. It is easy to see that the inmates are going to use this as yet another method of gaining power (money = power).

There is also rising concern that this will lead to more staff involvement in introducing contraband. It is always hard for some to deal with an issue that becomes criminal for some but not criminal for others. It increases the ability of an officer to rationalize his or her actions. Investigators expect to see an increase of staff becoming involved in illegal activity.

Investigators cannot become involved in the politics of any changes made within their department. They are charged with detecting and prosecuting criminal acts, and they cannot let their personal feelings cloud their sense of duty.

This issue may become a large part of the criminal investigator's job.

Prescription Drug Sales

This has always been a minor problem within the facilities. Many inmates are prescribed drugs for different ailments. Inmates have found that they can live without the drugs and make money. Most facilities have methods of insuring that the inmate takes his prescription drugs in front of staff. They have even crushed the pills and put them into juice that must be ingested prior to leaving the area. With the increasing numbers of inmates it has become increasingly difficult to monitor prescription drug intake. These large numbers of inmates have brought forth a need to speed up the medical delivery process. Inmates have been allowed to self-medicate, which has increased their ability to abuse their medication or sell their prescription drugs. It has become increasingly difficult to monitor the abuse of these prescription drugs, and because these occurrences happen within the facility, inmate to inmate, it is very difficult to detect. Correctional staff are the key to curbing this crime. Investigators often get cases where correctional officers find an inmate in possession of these drugs. The problem then arises in tracking the drugs back to their original recipient. Not many of these cases end up being adjudicated.

Clandestine Laboratories

When discussing secret labs inside prisons, most people say, "No way, not in a prison." Well, anything man can think, man can do. Although CDOC investigators have busted only one small methamphetamine (meth) lab at a western slope facility, they expect to see more of this. There is even a method of making meth without cooking. Labs do not seem to be able to make any large quantity, but the job gets done. During shakedowns of inmates, correctional staff have found hundreds of notes on how to set up a lab for making illegal drugs. These manuals are secreted into the facilities on a regular basis. With access to photocopy machines, inmates duplicate and pass on the formulas and sometimes make their money by selling these "cookbooks." Investigators have found the anarchist hand book, military manuals, and many other publications that are a direct threat to the security of prisons. Everyone wants to be a chemist. Unfortunately, there are new methods of cooking up illegal drugs that do not involve the use of an open flame. Many of the chemicals used are readily available within the prison walls. Investigators should be aware of the new and innovative ways to produce illegal drugs. These new methods will not be discussed in this book, which could serve as a resource for the convicts.

In addition to anticipating the creation of more drug labs, there is an ongoing problem with homemade booze. This has been going on forever. Some investigators feel that they would rather have illegal drugs in a facility rather than liquor because a drunk inmate is very dangerous.

To deal with these drug labs and home brew operations, it is important for correctional staff to know what to look for. It should be a priority to educate staff on what can be used to cook up some dope. Since the home brew operations are not unique and are known to the inmates, a few examples of what inmates use to make up their brew are discussed. Yeast is the accelerator that is most commonly used in creating drink. Facilities have made it very difficult to get a hold of this. The use of potatoes, tomatoes, any fruit, and bread is common. Some inmates use dandelion flowers and raisins. Inmates will try to get bread or other baked goods that yeast is used in to help them ferment their drink. There are literally hundreds of locations inmates can utilize to cook up their brew. An alert officer will usually find this contraband by nosing around, literally. Home brew gives off a very distinct odor. Like marijuana, once it has been smelled, it will always be a recognizable odor.

Urinalysis Screens as a Weapon

The district attorney in Fremont County, CO has been an advocate of anti-drug programs in his community for some time. His efforts have not only had a direct and positive effect on drug activity within the community, but have allowed criminal investigators to increase their efforts and success within the prison system. Not only does the district attorney aggressively prosecute drug cases, but he has been instrumental in creating new legislation that makes it difficult for prison drug dealers to survive. One of his efforts recently enacted into law was a statute that combines use to possession of drugs. This statute provides for inmates that have a positive UA for drugs to be placed in a rehabilitation program. If inmates have another hot UA, they can be prosecuted for use and possession of dangerous drugs. The CID intelligence unit writes up most of these cases, but also pass on the information to the prison investigation unit as intelligence.

Another benefit to this law is obvious. When an inmate has been determined to be using drugs, it is time to conduct an interview with him. Interviews do not always glean good information, but the chance is always there. It is a good bargaining chip.

Drug Deterrent Programs

The CDOC and the prison investigation unit have implemented some programs to deter drug activity within the prisons. These programs include but are not limited to random drug screening of staff and inmates, K-9 searches for drugs, drug check points, working intelligence cases, and visitor check points.

K-9 Unit

Upon request, the K-9 unit will go to facilities and search common areas and inmate cells for illegal drugs. The K-9 unit will also check visitor, vendor, and staff vehicles and the worksites for the inmates.

Random Urine Screening

The CDOC has had an inmate urine screening process for several years. This process is also utilized when there is suspicion that an inmate is under the influence of illegal drugs. Recently, the CDOC has implemented a random and suspicion drug screening program for all of its staff.

Intelligence Cases

An investigator will be handed much information concerning the use or distribution of illegal drugs within the prison. The investigation unit should take every opportunity to investigate these reports. Quite often, because the information is vague or incomplete, these cases tend to be placed at the bottom of the pile. The investigator should find time to investigate this information further.

Drug Check Points and Visitor Check Points

Investigative and K-9 units will often set up and implement a full-scale drug check point at a civilian worksite or at the entry to a facility in coordination with local law enforcement. These check points are usually set up during a visiting day. Be prepared to expedite these checks quickly so as to not disrupt the normal operation of visiting in the facilities. At these check points any and all contraband is confiscated. Depending on the contraband and the circumstances, the holders are either turned away, issued a summons, or arrested. These surprise check points have been widely accepted by prison wardens.

Prison Drug Prices

As previously stated, drugs are much more valuable inside the prison. This is what makes drug dealing appealing to the inmates. Just how valuable these drugs are inside the prison will probably surprise narc officers. The latest drug pricing from the Denver Field Division of the Drug Enforcement Administration is used to compare the prices inside the prisons. It should be noted that sales made inside the prison are usually small personal-use amounts.

A good rule of thumb is that drugs inside the prison hold a value ten times the street value. This varies in much the same way that supply and demand affect the prices of any goods.

Currently, 1 g of tar heroin can be purchased for about $135 in prison. Inmate drug dealers can still get $2500 from this 1 g of tar heroin. The tar heroin is broken into 50 pieces and each piece is put into a bindle. This bindle is called a paper, which is considered one hit. This one hit costs $50. So, 50 hits at $50 each thus yield $2500 per gram.

Marijuana is the most commonly abused drug in the prison system. It is sold in many different ways—anything from one joint to an ounce. The normal joint in prison is about the size of a toothpick with only a few flakes of marijuana inside. It is called a "pin joint." A pin joint is sold for anywhere from $1 to $3. Here is a breakdown of some of the marijuana prices in prison.

Amount	Description	Price ($)
Capfull	Chapstick capfull	25
Matchbox	A safety matchbox	70
Pin joint	Small cigarette	1–3
$\frac{1}{4}$ oz	$\frac{1}{4}$ oz	100–400

As shown above, the value of drugs in prison is high. Equally high is the expectation of violence. This violence comes when the drugs are not delivered, the drugs are not paid for, when someone snitches, or when different gangs try to control the drug trade.

Street Drug Prices

Many of the substances which are illegal on the street are not currently abused by inmates inside the prison. The following table lists the most frequently abused drugs in prisons.

Drug	Quantity	Colorado Prices ($)
Heroin (black tar)	$\frac{1}{4}$ g	40–90
	1 g	75–150
	$\frac{1}{8}$ oz	300–650
	$\frac{1}{2}$ oz	900–1,100
	1 oz	1,800–2,200
Cocaine	$\frac{1}{2}$ g	50 (60–80% pure)
	1 g	80–125
	$\frac{1}{8}$ oz	190–225
	1 oz	800–1,500
	$\frac{1}{4}$ lb	4,200
	1 lb	10,000–12,000
	1 kilo	18,000–22,000
Crack cocaine	1 rock	5–20
	1 g	80–100
Meth	1 g	80–100
	1 oz	800–1,500
	1 lb	10,000–12,000
	1 kilo	18,000–22,000
LSD	1 DU	0.65–1.50
Marijuana (varies with variety)	$\frac{1}{4}$ oz	30–45
	1 oz	150–300
	$\frac{1}{4}$ lb	450
	1 lb	800–1,200
Marijuana sinsemilla	1 lb	1,500–3,200

Facts about Marijuana

- It takes approximately 100 cannabis seeds to weigh 1 g.
- One plant can produce as many as 100,000 seeds.
- Most cannabis plants produce a taproot which rarely extends more than 1 ft. Lateral growth is responsible for most of the roots.
- Plants usually germinate in 6 or 7 days.
- A plant will average $\frac{3}{4}$ lb of dried leaves. If picked throughout the growing season, a plant can yield 3 to 4 lb of dried leaves.
- Plants grown for sinsemilla will average 1 lb of material.
- Most drug-type cannabis matures at 20 to 22 weeks from date of planting. Plants should be about 10 to 12 ft tall at maturity.
- Cannabis is a hardy, annual weed. The temperature has to fall below 25°F to kill it.
- The cannabis plant is made up of 50 to 60% moisture.
- A 1-acre plot contains approximately 5000 plants if planted 3 ft apart. (The shape of the plot can increase the amount of plants.)
- A 1-acre plot can produce 500 to 600 kilos of dried plant material (clean, no stems).
- Many indoor growers use metal halide and high-pressure sodium lights; 1000 W covers an approximate area of 50 ft.
- Only about 13% of the plant's green, wet weight is dried (smokable) leaves.

Physical Signs of Marijuana Use

- Poor distance perception
- "Red" conjunctive
- "Glassy" eye
- Strabismus
- Flushed
- Slow, nonreactive pupil
- Slow, "giggling" speech
- Green tongue
- Swollen uvula
- Marijuana breath odor
- Marijuana smell in hair and on clothes
- Dry lips
- Elevated blood pressure
- Increased pulse rate
- Mild hand tremor

- Cannot do finger-to-finger test
- Overstep curbs
- Poor balance

Facts about Heroin

- Ten parts of opium make one part morphine base.
- One part morphine base makes one part heroin.
- One opium pod contains 80 mg of opium (8 mg of heroin).
- One acre of opium poppies produces 6 to 8 kg of opium (600 to 800 g of heroin).
- The opium poppy grows in various climates and soils.
- After scarification of the opium pod, hail, rain, or gusty winds can destroy the opium yield.
- The national average of Mexican heroin purity in 1993 was about 38%.
- The average street dose of heroin is 5 to 100 mg, ranging from 3 to 80% pure. (Prison dosages are about the same, unless it is tar heroin and then the dosage is slightly smaller.)
- Heroin was first marketed in 1899 by the Bayer company in Germany as a cure for opium and morphine addiction.
- The average purity of heroin purchased in 1-g quantities in Los Angeles, San Francisco, and San Diego in 1992 was 34%.

A diagnosis of "under the influence" for legal purposes means that there is physical evidence of heroin activity present: constricted pupils, nonreactive pupils, and muscle relaxation, plus laboratory evidence of heroin derivatives in the blood or urine.

It is a fact that heroin addicts need a fix every 4 to 6 hours. Withdrawals can set in within 8 hours.

Physical Signs of Heroin Use

- Pupil constricted
- Reddish sciera
- Nonreactive pupils
- Nodding of the neck
- Slow respiration
- Itchy skin
- Droopy eyelids
- Slow or slurred speech
- Sleepy appearance
- Slowed pulse rate

- Fresh needle marks
- Slow or staggering gait

Puncture Wounds

An investigator should know how to identify fresh puncture wounds. A fresh puncture wound (FPW) is a puncture that has occurred within 48 hours. An old puncture wound (OPW) is a puncture that is more than 48 h old.

A close guess can be made by closely examining the puncture wound.

- A wound that has occurred within 8 hours can be identified by oozing clear substance or blood. There will be no scab formation, and the wound will be slightly swollen and pinkish in color.
- A wound that is between 8 and 12 h old can be identified by soft coagulation, visible puncture wound, scab formation, swelling, and redness in color.
- A wound that is between 12 and 24 h old can be identified by soft coagulation, scab formation, swelling, and slight redness and discoloration.
- A wound that is between 24 and 48 h old can be identified by harder coagulation, scab, swelling, and light pink discoloration.
- A wound that is between 48 and 72 h old can be identified by a scabbed over, somewhat raised, bruise-type discoloration.
- A wound that is between 3 and 7 d old can be identified by the scab edge being visible and light brown in color.
- A wound that is between 7 and 14 d old can be identified by a scab that is scaling, raised at the edges, attached at the center, and dark brown.
- A wound that is between 14 and 21 d old can be identified by a readily deteriorating scab. The scab may have fallen off, leaving flaking and possibly just a small portion of scab at the center of the puncture wound.

Facts about Cocaine

- About 150 to 200 kilos of dried cocoa will produce 1 kilo of almost pure cocaine.
- Approximately 7000 plants thrive on 1 acre.
- The cocoa bush contains 14 different alkaloids.
- A mature plant can have a triannual harvest.
- One plant will yield approximately 4 oz of leaves.
- About 1 oz of leaves is equivalent to $\frac{1}{4}$ g of cocaine.
- South American indians chew 1 to 2 oz of leaves daily.

- A standard line of street cocaine is considered 100 mg or 0.1 g.
- As of 1994 the street purity of cocaine in Southern California was approximately 40 to 60% pure. (Kilo seizures are generally 95% pure.)
- A lethal dose of cocaine is 99 mg/kg.

A diagnosis of "under the influence" means that there is physical evidence of cocain activity present: dilated pupils and a hyperactive nervous system, plus laboratory evidence of cocain derivatives in the blood or urine.

Physical Signs of Cocaine Use

- Irritable
- Reddish sciera
- Reddish area under the nose
- Talks too fast
- Rapid pulse rate
- Tremor, excessive sweating, disorientation of time or place
- Appears extra alert
- Pupils dilated
- Powder or debris on nasal hair
- Rapid respiration
- Walks rapidly

Facts about Methamphetamine

- A standard dose of meth is 5 mg of pure drug.
- The melting point of meth is 170 to 175°C.
- It is manufactured in clandestine laboratories.
- Precursors include ephedrine, pseudoephedrine, phenylpropanolamine, and various analos of ephedrine, i.e., methlyephedrine.
- Ephedrine to meth yields:
  Theoretical 1 lb of ephedrine equals 1 lb of meth.
  Actual 1 lb of ephedrine equals 8 to 12 oz.
  One liter of pure meth oil equals 1 kg of meth.
- 1 lb of ephedrine will typically yield $\frac{2}{3}$ lb of meth.
- 1 gal of hydiotic acid will yield 1 kilo of meth.
- 1 lb of hydrogen chloride gas will crystalize 4 lb of meth.
- 1 l of uncut meth oil will yield 1 kilo of meth.
- Generally, the production of meth can be estimated by the size of the flask.
- The flask size is 10%.

- A 22-l flask × 10% yields 2.2 kg of meth.
- A 72-l flask yields 15 to 16 lb of meth.
- A 22-l flask yields 5 to 6 lb of meth.
- A 12-l flask yields 2 to 3 lb of meth.
- A 5-l flask yields $\frac{1}{2}$ to 1 lb of meth.

A meth abuser or "tweeker" may exhibit the following signs:

- Twitching, distracted by ambient noise
- Elevated body temperature
- Dilated pupils
- Rapid and disconnected speech
- Red or inflamed nostrils
- Dry mouth, excessive licking or grinding of teeth, and foul breath odor
- Weight loss
- Unkept appearance, loss of interest in personal hygiene, and body odor
- Possible puncture wounds or needle marks
- Rapid pulse rate, elevated blood pressure, and rapid and shallow breathing
- Shifting weight from foot to foot.

Inhalants

What Are Inhalants?

Inhalants are breathable chemicals that produce psychoactive (mind altering) vapors. People do not usually think of inhalants as drugs because most of them were never meant to be used that way. Inhalants include solvents, aerosols, some anesthetics, and other chemicals. Examples are model airplane glue, nail polish remover, lighter and cleaning fluids, and gasoline. Aerosols that are used as inhalants include paints, cookware coating agents, hair sprays, and other aerosol products. Anesthetics include halothane and nitrous oxide (laughing gas).

What Is Amyl Nitrite?

Amyl nitrite is a clear, yellowish liquid that is sold in a cloth-covered, sealed bulb. When the bulb is broken, it makes a snapping sound; thus, they are nicknamed "snappers" or "poppers." Amyl nitrite is used for heart patients and for diagnostic purposes because it dilates the blood vessels and makes the heart beat faster. Reports of amyl nitrite abuse occurred before 1979, when it was available without a prescription. When it became available by prescription only, many users abused butyl nitrite instead.

What Is Butyl Nitrite?

Butyl nitrite is packaged in small bottles and sold under a variety of names such as "locker room" and "rush." It produces a "high" that lasts from a few seconds to several minutes. The immediate effects include decreased blood pressure followed by an increased heart rate, flushed face and neck, dizziness, and headache.

Who Abuses Inhalants?

Young people, especially between the ages of 7 and 17, are more likely to abuse inhalants, in part because they are readily available and inexpensive. Sometimes children unintentionally misuse inhalant products that are often found around the house. Parents should see that these substances, are kept away from young children.

How Do Inhalants Work?

Although different in makeup, nearly all of the abused inhalants produce effects similar to anesthetics, which act to slow down the body's functions. At low doses, users may feel slightly stimulated. At higher amounts, they may feel less inhibited and less in control. At high doses, a user can lose consciousness.

What Are the Immediate Negative Effects of Inhalants?

Initial effects include nausea, sneezing, coughing, nosebleeds, fatigue, bad breath, lack of coordination, and a loss of appetite. Solvents and aerosols also decrease the heart and breathing rates and affect judgement. The strength of these effects depends on the experience and personality of the user, how much is taken, the specific substance inhaled, and the user's surroundings. The high from inhalants tends to be short or can last several hours if used repeatedly.

What Are the Most Serious Short-Term Effects of Inhalants?

Deep breathing of the vapors or using a lot over a short period of time may result in losing touch with one's surroundings, loss of self-control, violent behavior, nausea and vomiting, unconsciousness, or death. If a person is unconscious when vomiting occurs, death can result from aspiration.

Sniffing highly concentrated amounts of solvents or aerosol sprays can produce heart failure and instant death, regardless of whether it is the first time or the tenth time. High concentrations of inhalants cause death from suffocation by displacing the oxygen in the lungs. Inhalants also cause death by depressing the central nervous system so much that breathing slows down until it stops.

Death from inhalants is usually caused by a very high concentration of inhalant fumes. Deliberately inhaling from a paper bag greatly increases the chance of suffocation. Even when using aerosol or volatile (vaporous) products for their legitimate purposes, i.e., painting, cleaning, etc., it is wise to do so in a well-ventilated room or outdoors.

Figure 2.1 Shown are 27 hand-rolled marijuana cigarettes found inside the back brace of a medically unassigned inmate.

Figure 2.2 Marijuana evidence seized as part of a drug operation introducing 1 lb of marijuana biweekly at an inmate worksite. Drugs were sent to the computer shop.

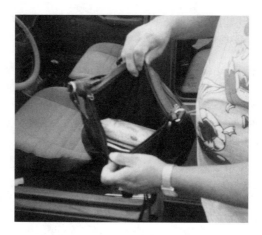

Figure 2.3 A cache of drugs found in the purse of a woman attempting to visit a correctional facility.

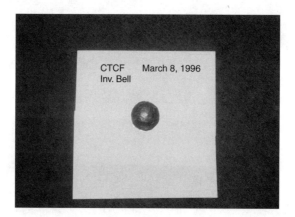

Figure 2.4 This tennis ball wrapped in duct tape contained marijuana and heroin. The ball was thrown over the prison walls during the night, to be picked up by an inmate yard worker the next morning. Alert officers found the ball and recovered the illegal drugs.

Figure 2.5 These dumpsters were utilized as a heroin drop location. Inmates working on outside crews would pick up the drugs. This drop zone was used for heroin. The drugs would then be swallowed or placed into a body cavity for introduction into a facility.

Figure 2.6 Drugs are commonly placed into balloons. These balloons are swallowed or hidden in a body cavity for introduction into a prison. These two balloons contained between $\frac{1}{2}$ and 1 g of heroin. (Prison value approximately $2500.)

Figure 2.7 K-9/investigator searching an inmate's cell for drugs.

Figure 2.8 K-9/investigator as part of a search of a typical prison living unit.

Figure 2.9 Investigators, K-9 unit, and facility staff conduct a search of all visitors and vehicles during a drug interdiction.

Figure 2.10 During this search the K-9 unit gave an alert for drugs. The entire van was searched and contraband was located.

All photos courtesy of the Colorado Department of Corrections.

Escape Investigations

3

General Information

Unlike the military, who insist that soldiers make every effort to escape when captured, the Criminal Justice System encourages the inmate to stay within the confines of the prison. There are serious consequences to consider when escaping from prison. These consequences include but are not limited to recapture and a new sentence to serve, confinement in a more secure facility, and the possibility of being shot.

The threat of these consequences, however, is not considered by convicts as a deterrent. All prisons in the state of Colorado as well as other states and federal penitentiaries have safeguards in place to curb attempts to escape. Unfortunately, no matter what methods are utilized to prevent escape, the convict will ultimately find a way. In prison convicts have 24 hours/day, 7 days/week, and 365 d/year to plan and execute an escape. Inmates do not need much of a reason to escape. Inmates with only weeks left on their sentence will escape for no apparent reason.

No matter what preventive measures are put in place, a number of escapes happen each year. It should be noted that in the past 15 years, the number of escapes in the Colorado Department of Corrections has decreased significantly.

When an escape happens, there are a number of things that occur before the criminal investigator is called.

- At first discovery of a possible escape, the security staff will search to insure that the inmate is actually gone.
- When it is determined an inmate can no longer be found, the escape plan for that facility is organized.
- Outside perimeter people look for signs or direction of travel for the inmate.

- The escape team is activated and usually the K-9 tracking unit is called.
- Outside law enforcement is notified, as well as on-call duty staff.
- Internal security staff conduct a search of every area within the prison for signs of the inmate. Convicts have been known to hide somewhere for days before actually leaving the prison confines.

Several of these things happen simultaneously in an effort to get a lead on the escapee. Once the criminal investigator arrives, what are his duties?

Duties of Prison Investigators

The job of the investigator is to investigate the crime and to assist in any way to capture the escaped felon. Ultimately, the investigator is responsible for putting the case together, filing it with the district attorney, and presenting it as the advisory witness. To do this, the investigator must use the tools available to him and combine them with his knowledge as an investigator. With the escape team activated and all the other staff doing their thing to catch the escapee, the investigator is not idle. He has a lot to do and a lot to offer in the apprehension of the escapee.

- When responding to the affected facility, contact the duty officer or other person in charge. He has the names of the security staff on duty, the cell number of the escapee, and any other information available. Be sure to interview the security staff to establish time frames. They will know when the inmate was last seen and when he was discovered missing.
- Search the inmate's cell. Get the inmates property list and check it against the property left in his cell. This gives the investigator an idea of how the inmate was dressed and what he might have with him.
- While searching the cell, look for correspondence. A letter may contain information of his planned escape. Although there is little chance of a letter describing the escape, the return addresses on letters are important. These addresses can be checked against the inmate's visiting and telephone lists. These addresses may become valuable later in the investigation.
- Interview inmates that the escapee associated with or bunked with and any inmates in the cell block he escaped from. One of his pals might be willing to give him up. The investigator might find that some inmates are willing to give him valuable information. Since the escapee is already gone, the inmate may feel that giving information is not really snitching.

Note that sometimes the smallest piece of information proves to be valuable. Follow all hunches.

Case History #9

An inmate named "Sergeant" was serving a life sentence for murder. He had pulled off a previous escape from a medium security facility. This previous escape was very similar to the Clint Eastwood escape in the movie *Alcatraz*. He made a papier-mache head using human hair and the whole works. Several years after his recapture, he manipulated his way into the Colorado Rifle Correctional Center, a 150-bed minimum security facility.

For a year, concern about him was very high and a special eye was kept on him. He and his case manager were working on a way to move him to community corrections. It seemed like he was not going to escape. He was working off grounds and had many opportunities to escape. However, nobody noticed his daily running and getting into shape, and nobody knew that he had clothing, food, and money buried at his worksite. The day came when Sergeant escaped and the Rifle Assault Team (RAT) was activated. The RAT escape team was responsible for lethal response and containment in the event of a major disturbance. This team was composed of seven hard-charging SWAT types. K-9 units tried to pick up his tracks. Sergeant had filled in the notches in his shoes and put a couple of pair of socks over the shoes so he would not leave notched footprints. The dogs tracked him in and out of streams, back and forth inside the perimeter, and finally back to the main stream going through the facility. He was tracked in both directions for miles as the team looked for his exit from the stream.

Sergeant's file was researched for background information. All his phones and letter records were checked. It was discovered that during the debriefing of his last escape he reported that he liked to live in caves. Near the Rifle Correctional Center there was a place called Rifle Gap. It led into a ravine that went for miles in a northerly direction into a large national forest. This was 1 million acres of mountains and woods. Not only were there caves in the area, but Sergeant had worked in that area before. With no tracks leading into the area or any other reason to check the area, it was decided to do it anyway.

While in the national forest, the RATs met up with a man who owned some property adjacent to the national forest. The man also had a cabin further up in the mountains and was worried that the escapee would hold up there. The man lived in the area and was concerned about his family. The team checked a few more caves and then went to the man's property. No sign of any activity was found at his cabin. The man said that further down his property, down a ravine, and into federal land there were a number of caves. He offered to guide the team to the caves.

About 3 hours into the trip down the ravine, the man said that about a half mile down, near the bottom of the ravine, a stream came in and there was a hard turn to the north. He said there were several caves on that side of the ravine. One of the hard-charging RATs stepped into the stream and found one notched footprint in a mini-sandbar in the middle of the stream. Sargeant was in the area, but it was getting dark. An observer team was set up for the evening and everyone regrouped.

Early the next morning, the RATs set out to check the caves in the area. Air support would be provided by a fixed-wing Piper Cub that could fly down into the ravine. A tracker agreed to come with the team. He was a Native American Indian who came highly recommended. He had a white German Shepard that he claimed was a tracker and attack dog. After about 2 hours of searching caves, one of the RATs found a cave with some evidence of occupancy. Sergeant's coffee cup was laying on a rock. The cup had S-E-R-G-E-A-N-T printed on it.

The team decided to assault the cave. All sorts of gear was found around the cave, but no Sergeant. Suddenly, someone discovered a small opening that looked like a chimney going up from the corner of the cave. Sergeant's feet were dangling out of the opening. His feet were quickly grabbed and he was pulled out. The hike back up the ravine was the hardest part of this operation, but that is a whole different story.

Investigative Tips

- Each inmate has a complete copy of his or her file at the facility where they are housed. This file is available and should be reviewed by the investigator. Check the file for names and addresses of relatives and friends. A visiting list and a telephone list for the inmate should also be included. Get a copy of the file for review.
- There is a high probability that the escape will occur after a visiting day. Check the visiting list and get information on recent visitors. Be sure to get the vehicle information on the visitor. Give this information to the escape team. They can watch for the vehicle. Any information on possible leads should also be forwarded to local and state law enforcement.
- The investigator will need to get a call detail report. This is a report that will list the dates, times, numbers called, and duration of each telephone call made by the inmate for the last 2 months. Pick up the tapes of these calls and review them for content.
- When reviewing these calls, listen carefully for coded messages. The inmate or the person he is calling for assistance will make reference to the escape, but it may be veiled in a coded message. The mere fact that the escaped inmate has called someone just prior to the escape may be an indication that he wants to see that person.
- Keep in contact with the escape team to relay any new information regarding the escape.
- The investigator should call anyone listed as a visitor, family member, or friend. Be sure to notify these people that the inmate has escaped.

Request them to contact an investigator or local law enforcement if the inmate contacts or visits them. Be sure to let them know that there are severe penalties for harboring a fugitive. You should contact the jurisdiction of each visitor and let their fugitive unit know that the inmate has a listed visitor in their area. Other jurisdictions are usually very cooperative and will assist the investigator in locating these visitors. (Visitor lists do not include telephone numbers, so request the local jurisdiction to contact the visitors.)

- If no valid information is obtained from any of these sources, contact the local law enforcement agency with the information and coordinate efforts to follow up on the information.
- Sometimes the inmate will have been working at a job outside the walls of the prison. Have escape team members check the area of that worksite. There may be a vehicle at that location that could be used in the escape. The inmate may decide to hold up at that familiar location until things cool down. At the earliest opportunity, check with the inmate's crew supervisor and interview him or her and other employees for possible information.
- As previously stated, be sure to keep in contact with the escape team. They may pick up tracks and be in pursuit at any time. Any new information should be passed to them. If the investigator has finished his initial information gathering, photographed the cell or point of exit from the facility, and completed all of his interviews, he may want to connect with the escape team and lend any assistance he can.
- The investigator may have picked up some leads that need to be followed up. Follow up on those leads, but make sure that the escape team or the command center is aware of what the investigator is doing.
- Whenever there is an escape, an escape packet is put together. Part of this escape packet includes a flier about the escapee. It contains a photograph of the escapee and information such as name, age, description, crimes, and other details. Be sure to circulate these fliers in as many public places as possible.
- Some states have their escape team, the command center, or even a centralized fugitive unit file the warrant for escape in the computer. Be sure that this is done. If it is not done by someone else, the investigator should write the warrant and enter it in the computer.
- When the investigator and the escape team have established that the inmate has left the area, it is time to start working the phones. Utilizing the information gathered and rereading the inmate's file, the investigator should contact everyone on the telephone and visitor lists again

and try to ascertain if the inmate has contacted them. Reinterview staff and inmates. Try to find out more about the inmate and his habits and friends. Be thorough and read all of the correspondence found in his cell.

If the investigator has gathered enough evidence to establish the location of the inmate but is not sure he has probable cause to write an affidavit for a search warrant, go with your gut feeling and write it up. The laws governing searches for escaped felons are relaxed enough that the warrants are easier to get from a judge. No one wants these people on the streets.

Although there are very few escapees that will "not be taken alive" and most will come easily when captured, always be careful. These inmates escape because they do not want to be in prison any more. Whether they walked away from work release or climbed the fence in a maximum security facility, they should all be considered dangerous.

Making an arrest on an escapee should be as tactically sound as any drug bust or undercover operation. Make sure the investigator does his homework and has a good operational plan in order. Always contact the local law enforcement agency; they will be glad to assist. A good operational plan will be well received by the local agency working with the investigator. They will recognize the professionalism and be more comfortable working with the investigator.

This is a short list of things to do when investigating an escape. Law enforcement is more an art than a science when working the street. When the investigator has an idea about something that can be done, then he should do it.

Case History #10

During an inmate's escape from a minimum security facility leads were not easily developed. The escapee was tracked to a creek and then lost. The dogs did not find a good scent. He was thought to still be on foot and probably had made it to the nearest town. Several correctional officers and local law enforcement were looking for him.

Finally, a lead was developed after his supervisor on an outside work crew was contacted. He worked downtown near city hall. His supervisor mentioned he had problems with this inmate, in that he was always talking to the local girls. He mentioned a young female that was always hanging around. This supervisor was on the ball. He had written down the license number of her vehicle. The plate number was run and an address obtained. She lived in a trailer park about halfway between the prison and the town. The trailer was located and surveillance was set up. The grounds near the trailer were searched for inmate tracks. (Note: The shoes of all inmates have the soles notched. This offers a distinctive track that can be identified from other civilian traffic.) No such tracks were found and it was decided to do a "knock and talk" at the trailer. The mother of the young girl answered the door.

As discretely as possible, the mother was advised that an escaped inmate was being sought and that her daughter knew the inmate. The mother was surprised but cooperative. She invited the investigators into the house to talk to the girl. During the conversation, the girl appeared nervous. This could have been from the presence of law enforcement, but it seemed to be more. The mother stated that the inmate was not there to her knowledge, but admitted that she had gone to bed early. She agreed to let the trailer be searched. Every precaution was used as a professional search was conducted in the double wide, three bedroom, two bath trailer home. By the time the last closet, in the last bedroom was reached, guns had been holstered. When the closet door was opened, a pile of stuffed animals could be seen inside. Everyone began to think that they had been wrong to suspect that the inmate might be in the trailer. It was then that a voice was heard coming from the pile of stuffed animals, "Don't shoot me." Inside this pile of stuffed animals was the face of the escapee. He gave up without incident and he was booked into the county jail.

The point of this case history is to tell you that whenever you are searching for a suspect, do not ever let your guard down. Do not become complacent.

Here is another case history that gives an example of some of the investigative techniques used and how they work.

Case History #11

It was not that the security officers did not notice the inmate running 5 to 10 miles a day or that he was doing the U.S. Navy SEAL workout every other day, it was just that they did not know he was formulating an elaborate escape plan. This inmate had planned his escape from custody for over 6 months. He had landed himself a job outside the fence, but on prison property. He knew the security was somewhat lax and that he would have 4 hours before he was detected. On the morning of his escape, he checked out of the rear gate of the Fremont Correctional Facility to go to work. He had left early that day, but had been frequently leaving early so as not to arouse any suspicion. He worked hard at his assignment and had the trust of his supervisors and the staff working the gate. No one suspected.

He had not expected that on this day his supervisor would come out early as well. Although it took the supervisor about 30 minutes to realize the inmate was missing, the 30 minutes turned into 2 hours while they tried to figure out where he might be. This was probably because his pattern of behavior was such that no one expected him to escape.

When the whistle blew and the escape team was activated, the inmate had a little over 2 hours head start. All of the procedures were followed. The K-9 unit was on track within 3 hours of the escape. It looked like the escapee was a runner. He had left through an area with no roads or access. It was about 3 miles to the nearest road in the direction he was traveling. His course zigzagged through water and he was making every effort not to leave any notched footprints in the soft dirt.

Unlucky for him, the best tracker in the state with his best blood-hound was on the escapee's scent. Lucky for him, his ride was waiting at that road that was about 3 miles from the prison. By the time the K-9 unit reached the road and lost the scent, he was long gone. The team stayed out looking for signs, but they knew all too well that he was on his way to freedom.

There were no letters or other communication or evidence found in his cell. Recent telephone calls had been researched, but there was no significant information. It was noticed that in the months prior to the escape he had called one number very frequently, but just prior to the escape he had stopped calling that number. The recent calls did not talk of the escape, but made references like "Maybe I'll be seeing you soon." All his relatives and the people on his visiting and phone lists were notified.

It was decided to pull up every call, especially the calls made to the number that stopped prior to the escape. The correctional facility had just started keeping a full 2 months of tapes on inmate calls. The escapee had made a lot of calls during these 2 months, and all of them needed to be investigated.

An elaborate escape plan was devised by him and a friend. During these calls they not only planned the escape, but the inmate talked about his military career in the U.S. Army Special Forces. He said that he was not going back, no matter what it took.

The telephone number he called did not match the name of the person he called. It did not take long, though, to find out that the inmate's friend lived with some friends on the north side of Denver. Based on these phone calls alone and coupled with the fact that the inmate did escape, a search warrant for the friend's residence was obtained. (At this time, an arrest warrant for the inmate's friend was not issued because a bargaining chip might be needed later to capture the inmate.)

After contacting the local law enforcement, investigators from the Criminal Investigation Division (CID) responded to the residence in north Denver. CID, along with the local law enforcement, executed the warrant. The inmate was not there. There was not any evidence that he was there and the inmate's friend was not there. The owner of the home did provide information on the inmate's friend, such as a last name, a physical description, and vehicle information.

As CID and local law enforcement were leaving the residence, about two blocks away, the inmate's friend was spotted as he was heading for home. They quickly got in behind him and followed him home. When they began to question him about the escape, he became very agitated. Even when the evidence against him was laid out, he still refused to cooperate.

Going into the "no more Mr. nice guy" routine and explaining fully that either him or the escapee would be going to jail today, he decided to cooperate. What really turned the tide were the recorded phone calls between him and the escapee. These calls described step by step details of the escape plan. CID and law enforcement knew it all and he knew they knew it all. He was given only one promise that could be kept. He would not be arrested today. He would be arrested later, but the district attorney would be advised of his cooperation. He still decided to cooperate.

He told the entire story which was verified by the recorded telephone calls. He said that the escapee was still in town, but he did not know where. He said the escapee called him almost every day. He was advised that, as previously said, somebody was going to jail today. If he didn't want it to be him, he needed to help find the escapee. He made a phone call to the place where he had last dropped off the inmate. He talked to a female and told her that if she could find him, have the inmate call him. He told her to tell the inmate that he had some money for him.

It was not 10 minutes later when the inmate called. The inmate wanted to meet him at a grocery store in the Cherry Creek Mall in Denver. It was agreed. The friend decided to fully cooperate and meet with the inmate. A plan was devised and the Denver Police Department was contacted. The Denver Police Department was very cooperative and assigned eight uniformed officers to assist in the bust. The "bust team" consisted of the eight officers and two CID investigators. An operational plan, covering presurveillance, surveillance, and backup, was put together.

The plan was simple. The friend would pick up the escapee at the store while a tight surveillance was run. Once the friend started toward an exit of the mall parking lot, the car would be trapped between several police cars and both the friend and the escapee would be taken down. Since the confidential informant (CI) (the friend) was driving, no one was worried about a high-speed chase.

After the "bust team" was set up in the mall parking lot, the CI drove in to contact the escapee. All eyes were on the storefront where the escapee was supposed to exit. The team could see into the store but did not recognize anyone inside the store. All of a sudden, this guy came crawling out from under a parked car and ran to the CI's vehicle. He jumped in and they were rolling before the team could react. The amount of traffic in the lot and on the street had not been anticipated and it was very difficult to box in the CI's vehicle. As it turned out, one Denver Police car did get in front of him, creating a traffic jam that caused the rest of the team to exit their vehicles about 40 yards from the CI's vehicle. When the team arrived, the Denver police had the CI out on the ground, but the inmate had not exited the car. He had a shotgun and two handguns pointed at him. He was being ordered to show his hands and exit the vehicle. This had every earmark of a suicide by cop. He reached into a paper sack that was on the floor. A crowd of about

50 people were standing around and the team did not want anyone to get hurt. So, an investigator immediately grabbed the escapee, threw him out of the car, cuffed him, and stuffed him in record time. The paper bag had a notebook and a compact disk inside. Later during questioning, he admitted that he wanted to die and did not want to go back to prison.

This case history should give the investigator an idea of how some resources work. The telephone system is a major asset to criminal investigations. The laws governing search warrants for escaped felons are such that an unearthly amount of probable cause is not needed to obtain a warrant.

The investigator needs to be in control of the investigation. Sometimes when the escapee is recaptured, the investigator may run into some difficulty. The inmate may have been picked up in another jurisdiction or even another state. There are only a few investigators and several thousand other employees who could do the transport. The escape team or some other unit from the investigator's department may be responsible for transporting the inmate back to the prison. This is reasonable and a good idea, especially from the manpower standpoint.

What the investigator needs to insure is that the transporting officers do not question the inmate. They can take down any spontaneous statements made by the inmate or answer any questions, but under no circumstances should they question the inmate. They might think that they could mirandize the inmate and then ask questions, but this practice will cost the investigator the ability to have a successful interview with the inmate. Cases have been damaged by transport officers questioning the inmate, receiving people questioning the inmate, and everyone he comes into contact with asking him questions. Everyone wants to know what happened, how he escaped, and why he escaped.

If someone other than the investigator transports the inmate back to prison, insure that they do not question the inmate. Make sure that the investigator is notified when the inmate returns so that he can be waiting and be the first to debrief and interview the inmate. It is the investigator's case and he needs to be in control of it.

Also remember to take naked, full body, front, top, back, and side photographs of the inmate whenever he is captured or turns himself in. What the inmate has done while he was gone is unknown. He may have been involved in a crime that caused him some injury that would assist in putting him at the scene of the crime. Make sure to get those photographs. Do not leave anything to chance.

An example of this would be a recent escape we had. The inmate had stolen a state vehicle upon his escape. He used the vehicle for 2 days before ultimately driving to Colorado Springs and turning himself in to the sheriff's department. He left the vehicle in the parking lot and walked in the front door. The escape team was notified before the investigators, responded to

Colorado Springs, and picked up the inmate. They also picked up the vehicle and drove it back to Canon City. They searched the vehicle and parked it somewhere near the prison on state property.

Here is what the escape team did and did not do that could have hurt this case. First, they did not log the mileage of the vehicle. Without this knowledge it might have been difficult to determine some valuable evidence of another crime. Second, the vehicle was not preserved for prints. Any prints of the inmate may have been covered by the prints and actions of the transport officers. The inmate had not been seen taking the vehicle or parking the vehicle in the sheriff's parking lot. No one could place the inmate behind the wheel of that car. Finally, by searching the vehicle prior to photographing and collecting evidence, they may have destroyed valuable evidence.

Never leave anything to chance. Do not allow other departmental agencies to step into the middle of a case. Preservation and collection of evidence is a very important part of any criminal case. The investigators in this case history were lucky. The inmate was very cooperative and gave a full confession concerning the theft of the vehicle and the use of a credit card.

Another thing to remember is that when the escape is over and the inmate is recaptured, the investigator needs to make some courtesy calls. The family and friends contacted should be called and told that the inmate has been captured. They are, after all, the family and friends and have an interest in the well-being of the inmate. The investigator should appreciate how he would feel if it were his family member.

By all means, without a doubt, call every outside agency that provided assistance. Let them know that their assistance was valuable and thank them. Let them know that help will be reciprocated anytime it is needed. It always helps to let these fellow crime fighters know how the capture was made and all the details. Cops are curious and will remember that call of thanks. It will make it easier for the investigator the next time he calls them for assistance.

Figure 3.1 Staged photograph of the actual capture of an escaped convict.

Figure 3.2 Actual capture of two escaped convicts by a K-9 unit and escape team members.

Figure 3.3 Aftermath of a nighttime capture of two escaped convicts. The capture was made by the K-9 unit and escape team members.

Figure 3.4 Items found on an escaped inmate. Inmates will normally take personal items because they do not intend to come back.

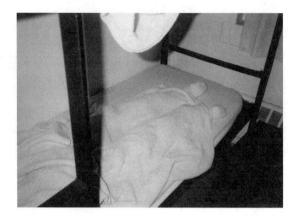

Figure 3.5 Makeshift dummy fashioned by the inmate to delay the discovery of his escape.

Figure 3.6a Dummy placed in cell by inmates trying to get another inmate into trouble.

Figure 3.6b Humorous head decoration put in place. Inmates were subject to administrative charges.

Figure 3.6c More levity, however, the laughter stopped when the inmates headed for administrative segregation.

All photos courtesy of the Colorado Department of Corrections

Solicitation Investigations

4

Types of Prison Solicitation Cases

In its most basic form, solicitation means to entice another to do wrong. It also means to accost for some immoral purpose, as in prostitution cases.

Solicitation cases are becoming more and more prevalent in corrections. In most early cases investigators became aware of an inmate wanting to have someone hurt or killed through his mail or telephone calls. The information was not usually sufficient to pursue a criminal investigation from inside the prison since most of the activity took place outside the prison. The information the investigators had would be given to another law enforcement agency.

Since the implementation of the Criminal Investigation Division (CID) in the department of corrections (DOC), investigators have become involved in a variety of solicitation cases. There are many types of solicitation cases within the prison walls. Some examples are:

- **Murder for hire**—These cases used to be within the prisons. Inmates would hire someone to kill or beat another inmate for wrongs committed. These wrongs could be for snitching, failure to pay for drugs or sexual favors, or any other reason felt justified by the bandit. Inmates have also gone to the streets to get even with a snitch, a bad drug deal, a gang problem, or any reason they felt was valid.
- **Introduction of drugs**—Inmates that are dealing in drugs do not want to get caught. They know if they become actively involved it will only be a matter of time before they are caught. They solicit others to do the work for them, therefore facilitating rather than doing the job. They solicit people on the streets to handle the money and then inmates and

people on the street to mule the drugs. Often, the drugs never touch their hands. They have inmates dealing for them within the prison and holding the drugs to keep the finger of suspicion pointed away from them.

- **Sexual exploitation**—Inmates will solicit homosexual favors and acts from those prostituting themselves. They will also solicit sex under the threat of violence or other devious means. Remember prison is a subculture where life becomes survival of the fittest or survival of those with the most power.
- **Theft**—Inmates who want something in another cell block will solicit inmates to steal those objects. If there is something they need at a work-site, they try to hire someone from that worksite to get it for them. Most often it will be something of value or other contraband. Equipment to build weapons is often solicited from inmates who work in the metal shop.
- **Perjury**—Inmates are master manipulators. If they see themselves at risk, they will do whatever is necessary to accomplish their goals. In matters as insignificant as a code hearing, they will force or solicit false testimony to beat the rap. In one particular murder for hire case, an inmate tried to solicit the investigator to obtain false testimony from two of his victims. (See Case History #19 later in this chapter.)

Means Used in Prison Solicitation Cases

There are usually reasons why individuals solicit someone to commit a crime. In prison the reasons are many and vary from case to case. Given the fact that law enforcement usually uncovers only about 1 to 10% of the crime, what is missing in the other 90 to 99%? The means used to solicit a crime are listed but not limited to the following:

- **Money or other valuables**—This is the most obvious, money for services rendered. You will get this for doing that.
- **Threats**—Inmates use the threat of bodily harm to solicit anything from an assault to sexual favors. They will threaten a young inmate to have sex with them and then they will turn him out. (Once the young inmate is submissive, they will let other inmates have sex with him for a fee.) Another threat begins by inmates giving free drugs to a potential inmate mule. Then they tell this inmate he has to mule drugs into the facility. They make him an offer he cannot refuse—do it or die. This usually comes with a preemptive beating. The introduction will either be on an outside crew or the inmate mule will have to use the "cry for help" to a friend or family and get the drugs during a visit. This method is used for "holding" drugs. Inmates will use a weaker inmate to hold their drugs. The weaker inmate will be

approached in much the same way. They know that if they tell, turn over the drugs, or lose the drugs the penalty is death. This is true even if the drugs are found during routine shakedowns.

- **Cry for help**—Inmates use this manipulative ploy on everyone they can. They use their families, friends, and any civilian or inmate to get what they want. Most often this ploy is used to get money from their families. They call or write home and tell their families that they are in trouble and need money right now or they will be killed. Most of these requests are false, but these inmates do not stop there. The inmate tells Mom, Sis, Bro, or Dad that if they do not bring in some drugs during visits he will be killed. This is often veiled.

Case History #12

During phone monitoring, an inmate was heard telling his little brother that someone was going to come to the house and give him a sealed package. He asked his brother to keister the package and bring it to him in prison. The younger brother, who had just been accepted to the U.S. Navy for some specialized training, became suspicious and asked his older brother what was in the package. The inmate told his brother that it was a gold ring from his girlfriend (actually his mule) for Christmas and that he could not get the ring into the prison any other way. He told his brother not to worry because he would not get caught and if he did there was nothing they could do to him. The younger brother agreed to bring in the package.

In a phone call to his mule, the inmate told her to wrap a teener of cocaine inside a $\frac{1}{4}$ oz of marijuana. He told her to deliver it to his younger brother and to tell him it was a Christmas gift.

Fortunately for this young man, the mule failed to get the drugs and failed to deliver the drugs before he entered the U.S. Navy. But had this case gone forward without knowledge that this lad was not culpable, he would have faced criminal charges for the introduction of illegal drugs. (Note: Since records of the inmate's phone calls proved that the younger brother was unaware of the drugs, he would not have been charged, regardless.)

- **Favors**—Inmates will solicit inmates and staff in return for favors already done. An inmate may set up another inmate or staff member by creating a potential danger to them and then coming to their aid, thus performing a favor. Later, of course, the trap is set by asking for a return favor.
- **Gang initiations**—In some cases inmates use their gang affiliations to accomplish goals. If they are close to the leader of a gang and want to have someone beaten or killed, they will solicit the job through the gang. If the gang leader sanctions the hit, they will sometimes utilize a new member and call it an initiation.

When working a solicitation case it is important to insure that the investigator is aware of the elements of the crime. Investigators need to meet all of the requirements in order to successfully prosecute the case.

Colorado Revised Statute 18-2-301 defines criminal solicitation, in part, as, "Except as to bona fide acts of persons authorized by law to investigate and detect the commission of offenses by others, a person is guilty of criminal solicitation if he commands, induces, entreats or otherwise attempts to persuade another person to commit a felony."

The identity or motive of the person solicited is irrelevant.

In working solicitation cases, as in most prison cases, the investigator will have to be very creative, that is, devious, sneaky, tricky, and all that stuff. He will do anything, legally, he can to close the deal (some of this behavior is displayed in the case histories). The reason for creating any deception and wanting to close the deal at any cost is that the investigator has the life of someone else in his hands. If he does not close the case or blows it in some way, the bandit will find someone else to do the job. If the investigator is not up to the job, then get an undercover officer who is able to do the job. None of these cases can afford to be lost. If a case is falling apart, the investigator needs to direct his attention to code charges or whatever it takes to show the inmate that he knows what is going on and if anything happens to the intended victim the inmate will be the prime suspect. Of course the inmate does not care what the investigator thinks of him.

Murder for Hire

Guidelines for Murder for Hire Cases

Use of Confidential Informants

It stands to reason that an investigator will need to work with a confidential informant (CI) in a murder for hire case. Bandits are not going to come to an investigator to hire a hit man.

- Be sure not to use any hearsay statements from the CI. The investigator has to be the person that the bandit asks for the service.
- Usually, when contact is made with the bandit, investigators try to keep the CI out of it. Make up a story or tell the CI that you do not want anyone knowing for sure what the investigators are planning.
- If the CI has to be involved, have him tell the bandit not to tell him anything else. Sometimes the only line of communication is through the CI. (Using the CI's phone to call the hit man for the bandit happens a lot.)

Case History #13

A CI reported that an inmate was making inquires about putting a hit on someone. Since he had been used often as an informant and was considered very reliable, the CI was told to go ahead and work the case. The CI, for his protection, was about to be moved because of some cases just completed. He wanted to do this one case before he left for parts unknown.

The inmate or bandit, wanted to do all his talking to the CI and did not want to talk to the "hit man" (an undercover officer). This is not acceptable and the bandit was pressured to contact the hit man. He was given an undercover name, address and phone number. The address was to a fictitious law firm so he could use legal mail and it would not be opened.

Finally, the bandit sent a letter to the undercover address. He wrote all about his problems with his case manager, his COPD (code of penal discipline—administrative charges) write ups, and how he did not like the food. He said in his letter that he wanted to be represented in his fight against the DOC. The CI said that the bandit was using this as a code for the hit. Well, this would not hold up in any court, so the undercover officer wrote the bandit a letter. In this letter he came right out and told the bandit, "Hey, I am not an attorney, I'm a hit man. I don't give a s--- what problems you have in the joint. If you want something done, you have to tell me what it is. When you do that I'll give you a price. When you pay me, I'll do the job."

The bandit wrote again and told the undercover officer that he wanted his services, but he did not want to say anything on the phone or in a letter. The bandit did ask what it would cost to do the job. This back and forth do-nothing writing did not seem to be working. However, the bandit did tell the CI that it was a CID investigator that he wanted killed.

About a week later the bandit's case manager contacted the CID. He said that the inmate had given him a letter from an attorney who wanted to do a hit for the bandit. According to the case manager, the inmate claimed to know nothing about this and thought he was being set up. It looked like this was the end of this deal, but not quite yet.

The inmate had the undercover phone number on his Colorado Inmate Phone System (CIPS) list. He called the number to complain about not getting a follow-up letter to his request for a hit. The undercover officer told him that it did not sound like he was serious and that if he wanted anything done, he needed to say who he wanted hit and exactly what he wanted done. He also needed to provide a description of the target and any information that would help to find and kill the target. So, the bandit names his ex-wife's new boyfriend, the district attorney (DA),and the CID investigator. When asked if he wanted all of these people killed, he said no, that he actually wanted the boyfriend beaten up and only the investigator killed. He said he would provide more information later and to write him with the cost of the hit and the beating.

So, the undercover officer writes to the bandit and gives him a ballpark figure on the hit, and tells him it is negotiable. Two days later CID gets a call from the DA. He said he received a letter from the inmate who was claiming to have been contacted by a hit man and that he was being set up by the DOC. Of course, the DA had known about this case from the beginning. CID decided to let the case drop because it was obvious that the inmate was not serious.

A few weeks later, the inmate surfaced again. He pleaded with the undercover officer to do the hit. He said that he got the money from his dying father and he really wanted the hit done. The inmate was advised that if he sent the money, the hit would be done. The inmate then asked for a letter on legal stationary. He wanted the letter to say that the fictitious law firm would represent him for a $5000 retainer. He would then pay the undercover officer to kill the investigator.

After all of this, a DA investigator from another city called the CID. The investigator said that his office was investigating a case where some attorney was planning to kill a CID investigator. The tip, of course, was from the inmate.

Obviously, this case did not pan out. There were too many problems. This inmate had some problems with the DOC. He may have even thought that he could manipulate this thing into something that would show he was a good guy or he may have even wanted to sue the DOC on some phony grounds. More likely, though, is the fact that he wanted a letter written to him from an attorney, giving a fee schedule for services rendered. He may have been trying to justify getting funds from his dying father for his own use. His intentions will probably never be known.

However, the case wasn't just dropped. A report and audio tapes of the inmate's request to have the investigator murdered were completed. This alone was enough of a preponderance of evidence to convict him on the COPD charge of attempted murder. He now sits in a maximum security prison.

Establish First-Hand Communication with the Bandit

In order to meet the probable cause (PC) requirements, the investigator will need to have first-hand communication with the bandit. The bandit needs to solicit the investigator to commit the crime.

- Set up communication on the telephone, either by providing an undercover phone number for his CIPS list or through the CI.
- If your bandit is sharper than the average guy, he will probably not want to talk openly on the telephone. The undercover officer and the bandit might decide to write letters. Tell him to write the investigator through legal mail so that it cannot be viewed by prison staff. The bandit usually agrees to this.
- When written communication with the bandit is obtained, it is imperative that the investigator insure that the letter was written by the bandit.

In order to have it analyzed, the investigator will need samples of the bandit's handwriting. The investigator can wait until the end of the case and get an exemplar, but handwriting samples can be obtained from the inmate's file. An inmate has to fill out many documents in the presence of his case manager. These samples are readily available. The investigator should get handwriting samples early in the case because sometimes the inmate will be smart enough to have another inmate write the letter for him.

- Some inmates may have access to a typewriter or computer. If so, the bandit's letter may be type written. If this is the case, have the paper and envelope preserved for latent prints and send them to the lab for analysis. If latent prints are found, the investigator can get the bandit's fingerprint card from inmate records for comparison.
- Remember that the investigator has to be asked by the bandit to commit the crime. Stay away from any comments that may resemble entrapment. It has to be the bandit's idea. This may be overly cautious, but it is better to be safe than sorry. Colorado Revised Statute (CRS) 18-1-709 states, in part, that "Merely affording a person an opportunity to commit an offense is not entrapment even though representations or inducements calculated to overcome to offender's fear of detection are used." Regardless, an investigator should stay as clean as possible.

Substantial Step

The solicitation case, as in any attempted crime or conspiracy case, has to include a substantial step toward the commission of the crime. In a murder for hire case, being paid for the crime is the final step before the killing takes place. Sometimes an agreement will suffice, but it has to be a strong agreement that will convince the jury that the suspect intended to cause the death of the victim. Along with this substantial step, it is always proper to offer the opportunity for the suspect to back out. By doing this, the investigator is insuring that the suspect *does* want to have this crime committed. In later case histories, investigators often offer the opportunity to back out several times.

Undercover Operations

Most solicitation cases can be worked from the investigator's desk. Unless the bandit involves someone from the outside to make payment or contact the hit man for further instructions, the investigator will be able to work this case from the comfort of his office. This is not always the case though. When working an undercover case, be sure to follow the rules of engagement.

An undercover operation requires good planning. Remember that prior planning prevents poor performance.

Case History #14

This is an operation where homework was not done. This case involved a bandit who was in jail for kidnaping his wife and family and engaging in a shoot-out with police. An inmate CI was temporarily housed at the same jail. The CI was located near the bandit. The bandit knew the CI was a convicted murderer and asked him to find someone to kill his wife.

To make a long story short, all the bases were covered and CIDreceived most of the probable cause through telephone calls between an investigator and the bandit. The bandit wanted to have a face-to-face meeting before he committed to the deal. It was agreed, but poor planning caused problems.

The sheriff's commander agreed to orchestrate a meeting between the undercover officer and the bandit. CID did not want anyone, even jail staff, to know what was going on. The visiting room was covertly wired for sound and the commander gave the undercover officer the routine needed to get into the jail. The jail watch commander was the only other person who would know what was going on.

When the undercover officer arrived at the jail, he used the information given to him to get into the jail. He told the staff that he just arrived from out of town and did not have any identification. He said he was the uncle of the bandit and needed a special visit because he was leaving town the next day. Everything was going smoothly. The undercover officer gave his personal information—name, date of birth, address, and phone number. Then, the staff began to ask further questions. Apparently the staff ran the name the undercover officer gave through the computer and came up with a warrant for his arrest. The undercover officer had to do some fast talking and had to ask to see the shift commander. The shift commander gave the staff the okay to let in the undercover officer but ended up irritating his whole shift. By the way, things worked out and the case was adjudicated.

Staff Investigations

The sad fact remains that staff sometimes solicit inmates for help in committing murder. They just get too close to the inmates.

Case History #15

When this case hit the local papers it shed a dark shadow on the DOC. Everyone hates to see one of their own turn bad. This case started when "Jimbob," a food service worker, complained about his wife. He complained to inmates constantly and mentioned that he wanted to kill her. He finally approached an inmate and actually made an inquiry. This inmate knew another inmate that he thought had committed a murder or two and he referred him. Jimbob contacted the inmate and asked him if he knew anyone that would kill his wife. The inmate happened to be a CI. He called CID and told them what Jimbob had said. CID asked the CI if this guy was serious and he said that he thought he was. The CI was told to tell Jimbob that if he was serious, he would try to find someone and would give Jimbob a number to call. Jimbob told the CI that he was serious.

Within a few days Jimbob called the undercover number. During the initial call, the undercover officer and Jimbob felt each other out and did not really discuss the murder. They had additional calls and Jimbob was really serious but needed to discuss price. He said he had a little problem talking on the phone and wanted to meet in person.

The undercover officer was quite sure that he did not know Jimbob and that Jimbob did not know him. However, the undercover officer thought he should do a sneak and peek to make sure that he had not met Jimbob. Investigators checked out Jimbob's schedule, got his vehicle information and his address. By the next morning, the undercover officer realized that they did indeed know each other. The undercover officer knew that he could not do the undercover work and was concerned that Jimbob had already heard his voice on the phone.

The Colorado Bureau of Investigations (CBI) had worked with prison investigators in the past and were always ready to lend a hand. One of their agents was contacted and he agreed to do the undercover work. A phone call meeting was set up and the undercover officer got himself hired to kill Jimbob's wife. Jimbob did not notice the voice difference.

To make sure that this was a quality case, a second phone call between Jimbob and the undercover officer was set up. The purpose of this meeting was to obtain further information on the wife, to detail what he wanted done, to get a price established, and to try to get a payday. This meeting went well and again the difference in the voice did not seem to matter. There were a couple of additional phone calls to set up the final meeting.

The CI informed CID that Jimbob had told him he was having more problems with his wife and she had filed for divorce. He had a military retirement and was vested with the state. Jimbob was concerned that he would lose at least half of his pension in the divorce along with everything else he owned. He complained that he had three children and the child support would be too high. The CI said Jimbob was so angry that it sounded like he was going to kill his wife himself.

A meeting was set for the next day. This needed to be the last meeting and an arrest made. CID was concerned that, if things did not go well, Jimbob would back out of the deal and possibly kill her himself.

Presurveillance was done and surveillance was set up at. At the beginning of the meeting Jimbob decided to take the undercover officer on a road trip. Everyone was prepared for the undercover officer to go with Jimbob, but the undercover officer needed to be the driver. This way he could keep surveillance with him and Jimbob would not lose the surveillance cars. CID needed to get all of probable cause on this meeting or the case might be weakened. Jimbob directed the undercover officer to his wife's boyfriend's house and showed her vehicle to the undercover officer. Jimbob told the undercover officer that he wanted her killed and wanted it to look like an accident. They discussed the problems with that and decided on making it look like a drug deal gone bad. Jimbob gave a description of his wife and her daily habits. He wanted it done while he was at work so that he had an alibi. While discussing the price, Jimbob did not want to front any cash. He said it was going to take a while to get the money together. He said that he did have an insurance policy on her and would pay $24,000 when he cashed in the policy. Normally, partial payment must be obtained before continuing, but the fact that he could kill his wife on his own was a problem. All the elements of the crime were present and CID felt that there was enough of a substantial step to make the arrest.

The bust signal was given. As the team moved in for the arrest the lights went on. A local television station had picked up the team's radio transmissions and figured out where the arrest was being made.

This was a case where substantial step needed to be developed without receiving any payment. Every case is different. The basic training academy teaches all staff not to develop any relationships with inmates. It teaches staff not to tell inmates about their personal problems and instructs them on how inmates will manipulate them. Staff is taught not to trust an inmate and they are given all the tools they need to survive. Jimbob did not listen and got himself hooked up with inmate pals. It is hard to believe that a staff member with all that training would resort to trying to hire a killer through a prison inmate.

All these cases have one thing in common: the opportunity to save some lives. These cases tend to become very complex. The following case history started out as one case, but turned into three cases. All three of these cases were companion cases done in one cell block with one CI. It was a nightmare of logistical planning and cooperation between several divisions of the department. These case histories demonstrate virtually every aspect of a successful solicitation case. They also show the complexity of the cases and how problems were overcome. Examples of undercover operations, surveillance, playing the games, getting the substantial step, mistakes made, and political problems are given.

This was a very high profile case where the lives of DAs and judges were at risk.

Case Histories #16 to #18

CID received information from a CI inmate that another inmate, called "IOU," was attempting to find someone to kill a DA. IOU was doing a sentence for sexual assault on a child. He was in his 60s and felt that he had been wronged by the system, yet he had pled guilty to the crime. The reliability of the CI had been proven on two previous occasions with convictions that followed.

Initially, all of the information concerning IOU's requests was second-hand hearsay from the CI. IOU did not want to talk directly to the hit man and would not write a letter. He just wanted it handled. The CI convinced him that he would need to talk to the hit man.

The first call was placed to the undercover hit man from IOU. During this call the only thing of value IOU said was that he wanted the work done but needed time to get the money together. He was unsure of how long it would take and needed to know how much it would cost. The undercover hit man told IOU that he would need more information from him in order to quote him a price. IOU said he needed to talk with his wife first and then he would call back.

Because of IOU's reluctance to talk on the phone, CID felt he must be serious about hiring a hit man to kill the DA. CID needed a plan to make him more forthcoming with his request. It was time to improvise, adapt, and overcome. The plan needed to be simple, impressive and real.

CID decided to use the normal attorney client mailings. IOU was told that the undercover hit man was a former black operational plan operative (the U.S. version of 007…) and had access to certain equipment. IOU himself claimed to have been in U.S. Air Force intelligence. CID told him that scrambling equipment would be used for the telephone and that he would be able to talk freely.

During the next telephone exchange IOU was told that the equipment was in place and he could talk freely. He explained that he had been unjustly prosecuted and he wanted the DA that had handled his case murdered. He went on to say that he was going back to court soon and he felt that if the DA was out of the way then he would get out of prison. He identified the intended victim as an assistant DA. He gave a description of her and even identified a vehicle he thought she was driving. IOU was told that the hit man would need $5000 to do the job. He was asked how he wanted her killed. Did he want her to feel a lot of pain, or did he have any special requests? Anyway the undercover hit man wanted to do it was fine with him, just so she ended up dead. IOU told the undercover officer that he would get back with him on the money and how he would pay for it. He ended the conversation with a request for a possible payment schedule.

This guy wanted to make payments on a hit! Remember, you need to do whatever you can to close the deal. If you do not, the bandit may find someone else to do the job and someone ends up dead. During this call IOU reported that he had worked intelligence and knew about all of the sophisticated equipment.

As part of the investigation you are, at some point, required to notify the intended victim. When you notify is dependent upon the circumstances of the case. Once you have enough reasonable suspicion to believe that the bandit is engaging in an attempt to have someone killed, it is important to contact the victim. The timing is essential. There are times when the intended victim is notified too early, causing the case to be lost. You do not want the intended victim to get angry and contact your bandit before your case is made and you do not want to wait too long in case the bandit is trying another way to commit the murder. CID advised the DA's office of the case involving IOU. CID knew that the DA would not contact the bandit.

During the weeks to follow IOU talked to his wife and wrote her letters. He told her that he had a new attorney and if he could get about $5000 together he could get out of prison. IOU was totally convinced that if the DA was murdered he would get out of prison.

The CI reported that IOU was dead serious and wanted to get this thing on the road. The CI was told to tell IOU that the hit man would consider payments if he would provide a promissory note and $500 dollars in the form of a downpayment. CID needed to get something or they would not have substantial step toward the commission of this crime.

IOU called his wife and told her that he was sure he would be home with her soon. He said that he talked with his attorney and it was a sure thing. He told her that the attorney knew they had money problems and he would take $500 down and a promissory note for the rest. He told her they could make minimal payments and that he would be coming home and making money to make the payments.

IOU called the undercover hit man within a few days. They discussed options and it was agreed that if he would send $500 and a promissory note for the rest, the undercover hit man would kill the DA. IOU agreed and seemed quite excited about the prospect. He said it would be only a matter of a few days before the hit man got his money. At this point IOU was told that if he had any reservations about doing this that now was the time to express them. He was told that once the promissory note and cash were received, the DA would be killed and there would be no turning back. His response was "just do it." The CI reported that IOU was writing his promissory note and would be mailing it the same day.

The CI said that he had more news. Another inmate, called "Watches," was trying to contact him to find a hit man. The CI was told to avoid him as long as he could without causing him to go elsewhere. The CI said that he thought that IOU had told Watches about what he was doing and that Watches also wanted someone dead.

This was the first time CID ever got a referral on a murder for hire. As interesting as it was, any conflict with IOU's case needed to be avoided and CID did not want to put the CI in any further danger. However, if Watches was not contacted, he might go elsewhere for the services. It seemed at that time that he could put off until IOU's case was further along.

CID could not believe it. That same day the mail room picked up a letter to the undercover hit man. Inside was a promissory note for $4500. It stated that there was a $500 up-front payment. It was for services rendered. Figure 4.4 shows IOU's promissory note.

IOU called his wife and told her to send the $500 to the attorney and to put a note inside the envelope. It did not appear that he cared much if his wife became involved in this crime. (It should be noted that CID was fortunate enough, through letters and phone calls, to know she was not involved. She became an unwitting accomplice.)

IOU, in his conversations with Watches, had told Watches that he was going to be getting out of prison when the DA was killed. According to the

CI, Watches was anxious to get in touch with the hit man. Watches was another convicted sex offender. He had been involved in a case of the rape of his two stepdaughters and had pled guilty to lesser charges. Watches was also under the impression that since his case was so similar to the IOU case that he too would be able to get out of prison. He wanted to get this going as soon as possible. He had already talked with his wife about a friend of his that hired this attorney that was going to get him out of prison.

It appeared that Watches was waiting to see how things worked out for IOU. When CID finished IOU's case, it would need to look like IOU was out of prison. This is the kind of secret that is not kept very well given the prison grapevine and all. CID started the planning and made contacts with offender services, wardens, and some security personnel. This was the beginning of another crisis.

Within a few days, the undercover officer got another call from IOU. He asked if his money had been received yet. IOU was told that the promissory note came, but the money had not arrived. He was again told that this would be his last chance to back out because once the money arrived the DA would be killed. He agreed that it had to happen. During this conversation IOU asked what it would cost to kill a judge. Without hesitation the undercover hit man told him that since he was a high official of the court it would be $10,000. IOU said that he did want the judge in his case murdered. He asked if he could make another promissory note for the judge, but use the same $500 as the downpayment. The undercover officer agreed. IOU was told again that once the promissory note and the money were received, the DA and the judge would be murdered and there would be nothing that could stop it, so if he had any reservations at all it was time to express them. IOU did not blink, he gave the okay.

At this point in the investigation CID knew that once the money arrived the case would be ready to take to the DA. CID also knew that once the case was finished IOU's trip to court and his release from prison needed to be orchestrated. CID did not have all the information though. Did Watches have contact with Mrs. IOU? Did their wives know each other? Can this be done without jeopardizing the case or endangering the CI?

Offender services, wardens, the inspector general, and the executive director were all involved in the decisions that had to be made. Involving all of these high level officials was, of course, necessary. Because the case involved so many areas, everyone had their own idea of what should be done. CID did not have the horsepower, as investigators, to insist on anything. So CID waited for "them" to decide. Both the executive director and the inspector general were Denver police officials. Knowing what it took to put a case like this together, they gave approval to a workable plan.

IOU was enthusiastic. He called again and was told that the money had arrived. He was told that the two targets would be eliminated and he just had to sit back and wait.

IOU apparently contacted Watches because the CI was saying that Watches was eager for the hit man's services. Watches had told the CI that he wanted the DA that handled his case killed. He also wanted his two stepdaughters to be forced by the hit man to change their testimony. Watches felt with these people taken care of he too would be freed from prison. CID arranged an initial call between the undercover hit man and Watches. Watches did not give any details, only that he wanted to use the undercover hit man's services but had to arrange funding for this and it could take a while. CID had been monitoring Watches' mail and phones and it did seem like he was preparing his wife for something.

IOU was told that he was going to be transported to court the next day. The CI said that he became very excited and was packing for court. IOU told Watches he would not be back because he was getting out of prison. He called his wife and told her that he would call her from the court-house to pick him up.

At 4:30 a.m. the next morning IOU was awakened and prepared for his trip to court. Everything was done the same way court trips are usually prepared. The computer messages were in place that indicated to *all* that IOU was on "Out to Court" status. Everything was the same. It was not until about 7:30 a.m. that the court bus picked up IOU. He was alone in the bus and a very happy man. CID had it planned that IOU would have no contact with any other inmates prior to his leaving. He ended up talking with several. Fortunately, he believed that he was leaving and it all worked out for the best. The inmate pipeline had the false information and it spread throughout the prison.

The transport officers were aware of the situation. They headed for the main gate of the prison complex. IOU was elated until the transport officers executed a left turn and headed for CSP. A look of surprise came over IOU's face as he complained that they had made a mistake.

IOU was admitted to CSP without any inmates and very few staff knowing about it. He was not placed on any paperwork. He did not even have a cell. He was moved into the bowels of the prison beneath the rest of the inmates. He was placed in a medical section with two 24-hours guards on him. Neither the guards nor the staff knew why IOU was there. CID intercepted all of his mail, incoming and outgoing. He was to have no contact with the outside world until CID solidified the case with Watches. If any of this had leaked out, the CI would most likely have been killed immediately. This covert secretion of an inmate had never been done before.

This tactic, however effective, put a major strain on the facility. Additional staff were needed to put a 24/7 watch on IOU. It was through the efforts and cooperation of facility administration and the inspector general's office that CID was allowed to continue this case.

This case could not have gone better. All the elements were there:

- **Communications**—Communications were both written and verbal and both were first hand with the undercover officer.
- **Motive**—IOU wanted revenge for conviction and he felt that the deaths of the DA and the judge would get him out of prison. The motive was revenge and freedom.

- Solicitation—IOU solicited for the murder of two court officials. His requests were complete. He stated what he wanted done and who he wanted done. He gave descriptions of who he wanted killed. He offered payment for what he wanted done and he even gave reasons why he wanted them done.
- The substantial step—CID not only had two promissory notes, but a $500 deposit for the killings. IOU was offered a way out on three separate occasions and he declined to back out on all three.
- Physical evidence—This came in the form of letters to his wife, two written promissory notes, taped telephone calls with his wife and the undercover hit man, and currency.
- Intent—IOU was given every opportunity to back out of the crime on several occasions and refused to do so. He fully intended to cause the death of an assistant DA and a district court judge. Also CID wanted to let him know why he was placed at CSP and to attempt an interview with him. An investigator went to CSP to interview him. The following is the general substance of that interview between IOU and the prison investigator:
  - CID has some information that indicates you may be involved in the murder of a judge and a district attorney. CID has letters and calls that give evidence to that. What CID does not have is the identity of the hit man. It looks like he is getting ready to kill these people. This is the last chance that you will have to stop this killing from taking place. If you do not, you will be a part of a first degree murder. If you stop it now there is a chance to help yourself. IOU, at least help CID stop this before it is too late.

  IOU responded by saying he did not know what the investigator was talking about. He had been given him virtually all the evidence CID had against him and the possible consequences if he did not give up the hit man. He had his last opportunity to save the lives of these people and chose not to.

In a criminal case, the case must be proven. CID had all of this evidence, but the evidence does not stand alone. This was accomplished in the following ways:

- Although CID knew the voice on the phone to be that of a person who said he was IOU, CID could not prove it without a voice analysis. Frankly, CID did not even know where to have that done. CID had not had any face-to-face conversations and could not even say that in their opinion it was the voice of IOU. What CID did was have a trusted staff member run surveillance on the telephone CID was using during at least one of the scheduled telephone conversations. CID could prove that IOU had a conversation on that phone and with the positive identification of that trusted officer CID could say that IOU was the one on the phone talking to the undercover operative.

- CID had the promissory notes and the letters from IOU. He had told CID that he had written the promissory notes. This may have been enough, but CID could not take any chances. CID went to his file and found documents he filled out in the presence of his case manager. These were taken and sent with the letters and notes to be analyzed. Bingo!
- The money order was easily traceable and was made out in the undercover name. It was sent to the undercover address and IOU reported that it was sent.
- This case made it possible to prosecute without divulging the CI. Everything was done between the bandit and the undercover hit man. Everything was corroborated in some fashion. It should be noted, however, that the CI was ready and willing to testify at the trial if it became necessary. His original agreement with CID was that he would not have to testify unless necessary and he knew that could be a possibility.

As stated before, CID already had one call into Watches. The CI had reported that Watches was not sure if he wanted to kill the DA. He did want the letters from his stepdaughters confessing that they had perjured themselves in court. It was not long before CID intercepted two letters from Watches to two different civilians. In one he told a female friend that he needed about $5000 to get some legal work done. He told her not to mention this to anyone. In the second letter he wrote to a male friend, called "Richie." He told Richie to burn the letter. He laid out his plans to hire some "really bad dude" to make the girls change their testimony. He also said that he was going to get the DA out of office to pave the way for his release. He told Richie that hit men had their ways and that the DA would be beaten up so bad that he would never be able to work again.

During this second investigation CID learned that a third inmate, called "Plowboy," a friend of Watches, contacted the CI with a request to hire a hit man to kill a DA and a judge. The CI reported that this inmate had told him that he had already made inquiries to a biker gang to get the job done. The CI wanted to know if he should work this case as well.

Things were getting a little confusing as it was, but it seemed as though this third case should also be worked. The CI was told to tell Plowboy that he would help him but he needed to wait a while. The CI was told to go ahead and give the undercover telephone number to Plowboy and tell him to call.

The CI called and said that Watches still wanted two letters from his stepdaughters and the DA killed or beaten, and now he also wanted the natural father of the girls beaten badly. The CI said that Watches wanted to make payments much as IOU was doing. Watches said that he had some antiques that he could put up as collateral. He also said that he had a very good watch collection that was worth a lot of money.

Mail and telephone conversations by Watches indicated that he was trying to get money together to do the job. Also, Watches was writing letters to Richie telling him that he needed his help to get money to pay a hit man. He told Richie that he was going to get letters from his stepdaughters and have the DA beaten.

Watches finally called the undercover hit man. During that call he reported that he wanted his two stepdaughters threatened into writing letters stating that they had lied in court. The undercover officer discussed methods of accomplishing this. Watches also said that now he did not want the natural father hurt or the DA killed. He said that he wanted the DA beaten so badly that he would not ever be able to work again. Watches was told that the DA was a very large ex-Navy SEAL (He was an ex-Navy SEAL). He was told that in order to beat the DA that bad it might be necessary to kill him. Watches said he did not care, but he was only paying for the beating. He was asked if he was sure he wanted that done because there was a very good chance the undercover hit man would have to kill the DA. He said that he would rather he not be killed, but it did not matter. Watches told the undercover officer that he would give him a collection of gold and silver antique watches that were valued at $7000. He wanted these held as collateral until he could get the cash. The undercover officer said okay and that the cost for the two girls and the DA would be $3000. Watches agreed and told the undercover hit man that his friend Richie would bring the watches to him. Watches was asked if his friend knew what was going on and he said yes.

During subsequent calls, the undercover officer talked at length with Richie and Watches about setting up the meeting. The meeting was set and CBI agents were requested to assist with surveillance and back up.

As planned the undercover hit man met with Richie. This meeting was audio and video taped. During the meeting Richie admitted his involvement and that he knew what was to take place. He presented the undercover hit man with 27 gold and silver antique watches. The meeting was terminated and Richie was allowed to go on his way.

CID had everything needed to file charges, but still had to execute a plan to move Watches in the same manner as IOU. Apparently Watches had contacted the inmate Plowboy and told him what was going on. The CI had reported that Plowboy had already contacted him and wanted to talk to the hit man about killing a DA and a judge. Plowboy was also doing a sentence for sexual assault on a child, involving his stepdaughter. He too thought the criminal justice system had failed him and he too had pled guilty to the crime. He was angry with the DA and the judge and thought that if they were dead he might be able to get out of prison.

CID learned that Plowboy and Watches were getting very close and had frequent contact. CID had to insure that Watches would not be able to contact anyone when he was arrested.

The same plan used with IOU was put into effect. Watches was checked out to court. No other paperwork was available to show where he was actually going. He went to CSP, just like IOU.

Similar to Watches' and IOU's cases, Plowboy did not at first want to talk in person to the hit man. All of the information CID had was directly from the CI. CID did not want to use the CI in court unless absolutely necessary. Plowboy told the CI that he did not want to do anything until he heard from Watches. He told the CI that he had told Watches to call or write to Plowboy's wife and tell her if he got out of prison. He wanted to see if the plan worked before he committed himself. The CI said that Plowboy was being very cautious.

The CI reported that Plowboy had talked with his wife about this. They wanted to do the same thing Watches did. They wanted to put something up as collateral and pay later. They offered some land and a Chevrolet Suburban.

Telephone calls and mail between Plowboy and his wife were monitored. During these communications they talked about hiring a hit man. They talked about waiting until Watches was out of prison to make sure things worked out for him. They seemed to have no difficulty in rationalizing the death of these people to suit their needs.

CID had Watches locked down and no one knew where he was. A letter was drafted to Plowboy's wife, called "Wanda". The letter told Wanda that Watches was okay and out of prison. During a phone call Wanda told Plowboy that she had received a letter from Watches and everything was okay.

Shortly thereafter, Plowboy sent a note to the undercover hit man telling him to contact his wife. The note said that he and his wife had talked and they wanted the hit done. (Taped telephone calls corroborated this.) The note said that Plowboy did not want to become involved and wanted his wife to handle it.

The undercover hit man called Wanda. During this call she said that she and her husband had talked it over and decided to have the assistant DA killed. She said that they would pay $5000 to have it done. She said that they wanted to put their Chevrolet Suburban up as collateral. She gave a physical description of the intended victim and where he could be located. She said that they would give the undercover hit man the title to the vehicle to hold until payment was made.

CIDs case against Plowboy was lacking in that there was no first-hand conversation about the killings with him. Wanda was asked if the title was in her name or both of their names. She said both. The undercover officer told her that he needed to talk with Plowboy to make sure he was okay with this agreement. He also told Wanda that he needed to get a feel for him because if he did not feel comfortable with him and her he would not do the job.

The next day Plowboy called. During this conversation Plowboy reported that he wanted the DA murdered. He offered the Chevrolet

Suburban up as collateral. He agreed to the $5000 price for the murder. He went into the reasons he wanted the DA dead. The undercover officer told Plowboy that once he had the title to the vehicle the DA would be murdered and if he had any reservations he needed to state them now. Plowboy said it was the only way and he wanted him dead. During two additional calls with Wanda, a meeting was scheduled to pick up the title to the vehicle.

The CBI again agreed to assist in the surveillance. The meeting was audio and video taped. Wanda showed up for the meeting with her two minor children. During the discussions it was apparent that she had wanted the judge killed as well, but settled for just the DA because of Plowboy. She was very explicit and indicated she wanted him killed with extreme prejudice. They discussed many ways of killing him, all of which would be very painful. She gave the title to the undercover hit man and also gave documents for a piece of property. She said that the money would be paid to retrieve these documents as soon as possible. Wanda was told that now that the contract had been paid for, the DA would be killed and if she had any reservations she needed to express them now. She did not. Wanda was allowed to leave.

After the warrants were secured, Wanda and Plowboy were served. Plowboy was interviewed by a prison investigator to see if he wanted one more opportunity to save the life of the DA. He elected not to.

All of these cases have been adjudicated and all five defendants have been sentenced for their parts in these crimes. It should be understood that when working a solicitation case you need to insure that you have all the elements of the crimes. You have to be willing to adjust to the circumstances. Your tactics may be dictated by these circumstances. CID would have rather worked these cases one at a time, but because of the circumstances the cases had to be worked simultaneously. A logistical nightmare? Yes. An easy task? No. A successful operation? Yes.

Investigator Tips on Solicitation Cases

A prison investigator must always be creative, particularly in solicitation cases. Sometimes the investigators find themselves in a position where it is difficult to rely on anyone for assistance, and they must be highly covert in working the case. In a very recent case which has not been adjudicated as yet, investigators had to resort to such covert actions.

Case History #19

In early 2001, a staff member was convicted of extortion. He attempted to extort a large amount of money from an inmate and was arrested during a sting operation. He was serving a 5-year sentence, which was the lengthiest sentence handed out to a correctional officer in the history of the CID.

In May 2001 this staff member, now an inmate, reached out to another inmate for assistance. CID referred to the former staff member as "Lil Abner." He considered himself a country boy, stating he was a born in the hills "redneck." Unfortunately for Lil Abner, he had contacted an inmate who was a CI. This CI contacted his investigator and told him that Lil Abner wanted to have the inmate/witness convinced to change his testimony. Lil Abner thought that if he could coerce the witness into changing his testimony and saying that staff talked him into perjuring himself, he would have his sentence overturned and become wealthy from a lawsuit he would file against the DOC. He had told the CI to find someone willing to go to extreme measures in obtaining an affidavit from the witness. CID told the CI to tell Lil Abner that he had an uncle who was high in the "Arian Brotherhood" and that his uncle had contacts in all prisons and could get the job done. Lil Abner was also told that this uncle had false identification (ID) in the form of an attorney and could visit with him if necessary. He was also told that because the correctional staff would think the uncle was an attorney, the visit would be private and they could speak openly. The CI also gave Lil Abner a phone number for "Uncle Bob."

The CI continued to have conversations with Lil Abner, but Lil Abner did not attempt to make contact with Uncle Bob. Within a week it appeared as though Lil Abner was having second thoughts. He told the CI that he had tried to call Uncle Bob, but inmate phone records did not corroborate this.

The CI told investigators that Lil Abner had written a letter to the CI's wife asking her to tell Uncle Bob to come and visit him as he did not feel comfortable talking on the phone with him. This letter was given to investigators and it appeared to be in the handwriting of Lil Abner.

The undercover officer had an undercover driver's licence, but needed to get some lawyer identification. The DA was contacted and he offered his lawyer registration card to copy for the operation. With some creative computerized graphics, a suitable ID was made up in the name on the undercover driver's license. Some business cards were made up and some stationary was created for future communications.

In late May of 2001, CID, with the cooperation of the warden of the prison gousing Lil Abner, arranged a meeting between Lil Abner and the undercover attorney. No one, with the exception of the warden, the security manager, and the local investigator, was aware of the visit. All standard procedures were followed for the visit. The DOC electronic surveillance expert had fashioned a briefcase with audio and visual capabilities to be taken in with the undercover officer to the visit.

As luck would have it, the video output was not operational. CID did, however, have audio and decided to go ahead with the visit. Lil Abner was called to an attorney visit and the equipment was activated.

When Lil Abner arrived he was greeted by the undercover officer who identified himself as Uncle Bob. During the initial conversations it was made clear that Uncle Bob was not a real attorney. Lil Abner was even shown the ID and explained the differences between it and authentic ID. This was, of course, to insure that Lil Abner could not later claim attorney–client privilege because he thought Uncle Bob was an attorney.

Lil Abner was very cautious and told Uncle Bob that he had just been "burnt" by an undercover officer. He even asked Uncle Bob if he was a police officer. Of course Uncle Bob said no and Lil Abner went into his story. He began to talk about his problems as an officer and gave an account of how he had been set up by staff and needed the witness to "tell the truth"—the truth as Lil Abner saw it. His story went into great detail of his life and correctional experience. Uncle Bob did not push the issue or talk of why he was allegedly there.

After Lil Abner poured his heart out, Uncle Bob told him that originally he only came to visit at the request of his nephew and had no intention of doing anything for him. Uncle Bob then said that Lil Abner had "touched his heart" with his account of what had happened to him and said that if he could, he would help Lil Abner.

Lil Abner said that he wanted the witness to change his testimony and provide an affidavit to the courts that would exonerate Lil Abner. He skirted the issue on every turn, though, and made it difficult to get him to actually say what he meant. He was told that Uncle Bob could find out where the witness was and could force him to write whatever Lil Abner wanted him to say. He was also told that the witness might not want to do this and would most probably have to be forced. He was also told that there was no guarantee that the witness would not go to the authorities. Lil Abner said that he did not know what to do then. Lil Abner did not want to come out and actually say what he wanted. Although it was understood that Lil Abner wanted the affidavit at any cost and knew that the only way to keep the witness from recanting his affidavit or going to authorities was to kill the witness, Lil Abner would not say the words.

Uncle Bob wisely changed the subject to payment. Lil Abner said that he was going to sue the DOC for millions of dollars and would settle for $4 million. He said that he would gladly pay half of his judgement to Uncle Bob for doing this. He tried to convince Uncle Bob that he would win the suit.

Uncle Bob continued the conversation for over an hour and it was finally agreed that the witness would be forced to write an affidavit and would then be killed to insure his silence. After the lawsuit was won, Uncle Bob would be paid for his services.

Lil Abner's intentions were understood between Uncle Bob and him, but it could easily be argued by the defense that there was no specific agreement and Lil Abner would walk away from his crime. A week after this meeting a letter was drafted from Uncle Bob to Lil Abner. The created stationary was used to insure that the letter had "Legal Mail" status (meaning that staff could not read the contents of the letter). This letter was written in a veiled context. The general substance of the letter was that the witness had been found. It indicated that the affidavit would be found and that the witness would be killed. No response from this letter was ever received.

Lil Abner did not take the letter to authorities or give any indication that he knew what was going to happen. Uncle Bob had seemingly overplayed his hand and not been specific enough. The DA's office was not satisfied with the case, even though there were taped conversations and writings that indicated a crime was being hatched between the undercover officer and Lil Abner.

Investigators were not initially aware of some time constraints. Because Lil Abner was an ex-correctional officer, he was slated to be moved out of state for his safety. The move was to take place soon and CID needed to develop this case further to insure a solid prosecution. The CI had reported that Lil Abner was trying to solicit funds to pay Uncle Bob and had told him that he received the letter from Uncle Bob and had destroyed it.

Nothing in the case had transpired until late June of 2001. CID decided that since Lil Abner had not reached out to Uncle Bob that one more letter would be written. A letter was drafted in very plain language to see if Lil Abner fully intended to have the witness coerced into writing an affidavit and ultimately killed. The general substance of the letter included Lil Abner being told that the witness had been found and some people had forced him into writing the affidavit. He was also told that the witness had to be beaten and threatened in order to write the affidavit. He was also told that the witness had not yet told anyone, as his family had been threatened, but the perpetrators were concerned that if he were not killed he would go to authorities. The letter also told Lil Abner that Uncle Bob wanted some assurance, in the form of a promissory note, that he would be paid . He was also told that Uncle Bob had talked to his nephew (the CI) who said that Lil Abner was not sure he wanted the witness killed. Lil Abner was instructed to write to Uncle Bob and inform him what his intentions were and where he wanted Uncle Bob to send the affidavit. He was told not to mention the murder in his letter, but rather to just mention a "Plymouth Fury" which would let Uncle Bob know that he did want the witness killed.

The letter was mailed on June 29, 2001. On July 3, 2001 it was learned that the letter had not yet arrived, but a letter sent to Uncle Bob from Lil Abner was mailed out on July 1, 2001. This letter has not yet arrived and this case continues.

In order to put together a solid case, investigators need to insure that all the elements of the crime are present before attempting to file the case. This case, on the surface, seemed to be substantial in the beginning, but unless a jury can be convinced that there was an understanding it will not succeed. This case is not dead yet. Investigators still work to see if they can successfully establish all the elements needed.

Figure 4.1 This bank of phones was used to make contact with undercover prison investigators to contract murders. There were three separate solicitation investigations originating in 1 month from these phones.

Figure 4.2 This table was used to orchestrate the murders of three DAs and one district court judge.

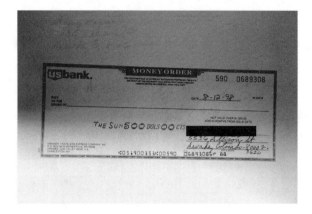

Figure 4.3 This money order was a down payment to kill a DA and the district court judge in Jefferson County Colorado.

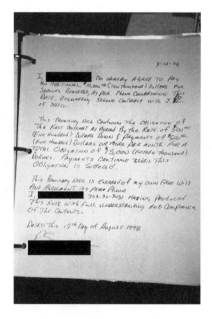

Figure 4.4 Inmate sent the alleged hit man a promissory note for the remainder of the fee for killing a judge and a DA.

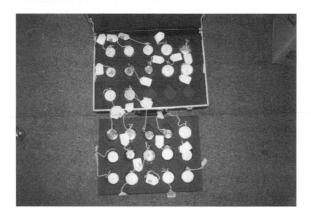

Figure 4.5 These 27 antique watches were paid to a hit man (an undercover prison investigator) for the maiming of a DA and the intimidation of witnesses.

Figure 4.6 Title to a 1990 Chevrolet Suburban given as collateral in a murder for hire case.

Figure 4.7 Title insurance papers for land given as collateral for murdering a DA.

All photos courtesy of the Colorado Department of Corrections.

Sex Offenses

5

Introduction

One might think that a criminal investigator in a prison setting would not have to investigate many sex offenses. After all, most prisons are all one-sex prisons and these guys are locked up. Like all crime, it does not stop just because that steel door has slammed shut. On the contrary, it continues and escalates. Prison is a subculture with a mind of its own.

Before analyzing the investigative process of the sex crime, it is important to know, at least an elementary level, statutory law. In Colorado the statutes governing sex offenses are very similar to those all over the United States. Only on rare occasions do investigators work any misdemeanor cases. Most investigations include felony sexual assaults.

Colorado Revised Statutes Related to Prison Sex Crimes

Colorado Revised Statutes (CRS) in the criminal code title 18 article 3 contains the statutes regarding crimes against persons. Part 4 defines unlawful sexual behavior. It is this part where investigators will find the elements of the crimes they will be investigating.

The most serious of the crimes would be found in CRS 18-3-402, titled "Sexual Assault in the First Degree." It states, in part, that

1. "Any actor who knowingly inflicts sexual intrusion or sexual penetration on a victim commits a sexual assault in the first degree." It goes on to enumerate the specific elements which must be present to constitute the first degree offense. Only one or more of the elements need to be proven in order to seek a conviction.

   a. The actor must cause submission of the victim through the actual application of physical force or physical violence.

   b. The actor causes submission of the victim by threat of imminent death, serious bodily injury, extreme pain, or kidnaping to be inflicted on anyone, and the victim believes that the actor has the present ability to execute these threats.

   c. The actor causes submission of the victim by threatening to retaliate in the future against the victim, or any other person, and the victim reasonably believes the actor will execute this threat.

   d. The actor has substantially impaired the victim's power to appraise or control the victim's conduct by employing, without the victim's consent, any drug, intoxicant, or other means for the purpose of causing submission.

   e. The victim is physically helpless, and the actor knows the victim is physically helpless and the victim has not consented.

2. Sexual assault in the first degree is a class 3 felony, except as provided in subsection 3 of this list.

3. Sexual assault in the first degree is a class 2 felony if it is attended by any one or more of the following circumstances:

   a. In the commission of the sexual assault, the actor is physically aided or abetted by one or more other persons.

   b. The victim suffers serious bodily injury.

   c. The actor is armed with a deadly weapon and uses the deadly weapon to cause submission of the victim.

This is an encapsulated version of the statute. There are statutes written for each different crime. The elements are different for second degree and third degree sexual assaults. Part 4 of the statutes in Colorado describe the elements for each sexual offense. This is presented for the novice reader and to reinforce the investigator's need to refer to the statute book whenever investigating any crime.

The Who, What, When, Where, Why, and How of Prison Sex Crimes

In civilian life many sex crimes go unreported, but in prison, *most* sex crimes go unreported. Usually an investigation into a first degree sexual assault will be initiated by a third party reporting a serious injury or a homicide. In these cases it is unlikely that the victim will be cooperative. He already knows what can happen if he cooperates. The victims are most often weaker, smaller, younger, immature, or homosexual. The crime can be a result of retaliation, sending a message, or even drug related. The victims have been taught the prison code by the more experienced inmates. The code calls for silence. It demands that the inmate not "snitch" on anyone—be quiet or be dead. It calls for taking care of matters alone and in most cases these victims cannot take care of the problem themselves. The victim will often resort to suicide or some other acting out that will cause them to be removed from general population and out of reach.

The perpetrators can be anyone. Sexual predators are not necessarily housed separately. Any predatory criminal can become a sexual predator. This is a subculture with its own rules. The main rule is that there are no rules. Power rules. Survival of the fittest. There is no moral code, anything goes. The self-gratification gained from these sex crimes outweighs any punishment the perpetrators might receive. The inmate knows that he is not likely to be prosecuted for a sex crime committed in prison.

Having homosexual relationships in prison is not considered by the straight inmate as being homosexual. After all, there are no women and the inmates need sexual relief. They can easily rationalize their actions, even if these actions include the commission of a criminal act to gain satisfaction.

Case History #20

In 1985 the Rifle Correctional Facility was a 150-bed minimum security facility with a total of 26 staff. With the limited number of staff, everyone had more than one specific duty. It bred closer relationships between the inmates and staff, which was not necessarily a bad thing. In fact, the staff knew more about what the convicts were up to than in other prisons.

One particular inmate was in prison for the third time and was currently serving a 12-year sentence for second degree murder. He had no sex crimes noted in his file. He was extremely homophobic. He would often make remarks about homosexuals and stayed away from anyone he thought to be homosexual. It almost seemed as though he protested too much.

A known homosexual inmate was being transferred to the facility. He had changed his name from masculine to feminine. He had successfully sued the department of corrections and forced them to allow him injections that would enable him to grow breasts. The inmate population found out that this inmate was being transferred.

On the first evening of his arrival, after the new inmate had eaten dinner, he sat outside the dining hall in a provocative pose. The other inmates were particularly well-groomed and hovered flirtatiously in front of the new inmate. Among them was the inmate who had repeatedly expressed homophobic sentiments.

A few days later this inmate and the new arrival were missing during two consecutive inmate counts. The facility, which had no fences, was in the middle of nowhere with no fences. An alert security officer found some footprints that led off into a wooded hillside. He followed these tracks and came upon the two inmates engaged in sexual activity.

During an interview, after his administrative hearing for sexual misconduct, the homophobic inmate remained in denial. He asserted that he was not a homosexual, that homosexuals were bad. He was merely exercising his right to sexual gratification and because he needed it, it was okay.

This is a common reaction to "straight" inmates being caught in homosexual acts. If they need "it," it is okay and there is no harm done.

Another problem with the reporting of sex crimes is that inmates rarely report the crime in a timely manner or even report it at all. It is not known exactly why this is, but it may be that they are waiting for an opportunity to speak with staff when the bandit is not around or will not hear about it. In any sex-related crime, physical evidence is necessary to prove the elements of the crime. Rarely will you get a reported sexual assault prior to the victim taking a shower, changing clothes, washing clothes, or otherwise destroying all the physical evidence.

As seen during the course of this book, inmates are not reliable witnesses or victims. Because they are convicted felons, they are easily discredited in court. Because of this there has to be a significant amount of corroboration. This becomes nearly impossible when all of the physical evidence in a sex offense is destroyed.

Unlike most victims, the investigator cannot rely solely on any inmate testimony. There are almost always underlying reasons for inmates to report the crime. Not that any investigator should rely on polygraph exams, but sometimes it is necessary to submit the victim and the suspect to polygraphs before spending too much time on a case.

You will be caught in a conflicting situation. The investigator's duty is to investigate all reported crime. The victims will often be convicted felons who are not known for their truthfulness. The investigator still has to do his best to determine the truth.

False Reporting

A great number of sex offense cases will be falsely filed by the alleged victims. Some examples of these reportings can give the investigator a partial understanding of the reasons.

- **Failure to pay**—Some sexual assaults are actually consensual sex acts with a promise of some repayment. The victim does not get paid and he reports the rape. Even when your investigation reveals the truth, the problem remains. Now the inmate needs to be protected or moved because he has violated the inmate code and could be sentenced to death.

- **AIDS**—In a recent case an inmate had consensual sex with another inmate. All was well until yet another inmate told the original inmate that his partner was known to have AIDS. The case was resolved rather quickly as the alleged victim could not keep his story together. He did make to it the medical ward and insist that he be treated for AIDS. He finally admitted that the sex was consensual, but he was in fear of the AIDS virus. He was tested for AIDS and the results were negative. His sex partner was not known to have the AIDS virus.
- **Sympathy or need for attention**—Some of the cases brought to the investigator will be the result of the inmate's need for attention. There are no statistics to bear this out, but inmates sometimes need to be the center of attention. For whatever reason, they will report being a victim of a crime. In prison the crime is usually sexual assault.
- **Guilt**—An inmate may not have any homosexual tendencies, but for one reason or other he agrees to have sex with another inmate. He then may have extreme guilt for this act and report it as a crime. It may be that he feels paranoid and thinks that someone knows what he has done. He does not want to be labeled as a homosexual, so he reports a rape.
- **Anger and revenge**—This will happen between inmate lovers on occasion, but it extends beyond that. There have been cases where a business deal has gone wrong or a new lover is involved. The jilted inmate may report a rape to get even with his ex-lover. Inmates will report a rape, knowing there is no evidence, to teach a lesson to another inmate. The reporting inmate knows that nothing will happen to him because investigators do not prosecute misdemeanor false reporting cases.
- **Medical treatment**—Much like the inmate that was actually afraid his partner had AIDS, inmates will report a rape in order to gain access to medical or mental health treatment. This assistance is always available for inmates and the rationale for this type of reporting is beyond most investigators.

The fact is that there are more and more false reports of sexual assaults than actual incidents of rape. The investigator needs to be aware of this and to keep an open mind during his investigation. Investigators have a tendency to want to believe the victims, but they must always keep an open mind. Things are not always what they seem. Remember also that a great number of these stories will be very believable. The investigator may spend a lot of time trying to substantiate these stories, only to conclude that there was not a sexual assault. Although there was no crime or enough evidence to pursue the case, the investigator may never know what happened or why the inmate went to such great lengths to lie.

Case History #21

An inmate reported that he had been raped. In his allegation he stated that he woke with semen on his belly and a sore anus. He said that he thought he was raped during the night. He said that he showered and washed up before he went to his morning meal, after which he reported the incident to security staff. He said that he had a feeling that this had happened in the past and that his cell mate must have drugged him with Valium. He said that he had observed another inmate hanging around his cell acting suspicious and that this must be the suspect. He could not explain how this inmate was suspicious and reported that they had no verbal communication. He said that when he observed this inmate he became suspicious and did not ingest any food or drink during the day. He said he did have some peanut butter that was locked in his locker so that no one could tamper with it.

The victim made several different statements to different people. He had a story for security staff, a story for medical staff, and a different story for his case manager. He said he was not conscious during the rape, but he knew that the suspect was HIV positive.

All of the victim's bedding and underwear he stated he was wearing at the time of the rape were taken into evidence. His cell was photographed and the locking devices were checked. The security staff was interviewed to see if there had been any inmate movement during the night. The suspect was not seen leaving his cell at anytime. The victim was questioned as to how the suspect had entered his cell. At that point he said he was not sure how the suspect got into the cell because he was asleep when the rape occurred and his cell mate would not have let in the suspect. He said that when he woke up he had a pain in his rectum and knew he had been raped. He was asked how he knew who the suspect was and he reported that the guy had made previous advances toward him.

The victim was taken to the hospital and a rape test was performed. The peanut butter was taken into evidence and the victim was given a drug screening test (blood and urine).

In this cell block the cell doors are self-locking when they close. Each inmate has a key to his own cell and can enter from the outside. No one without a key can enter the cell. There is no movement allowed after a certain hour or during the hours the rape was alleged to have occurred.

During the medical exam there were no signs of trauma found and there was no evidence of semen, hair, fibers, or other fluids. During the victim's exam, he reported that the suspect must have been wearing a condom.

The victim was housed in a double occupancy cell. His cell mate was questioned and he claimed to have no idea what the victim was talking about. He did not recall the victim having any problems with anyone. He said that he probably would have been awakened if someone had come into their cell because he had not slept well since he got to prison.

The victim's medical reports came back and there were no signs of any illegal or other substances in his system.

The victim was interviewed a total of five times. Each time he was interviewed his story would change slightly. He recanted his original suspect information with the fact that an unknown assailant had come into his cell. The case was closed with insufficient evidence to prosecute.

This case was typical of many false reports. The victim would not come off his story and this left a lot of questions. The lack of physical evidence and the continual changing of the victim's version of the rape were enough to cease the investigation. The problem is that there was no definite closure to this case. Many of the sexual assaults investigated in prison will end this way. The only thing an investigator will know for sure is that he is not sure what happened. This can be very frustrating.

These cases are not always easy to drop for lack of evidence. There was a very similar case in January 1994.

Case History #22

An inmate reported that staff should check on another inmate who had some injuries to his face. Officers responded to the victim's cell and observed that the victim had sustained injuries to both eyes and his left cheek. The inmate who reported the incident told officers that the victim had told him that he had done it to himself. Officers questioning the inmate were told by the victim that he would not give an explanation and he refused medical treatment.

The shift supervisor attempted to get the victim to seek medical treatment, but he refused. The supervisor gave orders to his staff to keep a watch on the inmate victim.

The next morning staff again approached the inmate to see if he would talk to them. The inmate agreed to talk to the staff. He said that the reason he had injuries to his face was that he was mad at himself and had beaten himself in the face as punishment. He then reported that two inmates had raped him. He named two assailants who had attacked him about 10 p.m. the night before.

The victim was taken to medical for an exam. The medical staff could not find any trauma and sent him to the local hospital to perform a rape test on the inmate. Just prior to his going to the hospital the victim was again interviewed. During this round of questioning he again stated that he had been raped at about 10 p.m. the prior evening. He said, this time, that the original reporting inmate was involved in the rape. He gave a more detailed report of the incident on this occasion. He said that he had not showered since the rape and had not had a bowel movement. He claimed that the rape happened in his bed. He said that two of the three inmates penetrated him and that they ejaculated inside him. The victim began to tire of the questioning and was released to go to the hospital.

All three suspects were interviewed. All three had alibis that of course were corroborated by other inmates. All three of the suspects cooperated with the interview and voluntarily gave hair and fingernail scraping samples. They all waived their rights to silence and gave voluntary statements.

During the interview of the reporting inmate, he showed signs of deception in his statement, but did answer all the questions put to him. In his account he reported that he was the cell mate of the victim. He said that he went to bed at 10 p.m. and was not awakened by anything. He said that the cell door was locked when he went to bed and he did not see anyone around the cell prior to his going to bed. He said that he did not know the other two suspects. (This was highly unlikely, but possible.) As it turned out, another of the suspects said he did know this inmate and he had visited the cell on that day. All of the suspects agreed to take polygraph examinations and were told that they would be interviewed again at a later date.

During the next few days the suspects and the victim were interviewed and reinterviewed. All the staff on duty was interviewed to see if any additional information could be found. The physical evidence was taken to the Colorado Bureau of Investigation for analysis.

Investigators found that the suspects were giving some conflicting statements and two of them showed obvious signs of deception during their questioning. All of the suspects denied the allegation and gave nontestimonial evidence freely (head hair, pubic hair, and fingernail scrapings). Two of the suspects had given alibi statements, while the third suspect could not give an accurate accounting of his whereabouts during the alleged rape.

The medical personnel reported finding no trauma other than the facial injuries sustained at the victim's own hand (according to him). The crime scene showed no obvious signs of a rape. No pubic hairs were found on the bedding and no seminal stains were found under a black light.

Investigators now had several conflicting statements from the victim. He originally reported a violent rape where he was held by two inmates and raped by a third inmate. He then reported that two of the three raped him while his cell mate stood by and watched. He then said that the cell mate raped him. He claimed at first that he did not fight the rapists. He then said that he read a book while being raped. Under pressure of additional questioning, he said that he was asleep and raped while he was sleeping, but still knew who had raped him.

After questioning staff at length, investigators determined that the cell mate was not in the cell at the alleged time of the rape. Two separate staff saw him sitting in the hall. The count officer found the victim in his room alone during the time of the reported rape. One of the staff members who knew the victim reported that he felt this inmate had some sort of mental problem and had made false reports in the past.

Investigators requested that victim sign a release of information form in order to obtain medical and mental health information. He did sign the document. Armed with this document investigators were able to determine that the victim was considered developmentally disabled.

As it turned out, the rape kit contained no evidence of rape or consensual sex.

This case is another example of the typical "reported" sex crime in prison. There was insufficient evidence to pursue any prosecution and many doubts existed in the minds of the investigators. This case remains a mystery. The suspects still maintain their innocense and the victim maintains he was raped.

Precautions Against False Reporting

There are some precautions investigators can take to insure they are not duped by a false reporter:

- Always interview the victim more than once. Sometimes the investigator might have another case manager or staff member interview the victim as well. Get statements from the medical people who treated him. They may have gotten a different story from him. If the inmate is making a false report, there will be significant inconsistencies in his statements.
- Most inmates want to insure that the rape is believable. They may include a beating they took while fighting off their attacker. Most often the injuries, if any, will not be consistent with the statement of facts. The injuries may be too old or too new in relationship to the inmate's reporting dates.
- In sexual assault there is always trauma to the affected area. Victims will report a violent sexual attack with penetration in the anal canal, but the medical personnel will not be able to find any trauma in that area.
- Be sure to interview inmates and staff in the area. The story given by the inmate may not bear out known facts by staff and inmate witnesses. Be sure to interview all staff that were on duty at the time of the incident. Quite often officers will know facts that they do not feel are important. Often they are not asked to write a report.
- The sexual assault medical exam (rape kit) performed will not yield any semen, hair, fibers, saliva, or blood.
- The crime scene will be void of physical evidence.
- The suspect will have a staff-witnessed alibi.
- The victim will admit that he has taken a shower since the event. The event took place 2 weeks ago. He is sorry, but he took all of his bedding to the laundry and mopped his floor, leaving no evidence.
- The victim is a 250-lb black belt in karate and the suspect who forcibly raped him is a 125-lb couch potato.

Although it is very important to realize that many of these reports will be false, they must be investigated to the fullest extent to determine all of the facts. The investigator will be faced with reports that they believe are bogus from the beginning. Do not fail to follow through. Some people have difficulty in putting their thoughts and facts in a reasonable order. Once all of the investigative leads have been exhausted, look at the overall picture and determine if there is a case. The district attorney will make the final decision on the case and will decide if it is a no-file case or not.

The Sexual Assault Investigation

When called to investigate a reported sexual assault, the investigator needs to get started right away. Physical evidence is very important in a case such as this and it does not have a long life. According to Willot and Allard at the London Metropolitan Police Science Laboratory, the longest time that sperm has been found is reported as follows:

- Vaginal swabs, 120 hours or 5 days
- Rectal swabs, 65 hours or $2\frac{1}{2}$ days
- Anal swabs, 46 hours or less than 2 days
- Oral swabs, 6 hours (9 hours on lips)

It should be noted that sperm on clothing, carpet, or other objects may be identifiable after much longer times because it has been air dried. These samples, however, may be tainted by other agents.

In most cases sent to the investigative unit, the victim will have made a statement to security staff or some other staff before the investigator arrives. Insure that the investigator obtains this statement before he interviews the victim. In some cases the victim may have already been examined by medical staff or at the hospital. Be sure to interview these persons prior to interviewing the victim. These statements can be very valuable in determining if the victim is a real victim.

Victim Interviews

After putting the victim at ease, get a general statement from him concerning the events that surrounded the alleged sexual assault. The investigator needs to give the victim the impression that he is not homophobic. The victim needs to know that the investigator sympathizes with his situation, being in prison, the inmate code, and other circumstances that make it difficult for him to talk. An inmate will often have the feeling that no one cares because he is just a convict. He needs to know that the investigator is serious about investigating the crime and bringing the guilty party to justice. Once an initial rapport is built with the victim, continue to be calm and matter of fact. Once the victim's initial statement is obtained, the investigator should begin to establish not only all the facts, but a time line of events. This time line will be beneficial in corroborating or disputing the victim's testimony. If there is a discrepancy in the victim's statement, do not, at this time, bring attention to it. The investigator will need to reinterview this victim after he has further investigated and interviewed other witnesses and staff.

Suspect and Witness Interviews

If the investigator has a real suspect in the case, there is a high probability that facility security staff have already locked him up and may have already talked with him. If this is the case, the investigator might as well hold off with his interview until he has a full overview of the incident. Find out what statements, if any, the victim has made and get the details of his arrest and interviews.

Once the investigation has been completed interview the suspect. By this time the investigator will have as many of the facts available and may be able to conduct a much better interview. (For information on interviews and interrogations, see Chapter 13.)

When dealing with inmate witnesses, talk to each one separately. The investigator needs to develop some rapport with each inmate prior to questioning. Remember that inmates do not normally like talking with the police and many will not cooperate in any way. One of the key things to remember when questioning any inmate is that the investigator has to ask the question to get the answer. Even the cooperative inmate will not volunteer information. The investigator must be very thorough when asking questions.

Do not forget to interview all of the medical staff involved in the case, including facility medical and the hospital medical staff. The investigator can gain a lot of information from them by asking the right questions. All doctors have a psychology background and may have some insight into the inmate's mentality during postincident treatment.

Remember, interview all available staff and be sure to ask them the right questions. Get detailed statements from them. The investigator will also need to get to these staff while the incident is fresh in their minds. They are a wealth of information. Quite often investigators and supervisors do not include all of their staff in these investigations. Use them, but do not abuse them. Keep them informed and a part of the investigation. No one likes to be left out. If any information obtained from any of these officers proves to be valuable to the investigation, call them and let them know how valuable their information was to the case.

The Crime Scene

The crime scene can produce some of the most important evidence in an investigation. It can substantiate or refute testimony of both the victim and the suspect. The physical evidence can put the suspect at the scene. The lack of physical evidence can point to a false report. Do not overlook any potential evidence. The investigator can never collect too much evidence, but he can fail to collect valuable evidence. (See Chapter 9 for information on crime scenes.)

Check Lists

In any investigation a check list is always valuable. It not only reminds the investigator of many things he needs to do, but it will stimulate his thinking on other things he might do. No check list can be all encompassing so do not try to put everything into the check list. If an investigator chooses not to use a check list, it is important that he keep some sort of chronological list of what he has done. The investigator can refer to that list from time to time and see if he has done everything he needed to do.

Remember that every case is different and these differences will cause the investigator to vary from his list. Below is a partial check list to illustrate a sexual assault case. The investigator should already know what elements constitute a sex crime, so those elements will not be needed as part of the check list. If the investigator does not know these elements, he either needs to get another job or to pull out his statute book.

1. Interview the victim.
   - Where did the crime take place?
   - Get a detailed account.
   - Did the suspect ejaculate?
   - Was there a weapon involved?
   - Were there any witnesses?
   - Did he know the suspect or can he identify the suspect?
   - Did he sustain any injuries or cause any injuries to the suspect?
   - Did the suspect say anything?
   - Did the victim clean up, shower, or have a bowel movement?
   - Did the suspect take anything from the scene?
   - Did the suspect leave anything at the scene?
   - What was the suspect wearing?
   - Get exact time frames and run a time line.
2. Work the crime scene.
   - Black light entire scene.
   - Collect all bedding.

- Vacuum the floor to collect trace evidence.
- Collect the victim's clothes.
- Take hair samples from the victim.

3. Medical
   - Insure that the rape kit is done.
   - Interview medical staff at facility and hospital.
   - Determine if there is trauma associated with the rape.

4. Interview witnesses and staff.
5. Photograph the victim.
6. Work the time line.
7. Interview suspect(s), get trace evidence from suspect(s), or get 41.1 warrant for the suspect (see Chapter 11 for information on warrants). Be sure to include in your 41.1 that a qualified medical staff person will collect the trace evidence.

Get the idea? Put as much as possible into the check list. It can be valuable in helping the investigator remember what he needs to be doing. Do not put off the interviews. Interviews need to be done as quickly and as thoroughly as possible.

Do not forget the tools at the investigator's disposal in the prison setting. Be sure to review all telephone calls made by the victim and any potential suspects in the case. Be sure to put a mail watch on them as well and monitor their mail. All criminals have a tendency to talk about their crimes. The only way they can communicate with the outside world is through the mail, telephone, or during a visit. Inmates also talk among themselves. This is why the investigator needs to interview all potential witnesses.

Figure 5.1a Sexual assault crime scene. The perpetrator entered the cell and forced the victim, at knife point, to drop his pants, telling him he was going to give him birthday present.

Figure 5.1b The perpetrator instructed the victim to lean over the sink while he penetrated him during anal sex. This was to remove them from view of the cell door.

All photos courtesy of the Colorado Department of Corrections.

Prison Undercover Operations

6

Introduction

The following article identifies the undercover cop and the role he or she plays in the investigation of felony crimes.

Shadow Cops*

Crime fighting is both science and art. "Shadow cops" are a prime example of artistic crime fighting. These warriors against crime are the unsung heroes of law enforcement. There is no area of law enforcement more dangerous or perplexing. The undercover cop is placed in harm's way both on and off the job, and he or she must be ready in an instant to become creative or die. The world of the undercover cop is lonely, with little recognition. The rewards come only in the satisfaction of a job well done and prosecution of the suspect. The shadow cop is misunderstood by his fellow officer, hunted by the criminal element and often criticized by his family and friends. The shadow cop works long and irregular hours, sometimes without a break. Unlike "James Bond," these officers are often ill-equipped and have to rely on their wits to remain safe.

Training deficiencies. Not much is written about these dedicated officers and very little structured training is available. Books or study guides are limited to prepare an officer for this assignment. Training manuals or seminars are not available. In addition there is not much in the way of written

* Reprinted from Bell, W., "Shadow Cops," Backup.Com electronic magazine, *www.backup.com*

policy for most departments. Strict written policy might disallow the use of the creativity that is needed to bring the case to a successful conclusion. The information available to young shadow cops is usually disseminated through word of mouth and actual on-the-job training. Anyone writing a "how to" manual for undercover cops would be arming the criminal element with information equal to the "cop killer" antiballistic vest ammunition.

Anything written usually becomes available to the general public, and persons who would utilize that information against these officers would have access. If the secrets of survival were ever to be printed, they would soon flood the Internet and be available to every drug dealer and domestic terrorist group in the country.

Training, if it can be called it that, usually comes after an officer makes the decision to work in a specialized unit that utilizes undercover work. Undercover cops rarely talk the trade, even with their trusted street cop friends. Initially, the rookie will get a list of critical do's and do not's which add little to the knowledge needed to be effective. These rookie shadow cops begin their training by going on missions in other capacities, watching the undercover officers working their trade. Premission and postmission discussions will bring out mistakes or creative ad-libs used by the undercover officer. Watching video footage and listening to undercover telephone conversations can give the new shadow cop an insight as to how a particular officer works. Every situation has specific needs and every situation differs from the last.

So you want to be a shadow cop?   There are no special requirements to do undercover work, only a desire to be part of the elite group of law enforcement officers that go one step further in detecting crime and putting the bad guys away. There are, however, a few things an officer needs to know before he enters shadow land. If you do not think you can do it, you are right, you cannot. Many officers feel that they have the look of a cop, and they do not think they could fool a bandit into believing their counterfeit personas. These feelings should not be overlooked and the officer might rethink his options. Trust your instincts. The truth of the matter is that no one looks like a cop and no one looks like a criminal. The test is in the individual ability of the officer to be believable in the part.

The shadow cop has to be ready to get into the role, whether he has to dress up, dress down or even smell the part. The shadow cop soon learns to walk the walk and talk the talk of the underworld. He must be willing to crawl through garbage to obtain evidence.

Officers who have decided to work in the shadows, must be prepared to give up a good portion of their personal life. Weekends and holidays go by the wayside when working an undercover case. The criminal element does not rest during the holidays and the hours they keep parallel that of a vampire. These creatures of the darkness work their trade hidden from the public eye in avoidance of the law and can rarely be depended on to be on time.

Undercover officers tend to be less supported by their departments. There seems to be a lack of respect for these undercover operatives. This may come from the separation and mystery of the job. When a suited detective walks into the department there is an air of respect. When they solve crimes, they are publically commended for their work. When the undercover officer walks into the department looking like a dirt bag, he is confronted by uniformed officers who do not know he is an officer. His work product is not commonly known within the department and there is no public commendation of his efforts. Working in an undercover capacity disallows the usual camaraderie in police work. You cannot hang out with your police friends as you once did. Your peer group grows further away from you as you continue your shadow work. You cannot confide in them what you are doing and you have to ignore people you run into while working undercover. The smaller your community, the harder it is to have any social life away from the job.

In addition, when you leave shadow work, you are either a hero or a zero. The heroes are those who are unfortunate enough to be injured or killed in the line of duty. The zeroes become strangers when they come back into the world of blue shirts. Most often they have to be retrained and have to develop a new rapport with fellow officers. Somewhere during their stint with undercover work they lose their identity as a cop.

Pitfalls and dangers for the shadow cop.   Police work has a number of pitfalls and dangers that are inherent to the position. The shadow cop, while still facing these problems, inherits a new list of difficulties to deal with. The shadow cop depends largely on his flexibility and wit in keeping himself out of harm's way. The following lists a few of the problems that are unique to the shadow cop. There are a few vague solutions offered, but remember that the vast majority of the methods actually utilized by undercover operatives will remain secret.

Danger #1—"Friendly fire."   When you think of "friendly fire," military operations first come to mind. The undercover officer must always be aware that there are many police officers out there that could mistake the undercover for a felon. According to a global survey of the largest cities in the nation, there have been 12 off-duty or undercover officers killed by police officers during the last decade. Although the experienced undercover officer is not likely to be killed by his brothers in blue, it remains a danger.

Undercover officers should never "John Wayne" or "Lone Wolfe" any assignment. Your team needs to know every move you are making. Always have backup and document every meeting, call, or other communication with the bad guys. Remember you may not be able to identify yourself as a police officer when confronted. Insure that there is someone else that can do that for you without "blowing your cover."

Danger #2—"Personality changes."   In order to convince your suspect that you are indeed a bad guy, you must play a role. Playing your role as a shadow cop often requires the perception of a personality change. The undercover officer has to seem to be what he purports to be. These changes can often carry over into other duties and your family life. It has been discovered that some undercover officers get into the part so well that they become the type of person they are pretending to be. These changes come slowly and are not easily recognized.

Staying in character is necessary only when you are on the job. Keeping close to your family is paramount to keeping your sanity. Drop your facade when you go home. During these undercover times it is very important to stay close to your family. Clean up and visit your station house occasionally. It is important to remember that it is not hard to become the "bandit" you are portraying and you need to have the "real you" available to your family and friends.

Danger #3—"Too close to your prey."   Undercover officers sometimes get too close to their prey. This comes with the social interactions that transpire during the operation. During these social interactions the undercover officer may inadvertently tend to divulge too much personal information that could cause premature discovery. Another adverse effect of getting too personal with your bandit comes twofold. First it may be difficult to close out the operation, knowing you have to arrest someone you have grown attached to. The other and worse effect is the feeling of remorse after the arrest. There sometimes is the tendency to feel guilty about arresting someone that you were so close to or even to begin feeling like a "snitch."

Always remember who you are dealing with. If necessary, read the suspects criminal history, reaffirming his criminality. Keeping in mind that this person is involved in felony crime, you can give him the impression that you care about him and you are friends, but never believe for one minute that you can trust the bad guy. Even while playing your role, keep your mind in the professional mode. If you feel you are getting too close to your suspect, talk it over with your boss or other team members. Getting too close will cause you to make mistakes that can have disastrous results.

Danger #4—"Becoming a criminal."   An undercover officer must always be aware of what is going on during the operation. It is possible to end up in the middle of some criminal activity. The undercover officer may become a witness to a crime or even worse get involved in the commission of a crime during the undercover operation. Although rare, it should be a concern to the alert undercover operative. There are times that you will not be able to affect an arrest during the crime for fear of discovery and possibly death.

This danger area is difficult to express without giving away the secrets of the shadow cops. Generally speaking, you never want to violate the law, departmental regulations, your morals, or your own integrity. Should you become witness to any crime and obviously cannot make an arrest, be sure to report it as soon as possible.

Danger #5—"Exposure."   Most undercover operations are a result of an introduction of the undercover officer by a confidential informant. Sometimes unwitting accomplices are used to gain the trust of the bandit. An unwitting accomplice is someone used in an undercover case without their knowledge. It is extremely dangerous for the undercover officer to use unwitting accomplices. In both of these cases there is a distinct danger of being exposed by your confidential informant or by the bandit checking the unwitting accomplice out. Confidential informants, although reliable to an extent, cannot be trusted with your life.

Common sense should always prevail. Keeping close contact and surveillance of anyone that knows who you are is important. The confidential informant may be only as good as the money he is paid, and if pressed too hard by the bad guys, he will give you up in a minute. Be aware of any changes in the personality of your confidential informants and the suspects. A change in the way they respond to you could mean that they may have some suspicion about you.

Conclusion. These are but a few of the dangers of being a shadow cop, and, for obvious reasons, methods of operation, procedure, and officer safety have not been fully disclosed. The intent of this article is to profile shadow cops and to commend them for the dangerous work that they do. Without the undercover operative, law enforcement as a whole would be significantly less effective. This article is not intended as a tell all on how to operate in the shadows of the criminal world. It is intended to bring awareness to the capacious work of the shadow cop. This secret society will remain a mystery to all but the men and women who have dared to work as shadow cops. Many tricks of the trade and methods employed to keep shadow cops safe were not disclosed here.

Shadow cops are some of the more dedicated officers in the country. It is a very difficult and dangerous job when doing the short-term undercover assignment. Try to imagine going deep undercover where you would have to live within the element and have no immediate backup other than a control agent that can only be reached when convenient. One mistake and you are gone forever with little chance of a prosecution against your killers. These are the true heroes of police work at any level. Be it local, state, or federal jurisdictions, the deep undercover officers are truly the bravest of all police officers.

The Criminal Element

There is only one rule and only one exception when considering allowing yourself to become incarcerated as part of an undercover operation. The rule is **do not ever do it.**

There are reasons why this option should not be considered. The criminal element is a fraternity. This fraternity begins with what is called grade school and escalates through college and on to post-grad school.

- **Grade school**—This criminal fraternity begins in the streets when the criminal is committing crimes. He meets other criminals in a network of conspiracy. This is especially true in drug trafficking. Since over 70% of the caseload in a prison is related to drugs, the intense network of individuals who know one another is an added danger on the street for the undercover officer.
- **High school**—The fraternity has now moved on to the courts and to the county jails. The criminals all know each other and have made both positive and negative connections within the criminal justice system. They know everyone either by personal contact or by visual observation.
- **College**—Somewhere along the line these criminals get convicted and are now serving time in a state penitentiary. They eat, sleep, and conspire together for the remainder of their sentence. They communicate daily and know everything that goes on in the prison. The criminal investigator is inside all of these prisons at one time or another. He will be known. When he arrives, the word goes out and all of the inmates know he is there. Many of them get a very good look at the investigator.
- **Grad school**—Once inmates have been paroled or discharged after serving their sentences, they begin to recommit their crimes. Grad school starts when they return to the courts, go through the county jail, and go back to prison.

Again, these people *all* know each other and they *know the criminal investigator*. It is never safe for an investigator to go undercover inside these institutions. The investigator's cover or life will be lost. It is not safe under any circumstances. The investigator must also understand that the staff that are protecting him may in some way let the cat out of the bag, may not know that he is undercover, or may be connected criminally with the convicts and may purposely expose him.

There are always exceptions to the rule. The one exception to this rule is a short-term undercover operation. This would normally only be conducted during a visit with a convict. Most often some sort of diversionary disguise is used. These particular operations are usually quite safe and normally effective. If the investigator gets burnt, at least his life is not in danger to any great extent. Like any operation, the investigator needs to do a lot of planning to execute an undercover operation in the visiting rooms.

Case History #23

This is an example of one. For this case it was necessary for an undercover officer to go inside a county jail as a visitor.

CID was working a murder for hire case. A confidential informant (CI) that was in the county jail getting ready to reenter the state prison system. He told CID that he had been approached by a county inmate (bandit) who wanted to have his wife murdered. A few phone calls were executed between the bandit and the undercover operative. The bandit was definitely interested, but wanted a face-to-face meeting.

CID knew that, for the success of the case, it was best to have only a few people aware of an undercover operation. So, a supportive shift commander was asked to set up the visit. CID went over the rules and found a few loopholes that could work in introducing the undercover officer to the bandit. The visiting room was wired and only the shift commander was aware of the visit.

CID planned the meeting as a special visit with an out-of-town visitor where there would be no other inmates in the visiting room. The special visit would be conducted as a window visit (noncontact behind glass with telephone communication only). The undercover officer effected a minor disguise. He wore a black watch cap, an army field jacket, a flannel checked shirt with the top button buttoned, and sunglasses. He dyed his hair darker and once more went over the visiting rules with the shift commander.

SWAT training teaches the five "P's": prior planning prevents piss-poor performance? Well apparently CID did not plan as much as they should have done.

The undercover officer entered the staging area for visitors and presented himself as Billy Martinez. The staff officer, unaware of the CID operation, asked him for identification (ID). The undercover officer told him (as suggested) that he did not have any ID and that he had just arrived by bus from out of town. This apparently was okay, but the undercover officer was asked for his date and place of birth. The undercover officer gave his own birth date and a town in New Mexico. Obviously, CID should have researched this prior to entry because Billy Martinez had an outstanding felony warrant. When the staff officer began to question the undercover officer further, the undercover officer knew something was wrong. He was doing okay for a while until he saw the troops gathering behind him. He quickly asked to see the shift commander. The shift commander arrived and in an attempt to wave the undercover officer through without blowing his cover, the shift commander managed to totally anger his entire staff.

At least it appeared that the undercover officer was going to get the visit. The staff called for the inmate and offered the undercover officer a seat until the inmate arrived. At about this time additional visitors began to arrive. The staff called for the undercover officer to visit, but as he was entering the visiting room he was stopped and told he could not wear the clothing he had on. The undercover officer had to remove his sunglasses (even after lying about the prescriptions lenses), his black watch cap, and his army field jacket. He then entered the visiting room to wait for the bandit.

The good Lord must have been smiling on the undercover officer and the bandit was not in jail for being very smart. He was an angry young man who thought that eliminating his wife as the witness/victim of his crime would stop him from going to prison. The case went well and CID managed to salvage the solicitation case.

At no time did our undercover officer feel that he was in any danger (except for the possibility of being arrested on a warrant) during this operation. This would not have been the case if he had attempted to go inside the jail, undercover, as an inmate. There would be no one to turn to and no where to escape danger.

Undercover work is done in many ways. It is done in the streets and inside the prison. Undercover operations inside the prison are done via telephone and written communication. On the streets undercover operations involve civilians who conspire with the convicts to commit crimes.

An undercover operation entails a lot of prior planning. When working with a CI, the investigator should always maintain control. These CIs often put together a plan that dictates who the undercover persona may be. It is always important to do research before entering into an undercover operation. Use the KISS system (keep it simple stupid) when putting together a plan.

Planning an Undercover Operation

An undercover operation, is usually planned after the investigator has gathered intelligence and is actively working the case. The investigative plan may only go far enough to establish probable cause that a crime is being or has been committed. It becomes necessary to establish that "substantial step" toward the commission of the crime before a case can be prosecuted.

This is when the undercover operation becomes a necessity. In order to conduct this operation the investigator will need, at some point, to have direct communication with the suspect. In most of these cases there is a CI that the investigator will probably want to protect. In order to establish this communication, the investigator will need to utilize this CI, but only minimally. An introduction needs to be made to the bandit, and the CI is the investigator's way in. The introduction can be made via mail, telephone, or visit. The least desirable is the visit.

In any undercover operation in which a CI is utilized, the investigator will need to have total control over what the CI is doing and saying inside the prison. Quite often a case goes bad when the investigator does not have control over the CI. Retain exclusive and frequent communication with him. Make sure that no one else is communicating with him about the case.

It is **important** to note that no officer or investigator should ever be forced into an undercover role. If an investigator does not feel comfortable in the role, he should not attempt it. No one is looking for an Oscar-winning performance in this type of work. Be as natural as possible. The bad guy can probably spot a performance. Keep it simple and give the appearance of honesty.

An undercover operative, no matter what the role, should never attempt to give the impression that he is a "real bad dude." The undercover officer should let the bandit know that he does not like violence or weapons. He needs to make the bandit feel comfortable and to be comfortable in his role. The obvious reason for this milder demeanor is that if things go bad, the undercover officer will have the element of surprise.

Although disguise is a method often utilized to alter an investigator's appearance, the best methods are very subtle changes. Keep the dress casual unless the cover is that of a professional, i.e., attorney, or it requires some other specialty dress. If the undercover officer wants to change his appearance, do it as subtly as possible.

During their first few outings most undercover operatives have the underlying feeling that they will be identified as "cops." The undercover officer has already been introduced as someone else, and the inmate wants to believe what he thinks he knows. If the investigator feels that he will be spotted as a cop, he should try a few additional changes. Police officers come in many varieties and there is no special look. One thing they all have in common, though, is that they are usually in pretty good physical shape and speak well. If an investigator wants to hide the fact that he is the law, he should try a slight limp. To ensure that he does not lose his limp in midoperation, he should put a wrap around his knee under his pants to keep the leg stiff. Another way may be to use a slight lisp or other false speech impediment. A particular phrase that is in poor English, e.g., "youse guys," has worked on occasion.

Undercover Operations Inside the Prison

There are times when it will be necessary to conduct the undercover operation inside the prison. This operation needs to be conducted as safely as possible. This means safe for the investigator and the CI. In these operations the identity of the CI will almost always become known to the suspects. Arrangements must be made for the CI to be moved prior to making an arrest.

Inside the prison undercover operations will almost always be conducted through the mail, telephone, and possibly during visits. Undercover operations inside the prison will often be a prelude to a continuing operation that extends outside the walls of the prison.

Mail

To communicate with the bandit through the mail, an investigator needs to establish an undercover mail drop and have some sort of address. The investigator will have to do this through his CI. Try to insure that the bandit initiates the correspondence. This is not always possible as bandits sometimes want to be contacted by the investigator. Inmates have the belief that most incoming mail is read, but outgoing mail is not. All outgoing mail is read, unless it is legal mail.

When the investigator is required to write first, it is important not to say too much in the letter. Sometimes codes are established, but be careful of using coded messages. Unless the investigator establishes cause to believe the bandit knows what the code is, it may be useless in court. If the investigator is using codes that has been established through the CI he will more than likely have to utilize the CI in the courtroom. Each case will differ in what the investigator says to the bandit. If the investigator has control over his CI, he can dictate what is said in these letters more effectively.

The undercover officer needs to have the bandit explain what it is he wants to have done or what crime the undercover officer is supposed to commit. This is sometimes difficult to extract from the bandit. Do not be overanxious to get the bandit to write about the crime. Take some time and establish a rapport with him. If the bandit is serious about committing the crime, he will tell the undercover officer what he wants done. Sometimes the bandit wants the CI to tell the undercover officer what he wants done. The undercover officer will need to relate to the bandit that he wants to work with just him and keep the CI and everyone else out of it. Develop trust between the undercover officer and the bandit. Without trust, the case will not proceed.

During this letter writing, the investigator can be planning the rest of the case. Although the investigator wants to expedite the case, do not be overanxious and do not scare off the suspect. This is sometimes difficult because the inmate wants his "instant gratification" and may lose interest if the undercover officer works too slowly.

Remember that these letters will be needed as evidence. These letters will have to be compared with known samples of the suspect's handwriting. Fortunately, there are several documents in the inmate's file that have been written in his own hand. These documents will be available to the investigator.

Telephone

It is much the same when talking with a suspect on the telephone. The investigator must get the conversation about the crime accomplished, but he will need to be careful how he does it. All inmate phones are taped 24 hours a day. There is also live monitoring of the phone calls. Since the investigator is on an inmate phone, he will not have to tape the call himself, but rather pick it up later. Do not pressure the inmate for information. He will find a way to let the investigator know what he wants.

When utilizing the telephone as a means of communication between the undercover operative and the bandit, remember that the taped conversation is not enough to present in court as evidence. The investigator will need to prove that the voice on the other end of the telephone is that of the suspect. Recognition of the voice needs to be proven. There are several ways to show that the suspect is the person on the other end of the telephone. Usually, the investigator will need more that a few conversations to prove his assertion.

- Each telephone call made by an inmate has a computer printout that shows the inmate used his inmate phone to make a call to a certain number. It shows the time, date, number called, and duration of the call. It identifies the inmate as the person authorized to make the call. (The suspect may use another inmate's phone and make a three-way call to the undercover operative. Unless the other inmate can be identified, no tape of this call will exist. The undercover officer should always tape the call himself at his end.)
- The suspect may identify himself during the conversation.
- The suspect may be using the CI's telephone to contact the undercover officer. If that is the case, the CI will witness the call as it happens. Do not rely solely on the CI for an ID.
- If the investigator knows when the call is going to be made, have a security staff member watching the inmate as he makes the call on the inmate telephone. This will positively identify the suspect.
- Some of these operations take several weeks and even months to complete. During this time the undercover officer may talk with the suspect many times. After these weeks of conversations, he will probably be able to recognize the suspect's voice. Be sure to contact the suspect as soon as possible after the arrest has been made and have a conversation with him. This may help the undercover officer to identify the voice during the conversation. Do not wait, do it while the suspect's voice is fresh in the undercover officer's memory.

Case History #24

CID had an interesting case where the suspect would not talk on the phone about the case. He wanted to have his requests made through the CI and did not want to talk about it on the phone. CID tried to explain to him that sometimes there is some miscommunication when you go through a third party. This was not enough to get the suspect to talk.

During one of the calls CID told him that they had some equipment that would enable a conversation without the department of corrections being able to tape the call. He was told to call the undercover officer back at a certain time and the equipment would be in place.

The suspect called back and the undercover officer told him that the equipment was hooked up, but that they needed to wait a few minutes for the "green light." Apparently the suspect had watched enough television and seemed to understand the workings of this equipment. The undercover officer told the suspect that they now had the green light and he could talk.

The suspect became very talkative at this point and explained how he wanted a judge and a district attorney killed. The suspect gave CID everything needed for the case. Recently, the suspect pled guilty to solicitation to commit first degree murder and is serving a 20-year sentence for that crime.

"Good tactics are tactics that work."

In any operation the investigator has to be flexible and has to do whatever he can to get the job done. If he does not get the facts needed to proceed with the case, then the bandit will find someone else to commit his crime.

Personal Visits

Whether the inmate suspect is contacted via telephone or mail, at some point the undercover officer may have to meet him in person. Some suspects must have a face-to-face meeting to solidify the agreement.

A face-to-face meeting is normally done through a visit. The suspect has to put the undercover operative on his visiting list or arrange a special visit. This can be difficult. An investigator probably has been at that prison facility in the past, so although the risk of injury is minimal during a visit at a prison, the chances of being identified are great.

If the undercover operative knows that he has not been in contact with the suspect or the suspect has never seen him, he may be able to pull it off. He will need to arrange a special visit, during a time when other inmates are not present. During a special visit there are fewer staff and no other inmates in the area. The undercover officer will have to arrange with the facility to have only a selected few staff present that are aware of what is going on.

Once an investigator decides to do the undercover work himself, he should insure that he plans fully for the visit. It may be advisable to discuss a diversion with the suspect that will make him think that the undercover investigator is very professional in his work. An example that has been used in the past is to pose as an attorney. This makes the operation a little easier. The investigator needs to convince the inmate that he is capable of pulling it off. The investigator tells the inmate that he has access to attorney credentials. He tells the inmate to ask for an attorney–client visit. This will enable the investigator to have a very private meeting that is not monitored by security staff. The inmate will then be able to speak freely about the crime.

There will be times that the initial undercover operative will not be able to meet face to face. There are any number of reasons for this: it may be a case where the operative cannot allow any staff to know what is going on, where he is too well known at the facility, or where he may personally know the suspect.

When this occurs a second undercover operative is necessary. Most likely, someone from outside the prison investigations unit will be needed. If the investigation unit has been successful in working with other agencies, this will be no problem.

Although this task may seem simple, there is always the chance that the new undercover operative may not be believable. This may be because of differences in the voice or mannerisms. It may be advisable for the undercover operative to tell the suspect that there is a warrant out for his arrest on a traffic mishap and he cannot come to the prison. He could tell the suspect that he needs to send another person to visit with him. For some reason this is almost always acceptable by the suspect, especially if a female undercover operative is sent in.

Precaution

If a new undercover operative is being used, be sure to follow a few safety precautions:

- Insure that the new undercover operative is familiar with the case.
- Show the undercover operative all the case notes.
- Have the undercover operative review all the telephone communications, listening for quirks or mannerisms (Quite often if there are specific mannerisms or sayings that the orignal undercover operative used, have the new undercover operative use them and the difference in voice will mean little to the suspect.)
- If there is any written communication, make that available to the new undercover operative for review.
- Make sure that the undercover operative has all the information on other suspects and players in the game. If *all* the information is not available, the undercover operative may be at risk of losing the case.
- In any undercover operation, insure that there is proper backup and make sure that the undercover operative is "wired for sound."
- Follow all the rules of safe undercover operations.

Case History #25

This murder for hire case is an example of sending in a second undercover operative for a meeting. This case was not done during a visit at the prison, but it does depict how to introduce a second undercover operative posing as the first. The case involved a prison staff member (bandit) who spoke to an inmate about murdering his wife. He told the inmate that his wife had a new boyfriend and was going to divorce him. He was worried about losing part of his military pension and department of corrections pension. He felt that the only way to prevent any of this from happening was to have his wife murdered. The inmate contacted CID with this information. The initial contacts were made via telephone. The case was progressing rather well and a meeting was set up at a highway rest stop. CID did not receive a photograph of the suspect until the day before the meeting. The assigned undercover operative knew the suspect and had talked to him several months before about another case.

CID had to place a different undercover operative into the mix. The second undercover operative reviewed all the taped conversations, notes, and reports regarding the case. The new undercover operative was made aware of everything related to the case.

When the new undercover operative met with the suspect it initially appeared as though the suspect was a little apprehensive. It only took a few minutes with the undercover operative to use things said during previous conversations for the bandit to become more at ease.

The new undercover operative was able to pull it off. He had a second and third meeting with the suspect and the case came together. The suspect was subsequently convicted of solicitation to commit first degree murder and was sentenced to prison.

It was the first time CID had to change up and send in another undercover operative. CID has had several cases since then where the operative needed to be changed in midstream. Being flexible is the key.

Undercover Operations Outside the Prison

In conducting undercover operations outside the prison walls, there are virtually no differences between the street cop version and the prison version. The only differences may be in how the case is originated: inside or outside the prison walls.

Every undercover operation is unique in some ways. The circumstances leading up to the investigation vary significantly, but the way the operation is run should always remain safe for everyone involved.

Gather Intelligence

Know everyone involved in the case. While gathering intelligence, be sure to do research. Anyone that becomes involved needs to be identified. Use any resources to identify new suspects: driver's license information, criminal histories, utilities checks, visiting records, and phone records. Know who they are, where they live, what they look like, what vehicles they drive, and any criminal history they might have. If possible, find out who their associates are and check if they have been in prison before. This is necessary for the safety of the undercover operative. It is possible that the undercover operative may have run across the outside bandit while he was incarcerated. The inmate suspect will most likely have set up the introduction for the undercover operative. If this is the case, check the inmate's mail and phone calls for information. If he has, for example, called the person to set up the meeting, the undercover operative will have the advantage of knowing what he has said. The conversation may give an indication of whether trust has been developed between the undercover operative and the inmate suspect. The undercover operative may find, as in many cases, that the inmate may embellish his trust for him in order to get this person to meet with the undercover operative and continue the criminal act.

Location of Operation

At some time in the investigation, the undercover operative may plan to meet with another suspect to solidify the case. The undercover operative may be buying drugs, selling drugs, making arrangements for a homicide, or arranging the commission of another crime. Always try to make the location familiar to the undercover operative. If the location is unfamiliar to the undercover operative, insure that he has time to find the location and decide if it is suitable for the safety of the operation. Allow enough time for the undercover operative to do some reconnaissance.

Preoperation Planning

Once intelligence has been gathered and the meeting has been set up with the outside bandit, it is time to do presurveillance. This will include having a team at the meeting location to do the presurveillance. They will be looking for the best place to set up and record the meeting. They will also be looking for countersurveillance and any other obstacles.

Another team will be running surveillance on the suspect the undercover operative is to meet. They will observe him at his location and follow him to the meeting place. They will record any stops or meetings and look for additional countersurveillance. Another team will maintain surveillance on the bandit's original location (home) to see what traffic or additional people may be at the home. They may have someone else that will follow the suspect to look for the undercover operative's surveillance.

Who Are You?

Whenever planning an undercover operation, the undercover operative will need to assume the identity of someone other than himself. Be sure to make it a very simple story. The simple things mean a lot. Make sure the undercover operative gives himself a name that he can remember. It is often a good idea to use his own first or middle name. This is where control of the CI is very important. The CI may want to go to extremes when putting together a cover story. The undercover operative needs to control the CI and make sure that he will not have to remember a whole bunch of facts. Make sure the CI does not give any physical description of the undercover operative in case other undercover operatives are used down the line. Although the undercover operative can be who ever he wants, do not ever try to pass him off as an ex-convict. All convicts know each other and it will create a lot of questions for the bandit that the undercover operative may have difficulty answering.

Basic Needs

The undercover operation should be no different than any other tactical operation. Be prepared for every event. This means a lot of preplanning. An operation plan should be in place that includes adequate backup. Audio and visual electronic surveillance should be used, if possible. There should be an audio and a visual bust signal, an audio and visual emergency signal, and an audio and visual signal to abort the mission. The reason for having both audio and visual signals is that the electronic equipment could fail. The undercover operative may need help and his signal for help may not be heard. All of these signals should be created by the undercover operative. It has to be signals that he is familiar with or wants to use. The undercover operative is in charge of the mission under all circumstances. It is his life that is on the line and only he can determine what needs to happen. He may see something or know something the other investigators do not know. The plan should include contingencies for every conceivable outcome. Insure that there is uniformed backup, medical assistance, and additional help available in case of an emergency.

Always have an investigator assigned to note taking. A chronological accounting of every event should be made. There are things that happen off camera or out of range of the transmitter that have to be recorded.

No two undercover operations are exactly the same. Many problems and changes may have to be made immediately. Be the most ready for an early bust signal or an emergency call. In the event that the bandit wants to move or change location for some reason, the general rule of thumb is not to move. If a move was not in the original plan, do not do it. Sometimes it could mean that the bandit does not trust the undercover operative or he has some plans for him. Normally, this will be discussed prior to the operation. The question "What if he wants to move?" will come up. There are considerations that have to be discussed. Is there enough surveillance for the trip to occur? Is air support available? Face it, when a move occurs control of the operation is lost. If the undercover operative is going to move, insure that he does the driving. This will insure that he will not lose his surveillance team and it will be more difficult for the bandit to discover the surveillance. It is very difficult to maintain surveillance of a moving vehicle and even more difficult if the driver of that vehicle is looking for a tail.

Many other questions are asked prior to the operation. What if the undercover operative decides to get into a car with the bandit and move? What if the undercover operative thinks he needs to move and the surveillance team really does not want to blow the case? What happens then? The answers to these questions are not easy, but the mission is not as important as the safety of the undercover officer. An immediate decision has to be made. The investigator must decide if there are enough surveillance teams to insure that the undercover operative will not be lost. This is a question that cannot be answered. The investigator needs to stop the move. There is an option that may work that will not ruin the case. If the investigator has a good operation going, he will have a uniformed backup nearby. Follow the suspect and the undercover operative while contacting the uniform car. Have the uniform car make a pretense stop and run both occupants of the car through the computer. If the bandit does not have a warrant, arrest the undercover operative on a traffic warrant and let the bandit go. The investigator has stopped the move and maybe, if he is lucky, saved the mission.

Vehicles, in general, are dangerous in these operations. It is a 3000-lb weapon. Always try to make the arrest prior to anyone starting to drive off in an arrest situation. If the undercover officer is in a moving car with the bandit, and the bandit spots the surveillance and tries to elude them, the investigator has a moving 3000-lb piece of metal that will put the undercover officer, the civilian population, surveillance teams, and everyone in danger.

When working an undercover operation there are occasions when the bandit wants to search the undercover officer for a wire. Do not ever let anyone search the undercover officer. If he has done his lead in properly, he can tell the bandit not to touch him. If the bandit does not trust the undercover officer, do not do the deal. There are many issues that may arise during a undercover operation. The undercover operative has to think quickly on his feet. Quick talking will keep him alive. The undercover operative should trust his instincts.

Going back to location for a minute. When setting up the location for the operation, a really good rule of thumb is never to go to the suspect's house. The undercover operative may have to be in the suspect's neighborhood, but he does not have to be in his house. There are exceptions, but try to make it a hard, fast rule. When the undercover officer is lost from sight, things can go bad.

Case History #26

Narcotic officers were working a young wanna-be drug lord. He was a tweeker (methamphetamine [meth] user) and was wired up. One of the narcotic officers was going to make a buy from him. The narc was wired and had plenty of cover. The problem was that the undercover narc had to go to the dealer's home to make the purchase. This was a relatively new group of narcs. The wire was checked and rechecked and the plan was laid out. If the wire went bad, the cover narcs would give the undercover narc a maximum of 20 additional minutes in the house and then they would hit the place. The cover narcs had no visual on the inside of the home as all the windows were shaded. The cover narcs checked for countersurveillance, but had to remain hidden. This place had a lot of traffic. A lot of things could have happened and the narcs knew it. There was concern about another buyer coming to the house and knowing that the undercover narc was a cop. The narcs had a few weak contingency plans, but did not expect what happened.

The undercover narc entered the house. The wire was working great and things were progressing smoothly. After about 5 minutes the wire stopped working. The cover narcs could not hear what was going on and sent officers to the doors and windows to see if they could hear anything.

Within 18 minutes the undercover narc emerged from the house. He gave the bust signal, indicating they were armed. The house was hit hard and fast. Arrests were made and a large amount of meth, some cocaine, and a little cash were confiscated. Some long guns and a .45 caliber semiautomatic pistol were also recovered.

Well, what the narcs did not know was that the wanna-be dealer was high on meth. Once in the house he quickly reached for the undercover narc to pat search him. He apparently hit the wire and caused the signal to be lost. The undercover narc began to resist and the suspect put a gun down his throat, screaming that he was a pig. The undercover narc kept his cool and kept talking. The wanna-be dealer searched him and did not find the wire. After some conversation, the undercover narc calmed down the suspect and they made the deal. The undercover narc came out of the house with the dope and gave the signal.

This was the last time this undercover narc went in anywhere unarmed. He made the decision not to go armed on this trip and it was the right one. He kept his cool, kept talking, and kept himself alive. He was lucky the wire was not spotted because things could have turned out differently. As said before, the undercover narc is in charge, but make sure you do not lose sight of him. During follow-up discussions he related how he kept talking and kept thinking. He said he was considering trying to disarm the suspect. He planned on throwing the bandit out the window to get the attention of the cover narcs. He could have done it, maybe.

Officer in Trouble

In any undercover operation, much like tactical operations, the investigator must improvise, adapt, and overcome. This does not mean that mistakes are made that put people in danger. Lose the case, not a fellow officer.

There is another issue that prison investigators, security officers, street investigators, and street cops in general must never forget. Not only are they always under the scrutiny of the public, but they are always potential targets for retaliation. The prison investigator is particularly vulnerable, in that the convicts know who he is and have access to personal information about him. The best way to illustrate this is to offer yet another article written for a national electronic magazine that illustrates the problem and offers some precautions an officer can utilize.

Officer in Trouble—When the Hunter Becomes the Hunted [*]

Dedicated police officers are tenacious individuals with the instincts of a hunter stalking their prey. Like the hunters, they utilize all of their knowledge, skill, and senses when going after criminals. Respected by their peers, congratulated by their citizens, and feared by the criminal element, these dedicated crime fighters put themselves in harm's way while protecting the population they serve.

One might think that, because the criminal investigated is safely in prison, the officer is immune to confrontations outside the workplace. But, remember the criminal network. There is likely to be someone the bandit knows on the outside who may cause harm to the officer. After all, each officer has the resources of his or her entire department behind them and the courts take a dim view of criminals acting out against officers of the court. Unfortunately, cases where off-duty officers have become victims are on the increase. This may be in response to the increasing violence in our communities. Today's criminal is more sophisticated, more violent, and more dedicated to criminal activity than ever before. When an officer has become a target, there have been a variety of responses by the individual officer and the departments they served. There are no specific guidelines or training offered to officers that experience such action.

A sad fact is, though, that many officers have suffered greatly by this lack of preparation. They may have underreacted by not doing anything or overreacted in some way that hindered prosecution or caused unnecessary grief to officer and family. In either case the results have sometimes been devastating.

A case in point was in the late 1960s or early 1970s a Detroit police officer had been involved in a series of fatal shootings. Each of these shootings were deemed justifiable but took on a different appearance when he became a target for a local militant group. There were "WANTED DEAD" posters placed throughout the city with his photograph attached. This officer did take precautions and did take the threat seriously. He did not seem to overreact and continued his work assignment. One evening while driving home, this officer

---

[*] Reprinted from Bell, W.R., "Officer in Trouble—When the Hunter Becomes the Hunted," Backup.Com electronic magazine, *www.backup.com*.

noticed a car following him. He had his police radio with him and called one of his fellow officers to respond should he need help. As he sped down the I-94 freeway it was obvious that the car was chasing him. The car began to ram his vehicle. He again called for assistance and continued on. Finally, another off-duty officer, assigned to his unit, came into view and radioed that he was ready to help. They decided to pull off the freeway and block the suspect vehicle in between their two vehicles. They accomplished this without incident and the officer got out of his vehicle and armed himself. He ordered the suspect, who was a rather large male, out of his vehicle. The suspect exited his car, screaming and charging the officer. The officer yelled several times to stop and when it was apparent he was not going to stop but continue his charge, the officer fired his weapon once, striking and killing the suspect. This officer was no longer the victim, although he initially felt that he had acted in self defense. The media frenzy that followed did not help his cause and incited the public against him. What was not immediately apparent was a terrible mistake he had made after the postshooting. This officer, realizing that he had just shot an unarmed man, (according to court documents) pulled a knife from his pocket and laid it near the body of the suspect. He made statements that the suspect was armed, which could not be corroborated by the other officer. In the end this officer was convicted and sentenced to prison. In retrospect it would appear that his fear overwhelmed his sense of good judgement and he made the mistake of his life.

The purpose of this article is to bring attention to the fact that a police officer can become a target and become the hunted. It may also serve as a resource for suggestions on what an officer might do if he or she becomes the target for retaliation. What the officer must do is be prepared for such an incident and act with all the professional, moral, and legal methods they would use during their normal course of duty. They need to insure that they not only protect themselves, but their family, friends, and neighbors. They need to use common sense and be guided by good moral judgement and law. In addition, this article illustrates some of the methods employed by other "hunted" officers in coping with and defending against these unwarranted attacks on their privacy, safety, and well-being.

It is important to understand that no matter what methods the officers employ to protect themselves and their families, anyone can be had. This is best illustrated by the fact that in recent years there have been successful attacks on the president of the United States. No one else in the free world has more protection and safeguards in place than the president, yet he too is not safe from the dedicated assassin.

One of the first actions taken in any threat, perceived or real, is to report it to your immediate supervisor. This action serves a dual purpose. First, you have notified, through your chain of command, a possible threat. Second, during your conversations you might realize that the threat bears no particular significance but remains documented.

Keep in mind that every threat should be taken seriously. In today's society people are capable of more violence than ever before. Discuss the threats with your peer group. Other officers may have experienced similar behavior and may have some insight into your particular threat.

Should the threat give the appearance of being genuine, an investigation should be commenced. If at all possible you should monitor the investigation throughout the case. Do not take the role of lead investigator when dealing with a personal threat.

It may be difficult, but you should never confront the perpetrator of these threats. This may be personal to you, but you must not act independently from your department. A threat is just a threat and does not become a matter for the courts until there is an overt act. Do not diminish your chances of a successful conclusion by confronting the suspect. Treat it as any other investigation. Use the tools available to you as a police officer and remain outside the on-line investigation. Should you get personally or emotionally involved, your chance of a successful prosecution is slim.

An officer should not wait until he or she becomes a target to build safeguards against the criminal element. The officer should always be prepared and aware. The first and very basic element of preparedness is honing your survival skills. Keep yourself in good physical shape, practice your defensive tactics, engage in strength training, and go beyond the required weapons training.

Being aware of your surroundings is always a must. Do not limit your awareness to on-duty hours. Always know where you are, escape routes, who is in the area, what you can do if confronted, what communications are available, and what arsenal is available. On-duty officers are almost always observant, but they must maintain their observations continuously.

In most homes, families engage in the practice of safety. They remove dangerous items from their children's reach and sometimes practice fire drills. They have emergency poison control, ambulance, and police numbers on their speed dial. They have fire extinguishers, smoke and gas detectors, and dead bolts on their doors. These families plan for the protection of their children by instilling practices like "never talk to strangers," "don't ever get into a vehicle with anyone," and "don't go with anyone except a trusted family member."

Most police families are the same. They tend to protect against the obvious, yet they fail to do any preventative planning for being a victim. Any officer should make contingency plans for a home invasion or other possible off-duty problems.

In discussions with officers who have been the target of "murder for hire" plots, there were many different methods they employed to safeguard against these threats. They obviously were dependent on the severity of the threat imposed. Some of these measures may seem extreme and all of these measures are offered as a suggestion only.

Countermeasures.   Many of these countermeasures should become second nature. While most officers are on-duty they are very observant and are always on the alert to crime and danger. Many officers run scenarios through their head while patrolling in the "what if" mode. Always looking for escape routes, what they might do and communicating the danger to fellow officers. This should be carried over into their normal routine off-duty as well. Becoming complacent can be the biggest danger to an officer.

- Always be aware of vehicles and persons at your back. Changing your routes to and from work and shopping is advisable. Plan for actions you will take if you are being followed. Always keep in mind that you should attempt to get backup when engagement of the suspect is imminent. If you suspect you are being followed, never take the suspect toward your home.
- Communication is essential. Always have a cell phone or other communication (police radio) in your vehicle with you and insure your family has the same ability. Keeping a cell phone in your home is advisable should your phone service be disrupted. (A home invasion may be preceded by disruption of phone service.)
- Have locks installed on your bedroom doors. During an actual home invasion, keeping your family in a locked room with communications and defensive ability is always a good idea. You may need to engage the suspects and this will give your family additional safety and time to call for help. Make sure you have a secret password for reentering the room your family is in.
- Make sure your locking devices on your home are satisfactory and in good working order. Insure that your home is locked whether occupied or not.
- Be very aware of your surroundings when approaching your home. Look for suspicious or out-of-place people and vehicles.
- If you do not have the ability to secure your vehicle in a locked garage and the threat is severe, sprinkling sugar, salt, or sand around your vehicle will help in determining if anyone has approached your vehicle. Sometimes invisible crime detection spray around the vehicle can be utilized. (This can be picked up under black light.)
- Install security lights around your home that are motion sensitive.
- Never answer the door unless you know who is there or you are prepared to defend yourself.
- Especially in the evening hours, keep your blinds closed and do not expose yourself or your family to open windows. In daylight hours always observe outside when passing an open window area. (If you can not see out [dark out-light in], people can see in.)
- You should always be careful what neighbors you might confide in. You do not want to upset your neighbors, but you need the extra protection of nearby assistance in identifying suspicious persons. In many cases other law enforcement officers may live near. These officers would be ideal to confide in. It may be advisable to join the neighborhood watch program rather than worrying your neighbors about your own difficulties. While working with the watch program you can suggest methods that would support your personal needs.

- Never enter into any pattern of behavior. For example, if you like to go for dinner on a certain day to a certain restaurant, don't. Change the day or restaurant when possible. Changing patterns makes it more difficult to become a target. There are routines that you will not want to change. Going to church is an example of a routine you would not want to change. Just be sure to watch your surroundings and utilize your skill as a police officer to insure the safety of you and your family.

Remember that how you react to the threat of danger is directly proportional to how your family, friends, and neighbors will react. Keep from creating fear and paranoia within your family by maintaining a professional demeanor and a positive attitude. Make sure they realize that the threat is most likely *only* a threat, created to instill fear and gain control of the officer. Let them know that these precautions are merely a means to better protect your family and not to disrupt your lives. Let them know that there are many people concerned for your safety and always on the lookout for any perceived threat.

Figure 6.1 Surveillance photograph of a meeting to discuss the murder of a district attorney. This vehicle was given as collateral for this murder.

Figure 6.2 During this meeting the undercover operative pretends to look around for police.

Figure 6.3 Actual surveillance photograph of an undercover prison investigator meeting with the "money man" to receive payment for the maiming of a district attorney and intimidation of witnesses.

Figure 6.4 This surveillance photograph of one of the suspects is where she spots the surveillance van. She later discounts it as a threat and hires the undercover officer to kill the district attorney.

All photos courtesy of the Colorado Department of Corrections.

Confidential Informants

7

Introduction

The use of confidential informants is common practice in every law enforcement arena. The general guidelines in using confidential informants are also universal. This commonality ceases, though, when dealing with an inmate in a correctional facility. It is hard enough to protect a confidential informant on the streets, but in the prison setting it is a life-threatening situation. In the "inmate code," "snitching" is taboo. Most inmates would give up information if it suited them, but the threat if exposed is real. The punishment by their peers is often death.

There are some general guidelines for the use of inmates as confidential informants. A confidential informant is any individual, not connected to law enforcement, that is willing to give information or actively participate in a criminal investigation. Most certainly, these individuals have a close connection with crime. The inmate informant, of course, is always connected to crime. These are persons who, under the direct supervision of a specific investigator and with or without expectation of compensation, furnish information on criminal activity or provide a lawful service for a law enforcement agency.

Other sources of information also come into the prisons. Sometimes family members of inmates will call with information for a variety of reasons. Sometimes information comes in the form of an anonymous letter or telephone call. Anonymous complaints should not be considered reliable. In the streets, officers never act on information without verifying or corroborating it. It is even more necessary in the prisons to verify and corroborate any and all information received from inmates or family and associates of inmates. Remember, inmates and their pals will set up an investigator in a heartbeat.

The obvious reasons for using an informant are to gather information and take the case to a logical conclusion. If the investigator understands the inmate mentality, he will have a better chance of using the informant and not being used by the inmates.

Information from the Informant

Some typical information inmates have offered in the past follows:

- Basic intelligence on a wide variety of crimes.
- Who the perpetrator or perpetrators are.
- Motive for the crime.
- What groups are involved in the criminal activity.
- Where evidence can be found.
- When a crime is going to take place.
- Information concerning staff misconduct.
- Information about violations of rights or rules.
- General complaints about prison.

Reasons Convicts Give Information

When using inmate informants, try and determine what their motive is for giving information. Wait for the inmate to give the information and then ask him why he is giving it. His motive probably will not satisfy the question, but it is not critical to the investigation. Investigators should be aware of some of the motives for coming forward.

Investigators have experienced a number of motives, some hidden. Frequently inmates will tell the investigator that they are tired of being in prison and now want to "go straight," that "I have always hated drugs," that "It's not right what they are doing," or that "I am afraid if they get away with it the guards will come down on all of us." The investigator would normally suspect that the reason is not valid with these responses. The following list of motives is taken from case histories and have actually been used by inmates. These are but a few and some remain a mystery. Looking at this short list may give the investigator some insight to the inmate.

- Inmates provide information to take the heat off themselves or to direct attention elsewhere.
- The target poses a threat and the inmate needs to get him out of the way.
- The inmate owes money or favors to another inmate.

- The inmate wants to create a protective custody issue by getting a "snitch jacket" put on him. This motive is usually disguised. Inmates have come forward with information that is of no value to anyone. Then they will go to their case manager and tell him that they have been working for the Criminal Investigation Division (CID) and need to be moved before they get killed. It usually is unfounded, and they are using the CID to get moved.
- Frequently, another inmate drug dealer passes information to get a rival dealer busted.
- Quite frequently, there will be bad blood between inmates and information is passed by the revenge seeker. It could also be a fear he has from a rival dealer or another inmate. (Remember that the fear the inmate has for this other inmate may be so strong that he changes his mind and sets up the investigator.)
- Inmates will want to be moved to a different facility or to look good for the parole board, and they will give information to show that they are a good person.
- As in the streets, inmates facing disciplinary action within the facility will give information for reduced charges. This occurs when felony street charges are forthcoming.
- Inmates give information because they enjoy the excitement of being involved in a dangerous situation.
- Inmates give information in order to acquire information.
- Inmates give information that is false in an attempt to set up another inmate, staff member, or even the investigator.
- Occasionally, an inmate will give information because he likes a particular officer.

Confidential Informant Safety

Whenever an investigator uses an inmate confidential informant, he should identify how far he wants to use him. If it is just information for intelligence purposes, the investigator will not put him in any jeopardy. If the informant is used where he will be actively participating in an investigation, the investigator must prepare for his safety. First put together the investigative plan. The warden of the facility and the security manager should be advised so they can be prepared for an emergency (they do not need any surprises). Offender services or whoever controls inmate movement and classification should be notified and the investigator must get prior approval to have the informant moved when it becomes necessary. The inmate should have a contact person inside the prison he can go to immediately if he runs into a problem.

These steps are a must. An investigator cannot wing it because of the danger to the informant and to the facility. Do not forget this.

Do's and Do Not's of Confidential Informant Use

In dealing with an inmate who is a confidential informant (CI), follow a list of do's and do not's:

Do

1. Do make the initial contact with the CI. It is usually not a good idea to meet with him at the prison.
   a. Contact him outside the prison using a medical or other ruse.
   b. Use the telephone to make contact.
   c. Use any means to ensure that no other inmates and few staff know of the meeting.
2. Do make the most of your future contacts via telephone.
3. Do stress the importance of truthfulness.
4. Do verify everything the CI says. Do not ever trust any information on face value. It will come back to haunt the investigator later.
5. Do be available at all hours in case of an emergency. That is why using the telephone is valuable.
6. Do be sure to ask the right questions. As in interviews, it is important to realize that a CI will give the information he wants to. He will know more and will not offer information unless the right questions are asked.
7. Do let the CI know that there is always the possibility that he may have to testify. If he balks at the thought of testifying, rethink using him.

Remember that when using an inmate informant, it is unlikely that the investigator will be able to remove him from any future steps in the case. For example, sometimes two or three additional undercover operatives are introduced during an investigation. This gives the appearance that someone other than the informant has given the bandit up. In the streets it is possible to introduce new undercover people, but it is more difficult in prison.

Understand that the informant will become known to the bandits at some point after the arrests are made. There is only one direction that the finger will point—to your informant! The informant needs to know this.

Do Not

1. Do not use an informant within the prison unless there is no other way to solve the case.

2. Do not continue to use an inmate informant if his cover has been blown.
3. Do not divulge any information to the informant that is not necessary for him to have.
4. Do not become too involved with the informant. The investigator can be friendly but not friends.
5. Do not make any promises that cannot be kept. Remember that the district attorney is the only one who can offer a plea agreement. The investigator can only advise that he will talk to the DA on the informant's behalf.
6. Do not refer to the informant by name or any other identifiable information. Give a number to the informant and use that.
7. Do not use the terms "informant, snitch, stoolie, or pigeon" or other terms in the presence of the inmate.
8. Do not fail to consider the motive and interest of the informant when estimating reliability.
9. Do not permit the informant to break the law.
10. Do not, if there are any promises or contracts, fulfill any promise until there are verifiable results.
11. Do not overuse an inmate informant. It is easy to do when the information is pouring in and the results are good.
12. Do not fail to verify all information received from the informant.
13. Do not ever permit the inmate informant to take charge of any aspect of an investigation. Always maintain control. If the investigator has an informant he cannot control, gain control or dump him.

These are just a few of the guidelines the investigator should adopt when using an informant. Remember that the security of the facility where the inmate is housed is of utmost importance. Never do anything within a prison that would breach that security. That is why it is important to work with the warden and his staff at a facility.

Because of the danger to inmates and staff, an inmate will rarely, if ever, be used in an undercover capacity. Only on rare occasions will an investigator send an undercover informant into a facility or use an unwitting accomplice in the prison environment. However, sometimes extreme measures have to be taken in a prison investigation.

Case History #27

CID had a case not too long ago that involved a staff member bringing drugs to inmates. A CI came forward with the information. This was a case where the informant claimed to be rehabilitated from drugs and now was against drugs. His motive was never confirmed.

The staff member would only talk with the inmate that was getting drugs from him. The other inmates receiving drugs would not talk to each other about the drugs. The CI was asked to gain the trust of the staff member and talk about drugs with him. Within a few days, the CI reported back that he had been talking with the staff member. He told the staff member that things were dry and he had not been able to score drugs with any of the inmates and was wondering if he could help him out.

The CI reported back that it did not seem as though the staff member was going to bite. The CI was told to go back and tell the staff member that he had some drugs available through his uncle, but had no way of bringing them in. He was then to offer money to the staff member to bring in the drugs to him. The staff member told the CI that he was not a drug dealer.

What was interesting was that the staff member did not report the request to bring in the drugs to his supervisor and did not write an incident report on the request.

CID tried several other approaches with the CI making different requests of the staff member. The staff member never agreed to do anything, but never reported the inmate. In the mean time, the CI reported that the staff member had just brought in another load of drugs to another inmate. CID could not corroborate this information, because, if a urine test was done on the other suspect, the staff member would find out.

One evening CID received a telephone call from the CI. He reported that the staff member had brought him a teener ($\frac{1}{8}$ oz) of marijuana and about 1 g of cocaine. The staff member said that since it was the holidays he thought he would help him out. The staff member told the CI that he could pay him with about ten tokens so that he could get a couple of sodas. (This facility used the token system of money exchange. Inmates would order tokens from the canteen and use them in the vending machines located about the prison.)

Well, this presented a problem. CID only had the inmate's word that the staff member gave him the dope. There was no telephone or written communication between the staff person and any inmate. The staff member would only talk with the person he was dealing with. The staff member would not take drugs on a reversal even if he did not have to pay for them. CID did not know his supplier and had virtually no corroboration on what the inmate (CI) was saying. (CID did have some hot urinalyses from that work area, but not enough evidence to support an investigation.)

Now CID had drugs allegedly from the staff member. The CI was smart enough to preserve the evidence for latent prints. Realistically, given the small size and material used to package the drugs, it was doubtful that any latent prints would be found. The drugs were picked up from the CI tested positive for marijuana and cocaine. The package was checked for latent prints. CID needed to be innovative, quick, and ready with a plan.

The staff member's supervisor was aware of the investigation and assisted wherever he could. On occasion, he allowed the CI to use his telephone to call the CID. Sophisticated surveillance equipment was not available. If CID did borrow the equipment, it would be near impossible to install without being observed by someone. An old mini-cassette tape recorder was available. The CI was instructed to engage the staff member in conversation. He was to ensure that they talked about the quality of the drugs (identifying them), and he was to pay the staff member the tokens for the drugs.

It was a comedy of errors: trying to get the recorder into the prison, getting it placed on the informant's body where it would not be seen, getting the staff member to talk with him about the drugs, and insuring the tokens he gave the staff member made noise on the table when the CI paid him.

It actually went much better that expected. The staff member had no problem talking about the quality of the drugs or about his own infrequent use of marijuana and cocaine. He thanked the CI for the tokens and agreed to bring in future drugs.

Future conversations between the staff member and the CI did not amount to much and it appeared that CID was pushing the envelope by leaving this informant at the facility. The staff member was called in for an interview and told that he would be directed to submit to a urinalysis. The staff member was confronted with the evidence and quickly wrote out a confession. His urinalysis came back hot for marijuana. The staff member was terminated and charged with introduction of contraband. The informant was moved out of the facility. In this case, since it was a staff member involved, the CI may never have received any heat from other inmates, but CID could not take any chances.

This was a case where CID had to change the guidelines and actually use the inmate in an undercover capacity. Keep in mind that the situation sometimes dictates tactics. "Good tactics are tactics that work." As in any case, investigators have to have the flexibility to operate. That flexibility is needed to ensure that the investigation is brought to a logical conclusion.

As previously stated, sometimes the investigator may have to divulge the identity of the informant. This usually occurs when the informant's testimony is critical to the case. That is why it should always be clear to the informant that he may have to testify. On the other hand, if the informant is used as little as possible and his testimony is not critical, the investigator has a better chance of protecting the identity of that informant.

Legislation Protection for Informants

There is some Colorado legislation that assists in protecting the confidential informant.

1. A defendant does not have an absolute right to disclosure of an informant's identity.

2. Defendants must make at least a minimal showing of need for disclosure.

3. The courts will weigh the following:

   a. Was the informant an eyewitness or ear witness to the criminal transaction? Is the informer himself available or could, in the exercise of reasonable diligence, he be made available?

   b. Are other witnesses in the transaction available to testify? Does the informer's testimony vary from other witnesses' testimony drastically?

4. *People v. Garcia* (Colorado 1988). Informants can be produced for an on-camera interview with the judge only. Only the defense is allowed to give the judge questions to ask.

5. Crime Stoppers, Colorado Revised Statute 16-15.7-104. Informers privilege protects the identity of persons who furnish law enforcement officers with information. It does not protect against disclosure of unnamed persons who give information to a confidential informant, who then give it to police.

6. Privilege can be used to protect the identity of persons whose safety would be jeopardized by the disclosure, but more than that bare assertion of danger is needed. (This should almost always be applicable to inmates.) *People v. District Court*, 904 P2D874P.2D (Colorado 1995).

Reliability of Informants

- An inmate's reliability can be shown by the fact that an investigator has used him in the past and the information given was proven to be truthful.
- The inmate has been an informant for another investigator or agency and again the information was proven to be truthful.
- The inmate has been a paid informant in the past and the information has proven reliable.

An investigator should develop his own network of informants to assist in gathering information. He should always treat informants with respect and always be honest with them. The investigator's demeanor is important in gaining the informant's respect. Even if their information is not valuable, keep the respect flowing. The investigator never knows when he might need the informant again. Do not go out and try to solicit informants, they will come to the investigator. While interviewing inmates, remember that they could be future informants. Keep in mind during interviews of the suspect that he may turn in some valuable information.

Case History #28

Not too long ago, an inmate attempted to give some information to an investigator. The information was bogus and could not be verified. The inmate irritated the investigator, who blew him off, and not too nicely. Anyway, about 6 months later the same inmate gave some really great information to another investigator. As a result, the investigator cleaned up some serious drug activity and is now working a murder for hire case. The first investigator did not follow the advice described.

It cannot be stressed with enough importance to keep control of the inmate informant during an investigation. The investigator will not be able to monitor the informant's actions or the actions of the bandits without letting too many people know about the investigation. Be sure to take precautions in protecting the inmate informant and the integrity of the investigation. This can be done by monitoring the informant's mail and phones. The investigator should already be monitoring the bandits phone and mail communication. If inside staff are working with the investigator, make sure they report any activity involving not only the bandit, but also the informer.

Remember again that inmates will never work a case with an investigator without a payoff. The reason may never become apparent, but believe that there is one.

Informant Procedures

The investigation agency should have some procedures and guidelines for its investigators when utilizing confidential informants. Inmate informants should have special rules as well. The use of confidential informants is important to the satisfactory completion of many investigations. Procedures should be established to provide for this resource within a controlled system in order to avoid abuse and to minimize any adverse impact. Investigators should take additional precautions when dealing with informants of the opposite sex and with informants whose sexual preferences may make an investigation more susceptible to compromise through alleged improprieties.

Investigators should be cautioned to avoid forming any type of personal relationship with a confidential informant. Among the suggested prohibitions are:

- Providing the investigator's home phone number to a confidential informant.
- Engaging in any sexual or sexually related contact with a confidential informant.

- Being related to or developing a personal relationship with a confidential informant.
- Socializing off duty with a confidential informant.
- Participating in any form of off-duty employment with a confidential informant.

There is the potential for any information provided to an informant to end up with the criminal element. For this reason, investigators should continually monitor and limit their informant's contact to a select few investigators and should provide as little information as possible concerning investigations and tactics to their informant.

Standards of Conduct for Informants

The potential for injury and for evidence being destroyed is increased when the informant is not in control of his own faculties. Rules of conduct should be established when working a confidential informant. Some suggested rules are do not use an informant if:

- He is under the influence of alcohol.
- He is under the influence of a controlled substance.
- He is under the influence of prescribed controlled substances.
- He is found to be in possession of a controlled substance.
- He has custody issues with another inmate.
- He has a history of being unreliable.

The investigator may find other rules necessary that will enable him to maintain control of his informant. Do not make the rules so strict that the informant may become ineffective.

Restricted Use of Informants

The investigating agency should restrict the use of certain informants.

- Persons under the age of 18 years should have written permission from their parents or guardian.
- Persons on probation or parole who have been proven unreliable in the past should be used with caution.
- Informants who have failed to meet set qualifications and who have violated any standards of conduct for the agency should not be trusted.

Documentation of Informants

It is necessary to document confidential informants. An investigator should maintain this file in a confidential manner. A personal information sheet might contain the following.

- Name
- Address
- Date of birth
- Aliases
- Telephone numbers
- Race
- Sex
- Height
- Weight ·
- Hair and eye color
- Occupation (if he is not an inmate)
- Driver's license information
- Vehicle information
- Employment information
- Family information

There are times when investigators develop confidential informants outside the correctional facility and this information is important. The investigator should take a recent photograph of the informant and keep it in the informant's file. If the informant is an inmate, all of this information is available from his file or the computer database.

Informant Questionnaire

If an informant is required to testify in a case, the defense is going to question the credibility of the informant and the investigator. For this reason, the investigator might want to develop a questionnaire for the confidential informant to sign and keep it on record. He should also identify his informant by a number assigned to that informant in any reports or writings.

Make a form that includes personal information and the identification number of the confidential informant. List the questions and have the informant answer the questions and initial each question by the response. Then have the informant sign the document and have a location for the investigator's signature as well. A witness might be appropriate as well.

Here are some suggested informant questions to be placed on the questionnaire:

- Do you understand that you are not privileged to violate any law while providing services for this police agency?
- Do you understand that you are not to disclose to anyone that you provide services for this police agency without the written approval of this police agency?
- Do you understand that you are not to carry documents or equipment that might give rise to the opinion by someone that you are a police officer?
- Do you understand that you are not to affect an arrest for violation of the law as part of your services to this police agency?
- Do you understand the law regarding entrapment and do you understand that you are not to participate in any activity that includes entrapment?
- Do you understand that you are not a law enforcement officer?
- Do you understand that you are not to use your services to this police agency to resolve personal matters?
- Do you understand that you are to stay in close and frequent contact with this agency's assigned representative while assisting this agency?
- Do you understand that you are not to carry any weapons while assisting this agency?
- Have you been read and do you understand the rules of conduct you must abide by during your time working with this police agency?

If the investigator keeps good records and insures that he has a resemblance of these suggestions, then he should be able to effectively answer any defense questions.

Disclosure of Informant's Identity

As previously mentioned, informants must be advised at the outset that their confidentiality cannot be guaranteed.

In extraordinary circumstances, the authority to guarantee confidentiality can be given for any state-initiated proceeding, providing the district attorney approves the issuance. Such guarantees shall be issued judiciously and honored regardless of the outcome of the case.

The disclosure of an informant's identity should be avoided whenever possible. Informant confidentiality shall be thoroughly discussed with the district attorney and any alternatives shall be given full consideration.

In situations where the disclosure of an informant's identity might adversely affect the outcome of a more significant investigation, the investigator should recommend to the district attorney the dismissal of the immediate case.

It should be known to investigators that currently the federal prosecutors will not honor the confidentiality in any federal criminal case. In a federal case the informant should be told.

No mention should be made in any public statement that an investigation depends upon an informant's information. This includes statements to the media that a particular arrest was based on a tip, unidentified source, etc. (with the exception of Crime Stoppers).

Understanding the Convict

8

Introduction

The transition from law enforcement to corrections can be quite a culture shock for street cops. The mentality in the prison setting can be an "us" against "them" situation. Street cops and law enforcement in general deal with a cross section of humanity and only run into felons occasionally. Correction officers deal only with convicted felons.

There are a couple of books that would help the investigator understand the nature of the convicted felon and give him a better idea of what to expect from these convicts.

The first of these two books is *Inside the Criminal Mind** by Stanton E. Samenow, Ph.D. Samenow and others did an in-depth study of criminal behavior. Samenow dispelled all the myths about why people commit crime. He found that people do not commit crime because of poverty, gender, racial background, poor education, peer pressure, cultural differences, mental deficiencies, or any of the many other reasons given to commit crime. He found that criminals just plain think differently than noncriminals. He found that they commit crime by choice. Although he believed in treatment for the criminal, he felt that the convict needs some tools to assist in a successful reintegration into society but that in order to succeed the convict needs to decide on his own to quit the life of crime. He did not believe in rehabilitation and felt that the convict has to be habilitated before he can become rehabilitated. This book is definitely worth reading to gain insight into the criminal mind.

* S.E. Samenow, *Inside the Criminal Mind*, Crown Publishing Group, New York, 1984.

Case History #29

The author's neighbor was a clinical psychologist for the department of corrections and they often tended to talk shop. The neighbor created many programs designed to rehabilitate the convict. The mentality of the inmate was not a topic on which the two neighbors agreed. The author was, and still is, a staunch believer in the Samenow theory.

The neighbor went to a seminar put on by Stanton Samenow. He had not read Samenow's book before attending the seminar. According to the neighbor, the seminar really changed his life. It changed his whole attitude on inmates and how to treat them. Just this one session with Samenow caused the neighbor to change everything he believed in with regard to the inmate mentality. The author's belief in Samenow's theory was reaffirmed.

The lesson learned from Samenow was that criminals commit crimes as a matter of choice.

The second book is *Games Criminals Play** by Bud Allen and Diana Bosta. This book was written by corrections officers for corrections officers. It deals with the types of personalities of the inmates and delves deep into their actions. It shows how manipulative inmates are and to what lengths they will go to get what they want. This book shows how the inmate will set up the staff member during this manipulation. This book not only identifies the problems, but shows officers how to protect themselves against being manipulated. Seasoned correctional officers exposed to this publication immediately recognized it as a factual account of the average inmate mentality. The search for power, the manipulation, the violence, and the arrogance are symptoms recognized by these officers.

The corrections investigation must always be cognizant of these attributes when dealing with convicted felons. These people, incarcerated or not, are dangerous and are very different that the perpetrators on the streets. There are many advantages to investigating prison crime, but there are significant differences that make investigating prison crime difficult.

It should be noted that both of these books are utilized in the Colorado Department of Corrections Basic Training Academy. They have become required reading for some positions as well.

What the prison investigator needs to know is that he will be dealing with a very violent suspect. Convicts are power oriented and prey on the weak. They are master manipulators and their response to any resistance is extremely violent. They try to impose their will on everyone they can and they use everyone. They will even try to use the prison investigator. They can and will stage an entire crime in order to cover up their own.

---

* B. Allen and D. Bosta, *Games Criminals Play*, Rae John Publishers, Sacramento, 1997.

"We" vs. "Them" Syndrome

Bobby Johnson, former chief of the office of special services, describes we and they, in part, as:

> Unlike most other areas of interpersonal relations between criminal justice system workers and their clients, the encounters we are going to explore carry none of the social niceties involved with what is currently termed as 'political correctness'. The situations we will be dealing with are Darwinesque, primal and ultimately distill themselves down to an 'Us' and 'Them' simplicity. In order to understand that relationship in its most fundamental aspect, we must understand and define who the 'Us' and 'Them' are in this relationship.
>
> Workers in the criminal justice system generally report their motivation for seeking employment in the field as being the need to 'help people' or 'make a difference.' While that motivation is appropriate and even commendable, it is inherently vague and not really definitive of the attitudes that contribute to surviving the work. Nonetheless, that reasoning begins to define who we are. In fact, were we to describe the perfect candidate, we would identify a person who is free of a criminal record, inherently nonviolent, well educated, mature, psychologically sound and responsible. Further, it would be nice if they came from a supportive family background, were stable in their relationships and essentially were driven by a strong sense of morals.
>
> HERE IS HOW 'US' TEND TO OPERATE.
>
> - We are bound by law.
> - We are bound by departmental policy.
> - We are bound by a code of ethics.
>
> Conversely, the offenders we encounter in our work most often have a violent criminal background, come from abusive if not broken homes, have little or no education or talent for personal relationships, and tend to be driven by panic, anger, fear, derangement, intoxication, or suicidal motivations. They tend not to be troubled by feelings of guilt or remorse and are prone to expressing themselves through physical violence. Add to that, the criminal population we deal with in DOC has a documented dedication to a life of criminal activity and behavior.
>
> HERE IS HOW 'THEM' TEND TO OPERATE.
>
> - They openly defy authority.
> - They oppose any constraints of civilized behavior.
> - They scorn any principle of ethics.

Johnson is keenly aware of the need for officer safety in the correctional atmosphere. In describing the confrontation with a convict, he said,

> Offenders contacted by officers during the commission of a crime are dedicated to a pattern of action they intend to see through to a conclusion. They will resist any actions of authority and will resort to the use of any weapon without hesitation, vacillation, or regard for the outcome of their actions. The action they take will be immediate and as devastating as they are capable of managing. Keep in mind that these offenders most likely come from the segment of society where the norm is to resist or defy any authority and whose principal means of communication is violence. Psychologically, many have fatalistic attitudes and expect to get shot or die as a natural risk of their lifestyle. Put very simply, they will assault, maim, and kill as an immediate reaction to any confrontation.

An investigator's perception of the inmate clientele is based on his personal experience within the system. What is important to realize is that this mentality is not only exhibited during the commission of a crime, but in their every day encounters with inmates.

Case History #30

It was visiting day at a medium security facility. The atmosphere in the visiting room was quiet and security was normal. A convict's mother sat down at her assigned table to await the arrival of her inmate son. Her son arrived and sat down at the table. The mother quietly asked her son, "How is everything going?" Without hesitation, without reason, without any consideration for the consequences of his actions, the inmate jumped up and smashed his fist into the face of his stunned mother. Before his mother or security staff could react, he punched her again, then calmly sat down.

Evidence Collection 9

Introduction

When working any criminal case, evidence is always important and often crucial to the case. Criminal cases in the prison setting often depend almost entirely on the physical evidence at the scene. Witnesses, victims, and perpetrators are quite often silent, making evidence even more important.

A criminal investigator in the prison must be able to identify all of the evidence within and outside of the scene. He must take proper steps to preserve the evidence and use the proper techniques to collect the evidence.

Investigation units often utilize the state bureau of investigation to work the crime scenes. This does not mean that the investigator does not need to be familiar with proper evidence identification and collection procedures. This chapter is designed to reacquaint investigators with a basic knowledge of crime scene management and collection of evidence.

As any investigator knows, the crime scene must be protected. This is often difficult in the prison setting. There are often emergency circumstances that prevent the line staff from securing the crime scene. Inmates that are not involved in the crime will intentionally destroy evidence. Staff members trying to regain control will inadvertently destroy evidence.

A major crime is not needed to have a crime scene. In some cases within the department of corrections crime scenes have been cleaned up before the arrival of investigators. In some cases staff did not realize that they actually had a crime scene. In most cases, however, a higher authority ordered the cleaning of all biohazardous materials. In other cases the evidence was actually preserved for investigators, but not handled properly. As an investigator, it is important to get involved in the training of all line staff.

Definition of Evidence

Admissible evidence is information (facts) or things which the "fact finder" (jury) is allowed to consider when deciding whether a defendant is guilty or not guilty. (Note that in a trial "to the court" the judge alone decides both the law and the facts.)

There are a few basic factors concerning evidence. There are always rules associated with presenting a criminal case, as well as rules of evidence. The purpose of the rules of evidence is to limit information or objects which a jury may hear, see, feel, etc. Courts and the legislature believe that a jury should "experience" only evidence which is relevant, reliable, not unduly prejudicial, based on proper foundation, and constitutionally gathered.

Relevance

While investigating a case, ask the following:

- What are the elements of the crime?
- What criminal state of mind must be proved?
- What defense is likely?
- Is there any way to ask questions of the suspect(s) or witness(es) which will help to:
  Prove the elements.
  Show the relevant "guilty mind" of the suspect.
  Disprove the defense.
- If there is any question whether the evidence is relevant, error on the side of trying to obtain it (with a warrant if it is a physical object).

Remember that when evidence is not gathered at the first opportunity, it is usually lost forever.

Reliability

Reliability is almost irrelevant to an officer. Get statements from everybody in sight and try to get the story from the "horse's mouth." Lock everyone into a statement as soon as possible.

Undue Prejudice

- If any other bad acts by the defendant are known, relate them to the prosecutor. (This is frequent in the prison atmosphere.)
- In court never refer to defendant's photograph as a mug shot.
- If there is any question about the admissibility of other bad acts by the defendant, be sure to discuss them with the prosecutor before they are mentioned in court.

Foundation

- Photograph and videotape all evidence.
- Document the who, what, when, where, why, and how of all evidence gathered.
- Mark and tag all evidence and preserve it properly.

Constitutional Violations

Know what probable cause is. Know the rules of search and seizure, statements, and identification. Know how things differ in the prison atmosphere from the streets.

Types of Evidence

There are many different ways to categorize evidence. The important thing to remember about evidentiary classification is the different ways the types of evidence get admitted into evidence so the jury can examine them.

Direct Evidence

Direct evidence is evidence which proves a fact directly. An example of this is when a witness testifies that he saw, heard, smelled, or felt evidence which goes directly to the defendant's guilt or innocence, i.e., "I saw inmate Jones stab inmate Smith."

Circumstantial Evidence

Circumstantial evidence is evidence which does not directly show the fact in question, but "implies" that the fact actually happened. There is no difference between the amount of evidence necessary to convict. The state's case can be based in whole or in part on direct or circumstantial evidence, i.e., "I saw inmate Jones go into inmate Smith's cell, heard a commotion, and then saw inmate Jones run out of the cell." A defendant can be convicted on circumstantial evidence alone.

Substitute Evidence

The rules provide for "substitutes" for direct or circumstantial evidence. Substitute evidence is evidence which does not have to be proved directly or circumstantially because it is a matter of common or "legal" knowledge.

The types of evidence the jury may see, hear, smell, and touch are often characterized as testimonial, real, documentary, or demonstrative evidence.

Testimonial Evidence

Most of the evidence presented is testimonial evidence. This is usually factual evidence of what a witness saw, heard, smelled, or felt that relates to whether the defendant did or did not commit a crime. Sometimes the witness may give his opinion.

- Factual testimony—Normally, a witness is limited to testimony about the relevant facts which the witness can swear he actually had personal knowledge of.
- Opinion testimony—A witness may be permitted to give an opinion if the witness is an expert and the court feels the expert is necessary for the jury to understand the facts. A lay person may give an opinion if there is no other way to relate the facts and if their opinion would be helpful in the jury's understanding of the facts.
- Expert opinion—When the facts are beyond the knowledge of the jury, an expert is permitted to give his opinion to the interpretation of the facts.

Real Evidence

Physical objects which are the original pieces of crime-related evidence are often classified as "real evidence." These objects may be admitted so that the jury can see, feel, hear, or touch them if the witnesses can testify that they are related to the crime and are associated with the defendant. It may take more than one witness to establish these elements. Examples may be the weapon used in the crime, fingerprints from the crime scene, or stolen property found on the defendant. Trace evidence, which includes but is not limited to hair, fibers, blood, etc., would be included as real evidence.

Within real evidence is what may be considered scientific evidence, i.e., fingerprint analysis, hair analysis, blood analysis, voice prints, polygraph, etc.

Demonstrative Evidence

Demonstrative evidence is used to explain the facts to the jury, but may not be admissible if the opposing side objects. The judge will decide this matter. This evidence merely helps the jury understand the evidence.

An example would be a crime scene sketch made by the investigator. The investigator then explains the crime scene by use of his sketch.

Documentary Evidence

Documentary evidence is recorded information.

- Handwriting
- Photographs

- Taped conversations
- Business records

Dynamics of a Crime Scene

Crime scenes tend to tell a story, the whole story. It is important for the investigator to be able to read that scene effectively. Crime scenes, as stated in a 1992 crime bulletin, have characters, a plot, a beginning, a middle, and hopefully a conclusion. The investigator needs the ability to analyze the crime scene and determine the who, what, where, when, and why to identify how the crime scene story unfolds. Recognizing the human behavior associated with the crime scene will reveal the modus operandi, personation or signature, and staging. Within the department of corrections the investigator has an advantage, in that his training and experience have taught him how these convicts think.

Modus operandi (MO) is used in the streets to identify a criminal from past crimes where the perpetrator had a certain signature to his crime. Certain similarities show up in the commission of each crime. These MOs develop over a period of time through successful completion of crimes and are refined over time as criminals learn from their mistakes. In prison, when there is a crime scene and a suspect, the investigator can utilize information from the convict's presentence investigation report (PSIR) or the actual case file. What the investigator may find, though, is that inmates tend to copy other inmates signatures in the commission of a crime within the prison. The investigator will also find that inmates are also limited, within the prison, as to what method they can use to commit their crime. They are limited by the physical plant, weapons available, close proximity to guards and other witnesses, and many other variables.

A problem arises in identifying a signature of a crime within the prison in that most violent crimes committed are acts of impulse and spur of the moment. Although contract assaults and homicides occur in prison, the methods used are limited by the same things. So in prison, do not look to solve the crime by use of the MO.

The signature aspect is not as prevalent in the prison system. Signatures are classified the same as the MO. There have been no serial offenders within the prisons. The crimes that are committed over and over again are the drug crimes and some property crimes. The signatures used in these crimes are also limited and most of the offenders utilize the same methods. They also tend to use the same people (mules) to facilitate these crimes. Crime scenes in violent crimes tend to be very similar in that they are committed in the same areas that other crimes are committed. Quite often violent crimes in the prison are committed by inmates that do not have a violent history, and trying to connect an MO or signature to a certain inmate would not be fruitful.

Staging occurs when someone purposely alters the crime scene prior to the arrival of the police or investigators. There are several reasons for staging a crime scene, including protecting the victim and victim's family, putting the police on the trail of someone else, or hiding any of a number of facts that point the finger toward the perpetrator. It is quite common in the prison setting. Most often the perpetrator will commit the murder within the victim's cell. Frequent inmate counts are conducted where officers are required to see every inmate. If they were to see the inmate laying dead on the floor in a pool of blood, the crime would be detected. If the perpetrator were to clean up his mess and lay the victim in his bed, the officer may not realize a problem until much later. Inmates committing murders in the cell block will often attempt to make it look like a suicide. That is why many prison killings are committed by means of asphyxia, either manual or ligature strangulation. The victim is then placed in a position that would resemble a hanging.

Be aware of your crime scene and be prepared to find some sort of staging. Remember also that the perpetrator will almost always take something from the scene or bring something to the scene. This evidence is always important to the investigation. All allowable property an inmate has in his cell is listed on his property list, which is easily accessible to the investigator.

Preliminary Investigation

James Davis, a crime scene expert, says that the investigator does not have to be an expert to collect evidence properly. He just has to follow the rules.

Remember the basics: watch where you step, wear protective clothing and shoe covers if possible, and always double the latex gloves (wear two pair at once).

Crime Scene Arrival

If the investigator is fortunate, when he arrives at the crime scene it will already be protected and will not be destroyed. Upon arrival, the investigator should do the following:

1. Provide first aid to injured.
2. Apprehend and identify the suspects and witnesses.
3. Protect the crime scene.
   a. From beginning to end, care should be taken not to disturb or destroy potential evidence. Protect as much of the crime scene as possible until control is regained.
   b. As help arrives set the perimeter of crime scene, marking it with crime scene tape. Mark the scene beyond the limits of what is suspected

to have the most priority. This needs to be done quickly to avoid contamination or destruction of evidence.

c. As the investigation progresses the physical size of the crime scene can be decreased. Remember it is easier to decrease than to increase a crime scene.

d. Remember that once the perimeter is set, protect it. Restrict the movement of everyone, including officers, inside the perimeter. Do not let anyone touch or move anything. Some exceptions include giving aid to injured, catching the bad guy, or moving evidence to protect it from the elements.

e. Common problems include premature moving or searching of bodies, touching surfaces that may yield latent prints or trace evidence, and walking in areas that may have shoe impressions. Supervisory staff will oftentimes enter the crime scene and contaminate it. Investigators should take command of the crime scene immediately, ensuring that no one enters or destroys evidence.

Preliminary Investigation

1. Do a walk through. Walk in a location or pathway that is least likely to destroy evidence left by the suspect. Once that pathway is established by the first investigator, others should follow the same path, entering only after obtaining permission from the investigator in charge of the crime scene. Move slowly, examining the immediate area of each step taken.

2. Do not be in a hurry.

3. Limit the investigator's activities in the phase to surveying the scene.
   a. Determine the scope of scene, formulating an investigative plan.
   b. Locate readily visibly evidence and take steps to preserve it.
   c. Record all observations through notes, an audio tape recorder, and photographs. (See Photographing the Crime Scene Section later in this chapter.)
   d. Mentally reconstruct the scene to develop a theory of what took place during the commission of the crime.
   e. Formulate a plan based on observations of the scene, witnesses' statements, and the initial theory of the reconstructed crime: develop a plan utilizing the available manpower and other resources. Remember to listen to the WHORE (witness had other reasonable explanation). Things are not always as they seem.

At any crime scene it is always desirable to use a more systematic approach. This is dependent on many outside factors such as manpower, nature and location of the scene, size of the area to be searched, and type of crime. The CBI teachings are simple yet effective:

1. Organize the investigation.
   a. Have one person in charge and make everyone aware of this fact. Insure that his direction is followed.
   b. Make assignments and make sure they are carried out.
   c. Have a plan prior to any action.
2. Work as a team.
   a. Although one person should be assigned to collect the evidence located in the crime scene, a second person is advisable to witness and record this information.
   b. One person should take all photographs and video.
   c. Review the investigation before leaving the scene. Have a conference with all personnel present to determine if everything possible was done.
3. Consider the use of a check list.
   a. The check list may vary for different crimes.
4. Document everything and note the times.

Crime Scene Searches

At street crime scenes caution needs to be placed on the legality of any searches, but in prison the rules are different. The standards set by the courts give prisoners almost no fourth amendment protection. The security of the facility is always the superceder. Remember, even though the investigator may search any area or person within or outside the institutional crime scene, another requirement is needed to make intrusive searches. A 41.1 warrant is needed, for example, to gather hair, blood, or other bodily fluids. (A 41.1 refers to Colorado Rules of Criminal Procedure which provides for a court order for nontestimonial evidence.) If, on the other hand, swabbing or fingernail scrapings are needed, the inspector would have to consider the suspect's ability to destroy the evidence and take the evidence. The investigator needs to recover evidence that can be destroyed.

Case History #31

A DA's office investigator recently reviewed a videotaped statement of a "big city" homicide detective. During this interview the detective suggested to the interviewee that he had gunshot residue on him. For the next 15 minutes the subject proceeded to wipe the areas of his hands with tissue conveniently provided by the police, destroying the evidence.

The investigator will probably have one opportunity to conduct a meaningful search, so take the time to do it right. Consider a method appropriate for that crime scene and always consider the priority evidence. Remember the search patterns; they are trite but right.

Search Patterns

A particular search pattern is not necessary, but an organized thorough search is essential.

Spiral Search

An inward spiral search begins at the perimeter and works toward the center of the spiral. Only one searcher is needed. This search pattern decreases the possibility of destroying evidence.

An outward spiral search begins at the focal point, or center of the scene, and works outward. This also is effective for one searcher, but be careful not to destroy evidence gaining entry to the center of the scene.

Strip Search

The strip search, also known as the parallel or lane search, is a method where the searchers line up shoulder to shoulder and proceed in parallel lanes all at the same speed. When an item of evidence is located, the entire line stops until the item is either tagged or photographed, measured, recorded, and collected. The search then resumes, making sure everyone proceeds at the same speed. (This might be good in a very large, outside area.)

Grid Search

This is a modification of the parallel search that provides double coverage. When the area has been covered with a parallel search, the searchers then go over the same area again at a right angle to the first search pattern.

Zone Search

The crime scene is divided into areas or sectors. Each searcher is then assigned to a specific area to search. When the search is completed, positions are changed and the area is searched again by another searcher. A building may be divided into rooms or a room may be divided into quadrants. A field may be divided into sections and so on.

Photographing the Crime Scene

1. Videotape the crime scene first.
   a. Always pan the camera slowly.
   b. Get a 360° view of the crime scene from the inside.
   c. Get a view of the entryway to and from the crime scene.
   d. If there are inmate witnesses in the area, be sure to get them on film (covertly, if possible).

    e. Be sure to include all walls, the floor, and the ceiling.

    f. Always get a close-up view of any potential suspected evidence. (If you do use sound recordings, ensure that everyone at the crime scene is notified to eliminate any non-professional statements from being made.)

2. Next take 35-mm still photos.

    a. Be sure to get overall and close-up photos. (Walls and floors may look alike, especially in a prison, so be sure to identify what is in each photograph.)

    b. Get one to one photos of suspected evidence (if the camera has macro ability).

    c. Be sure to take photos of all evidence prior to altering, moving, numbering, or collecting.

3. Locate and number all suspected evidence prior to collection. Photograph evidence again after it is numbered.

    a. Use cards, cones, or any other manner of numbering to number evidence.

4. Do crime scene sketch and take measurements.

    a. Sketch

- Make the sketch simple.
- Always put the door at the bottom of the sketch. This makes it easier for a jury to understand the drawing.
- Be sure and put the walls and the ceiling in the sketch. (See Figure 9.1 for example of sketch that includes door, walls, and ceiling.)

    b. Measurements

- Make all measurements from at least two adjoining walls on each item of evidence.
- Always handle the smart end of the tape only. (Do not let someone else call out the measurements to the investigator. This is his case and he has to have the answers.)
- When measuring a body, measure from head to all extremities and from the wall to each extremity.

The investigator needs to create good habits. Do things the same way each time, e.g., measure to the victim's nose.

Basic Evidence Collection

1. Collect all large evidence first, then go after trace evidence.
2. Make bindles (pieces of paper folded to contain small evidence) from paper or use envelopes. In some cases, use evidence bags and evidence plastic bags if appropriate for evidence.

3. When picking up trace evidence with tape, use the tape until it is not sticky anymore and be sure to log the location of the evidence.
4. Remember to shine the flashlight at an angle to the ground when looking for evidence. Shining directly at the evidence can cause shadow evidence to go unnoticed.
5. The collection of trace evidence is now more important than ever. DNA capabilities allow persons to be identified with the minutest sample.

Table 9.1 is a collection of evidence quick references that depicts the technique for collection, method of marking, preservation and packing, and investigative value. A more complete quick reference guide is usually contained within any evidence manual.

Death Investigations

Asphyxia

The physiological classification of asphyxia includes:

- **Anoxic or hypoxic**—Atmospheric oxygen cannot reach the blood, i.e., airways are blocked, lungs are in poor condition, or there is difficulty with the mechanics of respiration.
- **Anemic**—Blood cannot contain enough oxygen because of insufficient or poor quality hemoglobin.
- **Stagnant**—The circulation of blood is impaired, perhaps on account of focal pressure on blood vessels or poor pumping action of the heart.
- **Histotoxic**—Oxygen may be present, but the tissues cannot utilize it on account of low blood sugar or cyanide poisoning.

The practical classification of asphyxia includes:

- **Hanging**—Body weight provides the force on a suspending rope or ligature. Most hangings are suicides, accidents are uncommon, and homicides are extremely rare (except in the prison atmosphere). Suspension with the feet swinging clear of the floor is not essential since there is enough weight in the head and shoulders of an individual to produce asphyxia while lying, slumping, kneeling, or reclining. Hanging usually produces an inverted V-shaped furrow on the neck. After the application of pressure to the neck, unconsciousness usually supervenes in a matter of seconds; however, cessation of the heartbeat may not occur for up to as much as 20 minutes.

Table 9.1 Evidence Quick Reference

Specimen	Technique for Collection	Method of Marking	Preservation and Packing	Investigative Value
Latent fingerprints	Small transportable objects not processed at scene, pick up with forceps or gloves, handle in areas that would not have been touched	In area that would not have been touched	Place in box or paper envelope in such a manner that contact surfaces will not rub; do not use soft plastic bags; do not wrap in cloth; drain or thoroughly seal all liquid contents	Comparison with rolled prints for identification
Blood				
1. Porous objects	Photograph any stains before removal from item	Mark case information and location on outside of container	Protect from contamination	Determination as to source (animal, human)
	Protect at scene by covering with clean pan, box, etc.; mark with identifying information			
	Moisten clean cotton patch or filter paper with normal saline solution or distilled water			
	Handle only with tweezers			
	Soak up as much specimen as possible			
	Air dry and place in paper container			
	Small stains use no. 8 cotton thread			
2. Nonporous objects (dry), i.e., tile or smooth paint surfaces	Protect as above	Same as above	Same as above	Same as above

3. Wet	Scrape crust from surface with clean knife, razor blade, etc Use lightly moistened cotton patch as for porous objects; air dry Collect with dry cotton swatch to soak up wet blood and dry at room temperature	Note whether wet or dry at time of discovery	Package in paper container	Same as above
4. Fabric stains	See Clothing	See Clothing	See Clothing	Same as above
5. Control	Have control standards from victim or suspect collected by qualified medical personnel Collect at least 10 cc	Mark container Have collecting person initial container as well	Refrigerate (do not freeze) until transported to laboratory For mail, wrap in several layers of paper or styrofoam for insulation	Comparison to suspect or victim
6. General	Utilizing the cloth patch technique, collect swab from unstained area in case body fluids of a secretor were on the surface in addition to the specimen collected Never allow blood specimen to come in contact with a human body to guard against mixing blood groups with a secretor Whenever possible remove entire stained article to laboratory while protecting from contamination If item requires fingerprinting as well, handle appropriately	See Blood	See Blood	Used as control

Table 9.1 Evidence Quick Reference (Continued)

Specimen	Technique for Collection	Method of Marking	Preservation and Packing	Investigative Value
Clothing				
1. Victim, suspect, bedding, etc.	Avoid shaking to protect trace evidence Protect from contamination	Mark with ink in an inconspicuous location	Do not cut or fold through stain	Comparison with fibers and other substances collected elsewhere
2. Stains	Air dry stains by placing article on a piece of paper (avoid artificial heat, fan, etc.)	Place information on container	Package only dry articles Package only dry articles separately in a clean, dry paper and bag and seal Include paper used for drying or protecting stain If suspect is a secretor his blood group may be determined Blood stains: See Blood	Determine what the stain is and what it indicates Seminal stains are an important element of rape Paint stains: color and chemical comparison Used for comparison purposes
3. Gunpowder burns	Cover area with a piece of clean paper Fold so that area is flat			Gunpowder residue may be examined for composition Pattern (if recreated with suspect firearm and ammunition) can determine distance from victim when fired

Documents				
1. Letters, notes, checks, etc.	Use tweezers, but avoid grasping questioned document over an obvious smudge Protect for latent prints Do not handle or fold; if folding is necessary, fold at preexisting creases	Mark in corner on reverse side Mark envelope prior to enclosing specimen to avoid making additional impressions on article to be examined	Do not handle or fold Cellophane, paper, or plastic envelope	Comparison to exemplar to identify author Determine nature of alteration, erasure, or forgery Fingerprints Determine color and content of ink Interpretation of intended information Comparison to questioned documents
2. Exemplars	Collect a minimum of 15 from suspect author of document (single signature) on questioned check forms Have suspected writer use same or similar form and writing implement (pen, ballpoint, etc.) Dictate exact contents of questioned document Remove each exemplar from suspects view prior to dictating the next	Same as above	Cellophane, plastic, or paper envelope	Comparison to questioned documents
Fibers				
1. Lint, thread, rope, cordage, twine, etc.	Handle small pieces with forceps, making sure that none of the fibers adhere to them	Label container	Protect ends	Determine the source (animal, vegetable, synthetic)

Table 9.1 Evidence Quick Reference (Continued)

Specimen	Technique for Collection	Method of Marking	Preservation and Packing	Investigative Value
	Collect all available specimens Protect the ends from damage or unraveling		Package separately Use sealed container, i.e., pill box, glass vial, plastic bag, etc.	Coloring Comparison to known standards
Firearms and ammunition				
1. Revolvers	If cylinder is opened, process bullets and fired casings for prints	Mark the rear of the cylinder to show which chamber was under the hammer and number each round in clockwise sequence to indicate its position in the cylinder	After processing for latent fingerprints, seal in a heavy transparent evidence bag	Chamber marks on casing
	Always consider safety			Test fire to establish distance from victim (requires that type of ammunition used be known) Ownership history: serial number permits tracing from manufacturer to retailer and individual owners Fingerprint identification Determine if the weapon is operable

Type	Collection	Marking	Packaging	Value
2. Semi-automatics	See Revolvers Process the magazine and bullets for latent prints Note the position of safety and whether or not weapon is cocked	Use a metal scribe in an inconspicuous location on the frame, slide, barrel, and magazine	See Revolvers	See Revolvers
3. Rifles/shotguns	See Revolvers Pick up by edge of trigger guard or knurled portions of stock until after processing for latent prints Pick up by sling if one is attached On shotgun, note adjustment of choke (do not change)	Use a metal scribe in an inconspicuous location on frame	See Revolvers	See Revolvers (Note: Shotguns do not have rifling)
4. Bullets (fired)	Protect rifling marks which may be present by handling them with fingers or tweezers with tips taped Do not damage with knife or probe	Use metal scribe on the base of the bullet If the bullet is small caliber, mark container	Package individually in a small pill box with cotton or tissue to protect rifling marks Wash off blood (if blood type needed, request that this analyses be performed as soon as possible)	Can provide investigative leads by determination of make, caliber, and type of firearm Can be compared to one fired from suspect weapon for a positive identification of weapon used
5. Cartridge (not fired)	See Bullets	Do not mark on sides Metal scribe on nose	See Bullets	Chamber marks can be compared to suspect casing or bullets

Table 9.1   Evidence Quick Reference (Continued)

Specimen	Technique for Collection	Method of Marking	Preservation and Packing	Investigative Value
	Avoid damage to bullet or casing	If removed from revolver, include numbers which correspond with chambers		Comparison to bullets fired
	Process for latent prints			
6. Cartridge (fired)	Use taped tweezers at open end	Metal scribe inside mouth or as near as possible	See Bullets	Comparison of firing pin, chamber, and extractor marks to those from the suspect weapon
	Avoid scratching			
	Process for latent prints			
7. Shot shells (fired)	Use tweezers at open end and protect the brass base	Write on paper portion	Roll individually in soft paper and place in evidence envelope	Gauge of gun
	Process for prints		Do not scratch base	Comparison of firing pin, chamber, and extractor marks to those from the suspect weapon
8. Shot pellets	Avoid damage	Mark container	Package in small pill box with cotton or soft paper	Comparison of size and composition with shells in possession of suspect or in suspect weapon
	No special precaution			

9. Wadding	Use tweezers to keep intact and avoid damage	Package in small pill box; do not tear or damage	Determination of gauge of shotgun and make of shell
Glass			
1. Fragments and particles	Photograph in place	Mark container	Fracture lines may be matched
	Pick up with fingers on edge of large pieces and tweezers for smaller particles	Place case information on sealed container	Refractive index, density, and elemental content identification
	Process for prints		Headlight lens from hit and run may be matched to source
	Collect all of specimen (headlamp glass)	Use sealed container to prevent loss of specimen	Year and make of vehicle or replacement lens may be established
			Direction of breaking force
2. Standards	Collect control specimen from area around break (entire remainder of pane, bottle, etc., if possible)	In the case of a window pane, indicate inside and outside on glass with scribe or ink prior to removing	Comparison to above
		Same as above	
Hairs			
1. From scene	See Fibers	See Fibers	Determine the source (human and animal)
	Comb pubic area of sexual assault victim or suspect	See Fibers	Hair color, race, comparison to known standards

Table 9.1 Evidence Quick Reference (Continued)

Specimen	Technique for Collection	Method of Marking	Preservation and Packing	Investigative Value
2. Standards	Pluck from various areas of suspect and victim; different areas of head, body, and pubic area; 10 each from top, back, and each temple of head and also various places in the pubic area	Same as above	See Fibers	Used for comparison to those collected from scene
	Do not cut		Package in groups separated according to area of collection	
Impressions 1. Footprints and tire prints	Protect from damage or modification	Place case marker in photograph with ruler	Seal evidence envelope	Comparison to size, pattern, and irregularities of wear
	Photograph using side (oblique) lighting; camera on tripod; film plane parallel to print surface with ruler in picture to show proper perspective	Mark back of photograph		Positive identification depends on unique irregularities
	Photograph to demonstrate condition at time of discovery			Compared to suspect's shoes or tires to place him at scene
	After photographing, plaster of paris casts can be made	Scratch case information on back of cast before the plaster sets fully	Pack in paper inside cardboard box, wooden crate, etc. to protect from breakage	
	Fill entire print			

Type	Collection	Handling	Container	Remarks
	Pour gently to avoid destruction of impression Use reinforcing metal strips or sticks Use metal or wooden form around impression to contain plaster Preserve soil for comparision			Check for sugar or abrasives
Crankcase oil gasoline	Oil: approximately 1 pt from lower crankcase, directly from pan if removed; also collect filter Gasoline: collect from bottom of tank, especially any water in tank; also collect fuel line filter	Outside of container	Leakproof jar or vial	
Gunshot residue (Primer residue on hands)	5% nitric acid solution on plastic shaft cotton swabs	Note the surface swabbed on the outside of the individual containers Label each of subject's kit with name and case information	Package all the individual plastic containers for one subject together as a kit	Determine if primer residue is sufficient to indicate the discharge and/or handling of a firearm
Bloodspatter interpretation	Collection of actual object or surface Color photograph using 100 ISO film showing measuring device in photo	Note location from which object or surface was removed	Refer to serology section	Possibility of determining location and activities, etc. varies with each case

Table 9.1   Evidence Quick Reference (Continued)

Specimen	Technique for Collection	Method of Marking	Preservation and Packing	Investigative Value
Tool	Do not touch against suspect's impressions	Metal scribe or sting tag or ink on other than working surface	Protect working surface	Microscopic examination for trace evidence to connect the tool with the scene or point of origin: i.e., suspect obtained tool from garage where employed
	Protect working surface for trace evidence which may have adhered and protect from damage		Package individually in plastic or paper to preserve trace evidence and protect against contamination	
	Handle by sides after processing for prints		Note: Do not use plastic if laboratory is to process for latent prints	Comparison with tool marks
Tool marks	Photograph from a distance and close up	Mark in an area of no evidential value	Protect mark with a soft paper	Identify type of tool
	Include a rule for proper perspective	Use a scribe or ink	Place in cardboard or wood container of appropriate size	Comparison with tool and trace evidence from tool
	Collect item or portion of item bearing complete tool mark		Protect from contamination	
	If necessary, an impression can be made using dental impression material	Etch information into back of impression material		

	Collection	Marking	Packaging	Laboratory examination
Liquor	Collect in bottle or original container or place in clean, air-tight container Protect latent prints If "refill" case, obtain known standard for comparison	Mark container	Package in a manner to protect against evaporation, breakage, and leakage	Determination of alcohol content or refilled container Determination of proof
Narcotic or dangerous drugs 1. Liquid	Leave in original container	Mark container	Pack in leakproof container and protect from cracking and breaking	Identification of specific drug recovered
2. Tablets, powder, capsules, etc.	Examine container for prints Leave in original container If this is not possible, handle with tweezers or scrape or brush with paper, blade, or spatula and place in pill box or other sealable container, such as a paper bundle using "pharmacist's fold" All narcotics should be weighed; if in pill or capsule form, they should be counted or estimated if a large quantity Avoid contaminating surfaces if latent printing is desired	Mark container	Place in properly sealed pill box or other container which is adequate to prevent loss Note: If a small amount of suspected narcotic or drug exists, a presumptive "field test" should not be conducted as this may not leave sufficient quantify for lab analysis needed for court	May show that the material is not a controlled substance Identification of specific controlled substance found Results of field test kits are only presumptive

Table 9.1 Evidence Quick Reference (Continued)

Specimen	Technique for Collection	Method of Marking	Preservation and Packing	Investigative Value
Paint				
1. Liquid	Collect entire sample in original container or use spoon or similar device to transfer to a clean, airtight container	Mark container	Package protectively to prevent breakage or spillage	Determine texture, color, and content for comparison
				Sometimes the manufacturer can be determined
				Comparison to paint in suspect's possession or smears on suspect's clothing, etc.
2. Chips	Use tweezers or scoop with paper		Package first in paper fold then place in pill box or other rigid container	Large chips can be matched to fractured edge at suspected point of origin
	Do not break		Seal to prevent leakage	
	Collect standard from near all damaged areas with pocket knife, razor blade, etc.			Identification possibility improves with number and uniqueness of layers
	Obtain all layers			Whether automobile is a hit and run
				Possible determination of color, model, and year of vehicle

	Collection	Marking	Packaging	Remarks
3. Smears on fabric	See Clothing	See Clothing	See Clothing	See Clothing
Poisons	Collect in original container if possible Examine for prints Collect with eyedropper, tweezers, paper, etc. Collect any envelope, bottle, drinking glass, partial beverage bottles, etc. Collect all contents of medicine chest at scene of suspected poisoning Scrape up from floor with paper	Mark container Include location collected	Package in container which will prevent cross contamination, breakage, or spillage	Simplify autopsy Direct treatment Identification of poison by laboratory can lead investigator to its source
Safe insulation	Collect known standard from safe Collect from various areas	Mark container	Protect from spillage and/or contamination Seal in a pill box, plastic bag, or other sealable container Do not use regular envelope	Comparison to material found on suspect's clothing, shoes, tools, car interior, etc.

Table 9.1 Evidence Quick Reference (Continued)

Specimen	Technique for Collection	Method of Marking	Preservation and Packing	Investigative Value
Soil				
1. In footprint	Dig up only the surface sample that could have come in contact with suspect's shoes	Mark container	Same as above	Comparison to the suspect's shoes, vehicle, clothing, etc.
	Collect from various areas, especially those locations where suspect may have walked or driven		Package separately by area of collection	
			Do not remove from suspect's shoes	
2. Standards	Collect standards 4–20 ft surrounding footprints	Mark container and diagram showing location in relationship to footprint		

- **Manual strangulation**—Pressure is applied to the neck by the hands and fingers (a very similar situation is encountered when pressure is applied by means of the arms, as in certain police choke and strangle holds). Bluish discoloration/cyanosis of the face and small petechial hemorrhages in the skin of the face, scalp, and eye regions are common. Fractures of the neck cartilages and hyoid bone are common, but not always present.
- **Ligature strangulation**—A constricting force other than the body weight is applied to the neck. An object is placed around the neck and tightened. Most such deaths are homicides and a few are suicides. No V-shaped markings appear on the neck.
- **Smothering**—External openings for breathing (nose or mouth) are obstructed by an object or by virtue of the individual being within some form of container.
- **Choking**—Death results from obstruction of the airway. Deaths are mostly accidental and are associated with intoxication, senility, and natural illness such as Parkinson's disease. A "Café Coronary" occurs when an individual is very often in a hurry or has some other cause of muscular incoordination, causing the individual to choke on his food.
- **Traumatic asphyxia/crush asphyxia**—External compressive forces prevent effective breathing movements.
- **Drowning**—Immersion in water results in smothering with or without a degree of choking.
- **Asphyxiating gases**—A victim breathes an atmosphere which contains insufficient oxygen to support life or which contains poisonous gases at significant levels. The atmosphere contains 1% inert gases, 20% oxygen, and 79% nitrogen.
- **Sex-related asphyxia/autoerotic death**—Hypoxia (relative lack of oxygen supply to the brain) results in an increased "high" or "thrill" or appreciated sexual stimuli. If pressure is applied to the neck, a soft object is used to prevent marking of the neck. An increased stimulus can be obtained by using plastic bags or by solvent sniffing.

Blunt Injuries

- **Abrasions**—Focal destruction of the outer layers of the skin occurs by a compressive or sliding force. Abrasions darken when dry. The surface layer of the skin may be heaped up at one end of a sliding abrasion, indicating the direction of force.
- **Contusion bruises**—After a small blood vessel is damaged, blood leaks into the surrounding tissue.
- **Lacerations**—These are the result of blunt force, not the result of contact with sharp objects or instruments. These injuries are due to

crushing, shearing, tearing, or pulling apart of tissues. Bridging may occur.

- **Fractures**

Sharp Injuries

Injuries consistent with the use of a sharp object create incised wounds or stab wounds. Incised wounds are due to sharp things and extend along the surface more than they extend inward. Stab wounds are fairly long and are the result of a sharp object penetrating for a distance greater than the surface defect is long.

Penetrating vs. Perforating

Penetrating enters and does not exit, while perforating makes a hole.

Track vs. Tract

A track is detectable evidence that something has passed or is the course along which something has moved. A tract is a system of bodily parts or organs which collectively serve some function.

Cause, Manner, and Mechanism of Death

The cause of death is the injury, disease, or a combination of the two responsible for initiating the train of physiological disturbances, brief or prolonged, which produce the fatal termination. If there is a period of survival, sufficient to permit the development of serious sequelae, the initiating or proximate cause may be followed by intermediate causes such as pneumonia or pulmonary embolism.

The mechanism of death is the physiologic derangement or biochemical disturbance incompatible with life which is initiated by the cause of death. Examples are ventricular fibrillation and respiratory arrest. Mechanisms do not belong on death certificates. If you see "cardiac arrest" on a death certificate, the certifier has displayed a lack of familiarity with definitions.

The manner of death refers to the circumstances in which the cause of death arose (natural, accidental, suicide, homicide, and undetermined). This is determined by the coroner.

Basic Blood Spatter

It is important as an investigator to be aware of blood spatter identification. Investigators *will* encounter blood spatter in some homicide and assault investigations. If the investigator knows what he is looking for he will be less likely to disturb or allow someone else to disturb the evidence.

Impact

The velocity of the impact determines the length and pattern of the blood spatter.

- Low-velocity spatter is caused by the force of gravity.
- Medium-velocity spatter is caused by force that is greater than 5 ft/sec, but less than 25.1 ft/sec.
- High-velocity spatter is caused by any force that is greater than 100 ft/sec, usually from a gunshot. The slowest bullet travels at 500 ft/sec. Most bullets travel at about 900 ft/sec or greater.

The impact would be classified as medium velocity if the *majority* of the stains were 1 mm or greater. The impact would be classified as high velocity if the *majority* of the stains were 1 mm or less.

Direction

A blood drop striking an angled surface produces a teardrop-shaped pattern—the physical law of inertia.

The greater the angle of impact, the more elongated and narrower is the spatter. The pointed end of the stains show the direction of travel.

Remember the following points in reference to bloodstain patterns:

- The surface texture, not distance fallen, determines the degree of spatter (glass vs. paper towel vs. cardboard).
- Teardrop stains point in the direction of travel. Smaller and longer droplets have their pointed ends pointing back to the larger stains from which they originated.
- The smaller the drop of blood, the greater the energy of impact.
- The angle of impact of a bloodstain may be estimated by the geometry of the stain.

Prison investigators will not likely investigate a crime with the use of firearms, although it has happened.

Remember the following points about firearms and bloodstains:

- Backspatter usually occurs less than 3 in. from the muzzle to the target area, when blood is found inside of the barrel.
- The larger the caliber or gauge of the firearm, the greater the depth of blood penetration into the barrel.
- Penetration and concentration of backspatter occur less in recoil auto-loading weapons than in weapons where the barrel does not recoil.

- Higher energy loads will produce more backspatter penetration than standard ammunition.
- When double-barrel shotguns are discharged on body contact, considerable backspatter occurs in the dormant barrel due to the funnel effect.
- The majority of blood spatter pattern will be 1 mm or less.

What an investigator sees may not be what occurred. If flies or other insects are present at the crime scene, high-velocity blood spatter that looks uniform may be present. This could come from either the insects or flies tracking through the blood or from the regurgitated blood from flies.

If there is an addict present at the crime scene, or the crime scene was used to shoot up drugs, there may be medium-velocity blood spatter on the ceiling from when the addict cleared the blood out of the needle when shooting up. This may also occur when a paramedic clears blood out of a syringe at the crime scene.

Expiration of blood by a person who is bleeding from either an injury to the lung, airway, or mouth may look like high-velocity blood spatter.

References

Colorado Bureau of Investigation, "Physical Evidence Handbook," January 1, 1986.

J. R. Davis, Crime Scene Analysis Seminar, Highlands Ranch Co., 1998.

J. MacDonald and T. Haney, Criminal Investigation Seminar, Freemont County, CO, 1990.

Police Science Services, Inc., "Physical Evidence, A Professional Procedures Program," 1973.

Federal Bureau of Investigation, United States Department of Justice, "Fingerprint Identification," 1976; "Classification of Fingerprints," 1983; "The Science of Fingerprint," 1977.

Home Office, Scientific Research and Development Branch, "Manual of Fingerprint Development Techniques," London, 1986.

FBI Law Enforcement Bulletin, February 1982.

Search and Seizure Checklists, 2nd ed., Clark Boardman Company, Ltd.

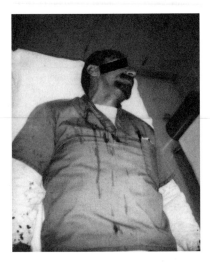

Figure 9.1 This assault victim was attacked with a mop handle while sitting in the inmate lounge. The first officers on the scene took photographs of the blood trail and the victim.

Figure 9.2 Table where the inmate victim sat reading. It would later be discovered that the suspect had blood spatters on him.

Figure 9.3 Blood trail of the inmate running to get medical attention.

Figure 9.4 The blood trail leaves the lounge. Unfortunately, when investigators arrived they found an inmate, under the direction of officers, mopping up this biohazard crime scene. Things got worse when investigators later found that the inmate that mopped up the crime scene was the suspect. Hence, an excuse for the victim's blood on his clothing and no prosecution of the case.

All photos courtesy of the Colorado Department of Corrections.

The Importance of Intelligence

10

Introduction

If an investigative division does not have an effective intelligence gathering and analyzing unit, this chapter provides some ideas on how to improve those areas in the unit. It may also assist investigators in evaluating their current system.

Intelligence is the key to proactive law enforcement. The gathering of intelligence is a must and should be an ongoing operation. The value of effective intelligence gathering and dissemination is a crucial part of any law enforcement agency. It is especially important to corrections, which deal only with convicted felons as their citizens.

Merely gathering information is not enough. The investigator needs to know how to analyze the information and when to disseminate the information. He has to put a value on the information and know how to act on the information.

A close relationship between the investigators and the emergency response teams is very important. This chapter explains why this partnership should continue.

Definition of Intelligence

One definition of intelligence is the gathering of secret information, as for military or police purposes: information that has been gathered for the guidance of policy.

Regardless of any written definition, intelligence is basically information. The gathering of intelligence is continual. It can be gathered passively or actively. In the criminal justice system this information not only needs to be gathered, but it needs to be analyzed and acted upon. The secret is in proper analysis and effective actions. If an investigator has information and does not act on it, in some manner, he will later be held accountable, either by the press or by his superiors.

Acting on the information may involve just passing it on to someone. The investigator needs to pass the information to someone or someplace where it will be valuable. Investigators tend to pass information up rather than out. Passing it up the chain of command is not always proper. It tends to be more a passing of the buck than passing intelligence to the entity that needs it. Most agencies are not very effective in the manner in which they handle information.

To better understand intelligence, the investigator must first realize that although intelligence is information, information is not necessarily intelligence. Information is unevaluated but relative material of every description derived from observation, communication, reports, rumors, imagery, and all other sources from which intelligence is produced. Intelligence is the product resulting from the collection, evaluation, and interpretation of information which concerns one or more aspects of a given incident which is immediately or potentially significant to the development and execution of plans, policies, and operations.

Passive Intelligence

Passive intelligence may be defined as a classification of intelligence which is data or information that originates from sources that the investigator is not actively pursuing. This information may not have any direct bearing on current issues within the department, but it is still valuable. There are many sources of passive intelligence.

- Information that is not regularly monitored but may draw attention because of the relevance of the topic. This could come from a newspaper article, a radio or television news report, or a magazine.
- Information that is received from people we know in the facilities. An officer may notice some activity that is out of the ordinary and thinks it noteworthy.
- Information that is developed during an investigation that does not contribute to that activity, but has implications outside of the investigation.

- Information that comes in a serendipitous manner, such as an officer overhears some talk of a crime involving inmates.

Passive intelligence is always an accident. It is always there and always available. The investigator must recognize it for what it is and act on it according to its value. The key is to **act on it**, whether it be a personal note, a talk with someone else, a report to other officials, a proposal, or an operational plan to deal with the information.

Passive categories of information gathering rely on two important practices that must become part of everything an investigator does:

1. Anyone connected with corrections must develop and pursue a heightened awareness of what is going on around them so as to develop a sensitivity to important issues.
2. All investigators must pursue and carefully maintain those relationships with all persons that facilitate the free and open exchange of information.

Both these principles need to be instilled in each investigator.

Active Intelligence

Active intelligence is the category of intelligence that investigators actively pursue through established resources or as a dedicated part of the investigative process. Active intelligence operations are generally done in collaboration with other parts of the organization whose practices should include constant checks and cross-checks.

An example of active intelligence gathering is when an investigator is getting ready to execute a no-knock search warrant. The investigator needs to know what he is going to be up against. He wants to know everything from what kind of door he will have to breech to gain entry to how many and who are the people inside. Are they armed? Do they have countersurveillance? Active intelligence is necessary whenever an investigator conducts an operation. This is especially true in the prison setting.

- Investigators gather intelligence as it relates to their specific investigations as well as the system at large. During an investigator's daily routine he will receive intelligence information from line staff, intelligence officers, and gang coordinators. This information will often initiate an investigation. By the same token, when conducting an investigation he may come across information that would be of value to facility intelligence officers, gang coordinators, and offender services.

- Intelligence officers within a facility will continually come across information that is of value to them or to investigations, gang coordinators, and offender services. These issues most likely will affect the security of their facility.
- Investigators and other staff will obtain intelligence working directly or indirectly with confidential informants.
- Other law enforcement agencies may obtain intelligence that will directly affect the operations of correctional facilities.
- Intelligence information is obtained through the constant monitoring of inmate mail and the inmate telephone system.
- Intelligence information may be gathered through the use of electronic surveillance.
- As a part of any special operations response team or criminal investigation division operation, intelligence may be collected through electronic or direct surveillance.

Every department of corrections should have in place dedicated intelligence gathering activities such as risk assessments or threat identifications that investigators might offer to the system as a special service to augment regular correctional facility security operations.

An investigator continually gathers intelligence to be analyzed and disseminated. He utilizes this information to develop criminal cases. Unfortunately, one of the problems with intelligence gathering is that it is not always maintained in a central location and is not always analyzed properly and disseminated. The investigator should take this into consideration and develop a plan to ensure that this is done. It will be beneficial to the investigator's unit and to the department as a whole.

Processing Intelligence

It is fundamental to any intelligence service that it maintain a central clearinghouse for all information. A single site means that all raw data is at hand and connections between similar bits of information can be identified and verified, inferences can be applied, and systemized pursuits to further develop information can be planned and executed to a logical conclusion. This can be accomplished through the use of databases and qualified personnel. The investigator needs to establish a standardized processing format together with a rating system for identifying the quality of the intelligence produced.

Intelligence processing should be no different on a daily basis than it would be at a command center during a critical incident.

Information or data received from any source is the raw material from which intelligence is produced. The process for conversion of the raw material into the finished product should include:

- Assessment of reliability of the originating source
- Assessment of reliability of the transmitting source
- Corroboration of any data from an independent source
- Application of logic to the details of the information

Refining the information, whose value or importance is judged to be worth the effort, should be done through whatever means suited to the nature of the topic, source, or transmitting persons.

Rating the processed intelligence should be limited to only three levels computed on how much the investigator can verify in the source, transmission, or corroboration.

- **High confidence**—Investigators have good reason to believe this information is true and free from unknown factors.
- **Low confidence**—Investigators have reason to believe that this information is probably true, but there may be unknown factors that may affect the quality of this information.
- **No confidence**—Investigators cannot corroborate, verify, or otherwise validate this information.

Another way of rating that is commonly used in the law enforcement community is:

- Very reliable: police officer, reliable informants, etc.
- Reliable: persons that are named in the report and are in a position to confirm the information
- Unreliable: persons that have provided incorrect or bogus information in the past
- Unknown: anonymous persons or others that do not have direct knowledge of the information

Adding other ratings would confuse the issue without serving a useful purpose.

Transmission of intelligence information is tricky. For example, where would the investigator send information concerning an escape? Would he send it to the affected facility? Would he send it to offender services? Would he send it to his investigative unit? The answer in this case would be all of the above and then some. The investigator needs someone in the intelligence community to identify where certain information should be disseminated to.

There will be many questions to be answered. The investigator will have to come up with the answers.

Case History #32

CID received information from the parole division of a possible escape attempt that was to take place within a few hours. The information was third hand, but all reports were considered reliable. Apparently, the parole officer of an ex-convict from the women's facility was told by the parolee that she was involved in a planned escape. The parole officer passed on this information to an investigator in another division, who in turn called CID.

The female parolee reported that, for about a year, she and an inmate had been planning the inmate's escape. The parolee and the inmate had been communicating recently by telephone and letters and the escape was planned for that very afternoon. The parolee told her parole officer that she wanted no part of the escape and wanted to help investigators.

A plan to stop the escape had already been devised by investigators and officials from another department. The plan and the case were turned over to CID, since the affected prison was in CID's jurisdiction.

According to the parolee, the inmate, and possibly another inmate, were going to attempt an escape from the prison. The inmates had already stolen a pair of wire cutters. They planned to leave at 4:30 p.m. just prior to a counting of the inmates. The inmates would leave via a fence at the rear of the laundry and meet with the parolee on a road about 1 mile from the prison. The parolee would have a car waiting and she would whisk them away.

The previous investigator and department officials had planned to let the inmates leave the prison and arrest them as they tried to enter the parolee's vehicle. It may have been a good scenario, but CID was not in the habit of using someone else's plan without researching all the possibilities. CID had 4 hours to decide what to do. As with any information, before anything is done, it needs to be corroborated. The parolee informant was interviewed by CID investigators. The interview revealed the same basic scenario and the parolee said that the she would drive her car to meet with the escaped inmates and assist with the investigation. The parolee also told CID that she had two recent telephone conversations with the escaping inmate. The telephone calls were reviewed and the information was corroborated. The parolee had given other information that could later be corroborated. CID checked computer information on the inmates that were going to escape. Both of these inmates were convicted murderers and were considered very violent and dangerous.

CID investigators decided not to let the escape attempt happen. Although it could have been a good operation, CID was well aware that there was room for error. Two very dangerous ladies were trying to escape. It was not known if they had weapons. There was a residential area between the prison and where they were to be picked up. The parolee had an extensive criminal record, and CID did not know for certain where her loyalties lay. (In fact, it was learned that the plan for capture was originally her idea.) The safety of the community, officers, and of course the inmates had to come first and the original plan was abandoned. CID had the telephone calls and the testimony of the parolee which was a beginning. The two inmates were immediately arrested and locked down in segregation while the investigation continued. CID notified offender services, security at the facility, and perimeter patrols. Extra patrols were initiated in case more inmates were involved.

The action taken was appropriate. No one was hurt and the escape never took place. The information was verified and corroborated before any action was taken and there was enough information collected to get arrest warrants issued. Escape materials were found in the possession of the inmates and the parolee agreed to testify. One of the inmates claimed to have backed out of the escape plot and was able to convince investigators that she did so. She too agreed to testify against the one inmate. It seemed like it should have been an open and shut case. Unfortunately, the inmate bandit that testified against the other was not well received by the jury. The parolee discharged her sentence and left the state. The jury took a liking to the defendant and she was found not guilty at trial. The good news was that no one got hurt and an escape was thwarted.

The intelligence process can be complicated and can easily run amok. Any intelligence gathering entity must be well planned and directed. The information must be efficiently collected, evaluated, collated, analyzed, disseminated, and re-evaluated.

Collection

The collection is the gathering of raw information and data in an organized fashion. To be effective, the collection effort must be planned and directed.

The investigator begins with target selection. First, establish a method of targeting which information will be sought out. Being able to anticipate and predict an occurrence before the fact is essential in the expenditure and deployment of resources. Thus, intelligence collection is a planning function which is closely related to the field of planning and research. Essentially, target selection involves the questions of why an investigator should spend a concerted effort on a target, when should he spend that effort, and how did he come to that conclusion.

Strategic intelligence is the long-range collection of information that reveals patterns and activities of organized criminal activity. The product of analyzing the problem—its size, scope, growth, influence, and projected impact on the investigator's organization—will weigh heavily on the target selection process.

Planning intelligence collection is essential. The investigator needs to establish who is to collect the information. Duplication of information is always a problem.

All overt means of collection should be exhausted before extensive covert operations are initiated. Covert operations, such as surveillance and controlled penetration (infiltrating an organization or group) informants, are often expensive, time consuming, and sometimes wasteful. Therefore, the cost must be honestly weighed against the probable return on the investment.

Evaluation

This process is when the information is categorized and interpreted for its validity, reliability, usefulness, and timeliness.

Collation

This is the process of compiling and filing the collections effort and the creation of a system for the rapid retrieval of stored information. It would be wise to set up a database for this effort. The system should also have the capability of rejecting of useless, nonrelevant, and incorrect information.

Analysis

This is the function that converts information into finished intelligence. It is analysis that assembles bits and pieces of collected data and puts it together in such a fashion that trends, patterns, and meanings are indicated.

Dissemination

This is the utilization of the product of the intelligence process. Dissemination is the reason that intelligence information is gathered and unless the gathered intelligence is utilized in an enforcement posture, the investigator's efforts have been wasted. Information in the files does not put the bandits away.

Reevaluation

This is the measure of effectiveness of the entire intelligence process. Reevaluation enables the investigator to refine the techniques of collection, evaluation, collation, and interpretation of data. Through this process, the investigator continually perfects the end product.

Categorization of Intelligence

1. *Indicative or premonitory intelligence* is intelligence that suggests new operations or developments.
2. *Tactical intelligence* is intelligence whose immediacy calls for direct action. This type of intelligence oftentimes is associated with major prison disturbances or serious criminal activity.
3. *Strategic intelligence* is intelligence that is collected over a period of time and is analyzed to indicate a new pattern of activity. This type of intelligence is utilized primarily in planning and resource allocation or to focus on a given area of investigation.
4. *Evidential intelligence* is intelligence that is factual and precise. It can be utilized for court presentation. This type of intelligence may often be of immediate tactical value or utilized in developing strategic intelligence.

Many necessary ingredients are needed to have an effective intelligence gathering community. A rapport needs to be built within the investigator's department as well as with other outside law enforcement agencies. The most important activity of the intelligence function is to form a liaison inside and outside the investigator's agency. This liaison not only gives the investigator wide-based coverage, but it also allows the investigator to build a mutual rapport, trust, cooperation, and personal contacts while continuing to collect information. There is no substitute for agencies working together. Today, no agency can "go it alone." The multijurisdictional approach to the problems of law enforcement is most desirable. Multiagency meetings increase personal contacts and the free exchange of information and ideas, which cannot be achieved in any other manner. Remember the basic principles of intelligence production: purpose, sources and resources, information conversion, unity of effort, and dissemination.

Access to Intelligence Files

All intelligence files should be stored and locked in a secure area within the investigator's department or intelligence unit. Any information maintained in a computerized intelligence information system should be maintained in a secure system that protects unauthorized attempts to access, modify, remove, or destroy intelligence information. Any backup tapes should be stored off-site in a fireproof safe.

Access to intelligence files should be limited to those individuals who have an absolute need or who supervise those with this need. The intelligence unit should identify, in writing, those who are authorized to access these files. The intelligence files should always be considered confidential.

Submission Criteria for Intelligence Information

As previously stated, there must be objectives and a purpose for the information gathered. Useless information gathering is senseless. It should be policy that information gathered should relate to the intelligence objectives and that files should be maintained only under certain conditions.

1. Information should not be collected on political, religious, or social views; associations; or activities of any individual or group, association, corporation, business, partnership, or other organization unless such information directly relates to conduct or activity and there is reasonable suspicion that the subject of the information is or may be involved in criminal conduct or activity or that the subject of the information could reasonably be considered a threat to the security of the facility.

2. Information should be collected anytime there is reasonable suspicion that the individual or group is involved in criminal conduct or activity or the conduct could reasonably be considered a threat to the security of the facility.

3. Reasonable suspicion is established when information exists which establishes sufficient facts to give a trained law enforcement officer or correctional officer a basis to believe there is a reasonable possibility that an individual or group is involved in criminal activity or activity that could be considered a threat to the facility.

4. The investigative unit should not include any intelligence information which has been obtained in violation of any applicable federal, state, or local law.

5. Information should be gathered relative to crime figures and criminal operations in order to identify crime patterns, conspiracies, or criminal associations or to develop probable cause to criminal acts and threats of the same.

6. Information should be gathered on violations of law, events, or conditions occurring in other jurisdictions which may pose a threat to life or property within the investigator's jurisdiction. This could generally pertain to organized crime, kidnaping, murder for hire, extortion, or acts of terrorism. It could also include conspiracies that involve inmates under the investigator's supervision involved in any criminal act in concert with civilians in another jurisdiction.

The criteria for establishing intelligence should be formulated by the investigator's agency and should preclude the gathering of information that is outside the objectives and purpose of his organization. In order to keep files current and efficient, information that was collected pursuant to the established criteria should be archived when the specific activity or threat which generated the collection has been abated or altered in a manner which would make void the original investigative objective or if the activity or threat was found to be false or nonexistent.

Review Process

There should be established review procedures which apply to the intelligence information received in the unit. These procedures should include a unit supervisor or designee that reviews each intelligence report received. This information should be correlated by the reviewer and placed into proper files. This reviewer should also be responsible for insuring that the information meets the submission criteria established by the unit.

Dissemination

Intelligence information should not be disseminated prior to the completion of the review process by the intelligence unit supervisor or designee. This would be to insure that all submission criteria have been met prior to dissemination.

The reviewer should then classify the information and disseminate it according to established criteria. The type of intelligence, of course, would determine where the intelligence is sent to.

- Ongoing criminal investigation
- Ongoing intelligence investigation
- Information required by court subpoena
- Threat information to a facility, law enforcement, government officials, or private citizens.
- Ongoing or new drug investigation
- Escape information
- Criminal information that relates to crimes outside the prison
- Planned demonstrations or other activity that would be a threat to a facility

Dissemination of intelligence information should only go to predetermined department of corrections personnel and law enforcement agencies on a need-to-know or right-to-know basis when it involves the performance of law enforcement activity.

Need-to-know is information that has been requested or is pertinent and necessary to the requester in initiating, furthering, or completing an investigation. It may also be information that is necessary to maintain the security of the facility.

Right-to-know is when the requester has official capacity and statutory authority to the information being requested or the information directly affects the security of the facility. Usually, it should be required that only the investigative unit pass the information to recognized outside law enforcement. A partial list of law enforcement agencies can include the following:

- Federal Bureau of Investigation
- state police
- any local sheriff or police department
- Internal Revenue Service
- U.S. Secret Service
- Alcohol, Tobacco, and Firearms
- Drug Enforcement Agency
- U.S. Postal Service
- Armed Forces Police
- Immigration and Naturalization Service
- Department of state, security division
- State bureaus of law enforcement

Nothing in an investigator's procedures should limit the dissemination of information to anyone when necessary to avoid imminent danger to life or property. This is particularly true when dealing with threat information. All threat information should be handled with first priority. Intelligence gathering is an absolute necessity for the prison investigator. The community the investigator polices is the underbelly of society, and without proper and efficient intelligence gathering he can do nothing but put out fires.

Affidavits and Warrants

11

Introduction

Although some of the following information has been covered in an earlier chapter, it bears repeating in the context of legal criminal justice procedures.

Inmates have the same rights as others under the constitution with a few exceptions. One is searches and seizures. Their person, their cell or any place else in the prison may be searched at any time without probable cause, warrant, or even reasonable suspicion. Their mail, both incoming and outgoing, is monitored, with the exception of legal mail. Every call they make or receive is monitored. All this evidence is admissible in court.

They also do not have freedom of movement, and visitation is controlled. Visitors and inmates can be monitored visually and audibly but must be informed of the surveillance. The equipment must be posted where everyone can see it.

All prisons have rules that are posted along with the obvious statutory laws. These rules may be enforced and do not necessarily coincide with typical rules outside the prison.

If an individual is thinking about applying for a criminal investigator position in the prison system, he had better be able to write an arrest warrant, a search warrant, and the affidavits to show probable cause. He will also need to be up to speed on 41.1 warrants and civil seizures. Most personnel in law enforcement already have this expertise. This chapter touches briefly on these documents for individuals who do not know what is necessary to produce a quality affidavit or warrant request.

Affidavits

In the strictest terms, an affidavit is a statement of facts that supports the issuance of a warrant. The affidavit also shows probable cause for a judge to sign the warrant. In preparing an affidavit there are certain guidelines that will insure that the warrant will be issued (that is, if there is probable cause in the first place).

Make sure that in the first paragraphs the criminal investigator identifies himself as a peace officer and that he has the authority to be writing the affidavit. It may be appropriate for him to give a very short history of his experience. This would be appropriate if he is not familiar with the judge or district attorney who will be reviewing his work. For example, "Your affiant, John Doe, has been assigned this case and is a criminal investigator with the Department of Corrections with 15 years of law enforcement experience."

Be sure to include that all the events described in the affidavit have taken place in the county where the warrant is being requested. Something that may help the investigator is that whenever a crime has been committed in more that one county, both counties have jurisdiction. So if the crime started in a prison in the investigator's county and part of the crime moves to another county, he can still seek the warrant in the county that he is familiar with. For example, "All the events occurred in the County of _____ unless otherwise stated."

List the statement of facts in chronological order, insuring continuity. Make the statements as short as possible without leaving anything out. If the affidavit has to be lengthy in order to show probable cause, then so be it.

Make sure to include dates and times and be very careful to include all the elements of the crime that have been allegedly committed.

To end the affidavit, of course, the investigator will need to explain in a paragraph how the affidavit lends to the probable cause for the warrant to be issued.

This is but a quick overview of the makings of the affidavit. The format differs from county to county and state to state. The investigator needs to become familiar with the needs of each jurisdiction. Remember also that the affidavit is the same whether the investigator is requesting a search warrant, an arrest warrant, a 41.1 warrant, or a civil seizure complaint.

Search Warrants

Probably the most important part of the search warrant is the location of the area to be searched. There is *never* a valid reason for searching the wrong location. A good investigator will never execute a bad search. He may find nothing, but he will not execute a search on the wrong premises.

When describing the place to be searched, include the street address and physical description of the property. Make sure the description is complete, giving cross streets and the number of houses from a known point. For example, "2222 North Nowhere Street. A single family dwelling, red brick with white trim, located on the northeast corner of Nowhere and Somewhere."

In addition, the investigator must include any outbuildings or vehicles that he may want to search. Near the end of the search warrant, the investigator will want to include what he is searching for. Be specific but in broad enough terms to insure that any fruits of the crime being investigated will be legally seized. Be careful not to make requests beyond the scope of the investigation.

Keep in mind that the evidence the investigator is searching for must be stolen or embezzled or designed or intended for use or which is or has been used as a means of committing a criminal offense or the possession of which is illegal or would be material evidence in a subsequent criminal prosecution.

This is a broad-based summary of search warrants and is not intended to be a know-all, tell-all resource. After all, investigators should already know this.

Additional Search Information

When an officer enters the world of prison investigations there are some unique differences when it comes to searches and seizures. These differences make the investigator's life a little easier, but they only apply within the prison walls.

There is little expectation of privacy when a criminal is sentenced to the department of corrections. Because of this lowered expectation of privacy, it is clearly legal to search any inmate, inmate's cell, or any common area of a prison facility. These searches are considered a matter of security: Security for the facility, staff, inmates, and the public. This capability gives the investigator an advantage during an investigation within the prison walls.

Another security issue is the inmate mail and telephone system. All inmate mail is subject to search and scanning, both incoming and outgoing. Since a portion of the inmate population is always involved in criminal activity, it is a matter of security to review the mail. This capability ends with the inmate's "legal" mail. Any mail from or to the criminal justice system is not subject to search. Incoming legal mail can be opened in the presence of the inmate and checked for contraband, *not* content.

The Colorado Department of Corrections has an inmate phone system. It is called the Colorado Inmate Phone System (CIPS). Each inmate presents a list of 11 telephone numbers he is allowed to call. The inmate signs a waiver and submits his list. This waiver notifies the inmate that all of his calls are subject to random monitoring and all calls are taped. The inmate is given a personal identification number (PIN). The inmate can now call any of his numbers by dialing his PIN number and the number associated with each telephone number. He can only call the numbers on his CIPS list.

An investigator can see the value of this system in conducting investigations. Inmates frequently use the mail and telephones to facilitate criminal activity.

In addition to this, all visitors entering Colorado prison grounds are required to sign a consent to search. This consent to search waives the right to privacy and allows for searches of their person, property, and vehicles. The waiver and large posted signs inform visitors of this.

This consent to search form is also utilized with all correctional staff. Every staff member is required to sign this form as a condition of employment.

Even though investigators have the ability to conduct these warrantless searches, they still need to write search warrants. Much of the crime that originates within the facility walls reaches out into the community and throughout the state. Additionally, some searches of inmates and visitors are intrusive and a warrant is required. Some of these searches include, but are not limited to, body cavity searches and strip searches. (A strip search does not need a warrant, but there are circumstances where it is advisable.)

Here is a short list of regularly sought warrants:

- Home and building searches
- Vehicle searches
- Visitor and body cavity searches
- 41.1 searches for trace evidence
- Bank record searches
- Telephone record searches
- Mail covers

In the past, telephone conversations were between two parties and the investigator knew the address where the call originated. With the advent of call forwarding and three-way calling, the investigator cannot rely on this originator information any longer. He cannot determine where a telephone call was made from anymore. The investigator will have to continue with his investigation and get more probable cause to request a search warrant based on telephone information.

Arrest Warrants

The same affidavit information is required to show probable cause. The investigator needs to identify the statute that is violated in his affidavit and show probable cause. When writing the warrant the investigator will also need to have a positive identification and physical description of his subject. The only exception is a John Doe warrant. In a John Doe warrant, if the investigator knows who the suspect is but has not positively identified him, he can get his warrant. Be sure that he or another investigator who actually knows the suspect are the only ones who attempt to serve this warrant.

41.1 Warrants

A 41.1 warrant refers to rule 41.1 of the Colorado rules of criminal procedure that authorizes an affiant, or any other peace officer, to take nontestimonial identification from a suspect. This nontestimonial identification evidence can be hair, blood, urine, saliva, semen, or fingernail scrapings, but it is not limited to these samples.

The affidavit is the same as requesting any other warrant, in that the investigator needs to have probable cause to have his request approved. This probable cause shows that the suspect has committed a specific violation of statutory law and the results of the specific nontestimonial identification procedures requested will be of material aid in determining whether the suspect named and described committed the offense.

Civil Seizures

Quite often suspects use personal property in the commission of felony crimes. They will use their homes, vehicles, boats, planes, money, or other personal property. When they choose to use their personal property in the commission of crimes, this property may be subject to seizure. This is done through a misdemeanor nuisance law. Sometimes the investigator opts to seize such property. Although this property is not part of the crime, it is charged under a separate offense. It is always important to prove ownership of such property and to insure there is no lien against the property. If there is a lien against a property, the investigator will need to determine if the value of the property is such that he will be able to pay off the lien. This lien becomes the investigator's responsibility when seizure is accomplished.

In Colorado, as in most states, there is a lot of paperwork to fill out in attempting a seizure. The investigator has to file a seizure complaint, seizure affidavit, motion for temporary restraining order (TRO), the temporary restraining order itself, and a seizure summons.

Seizure Complaint

In the seizure complaint the investigator must get a civil action number to be used on all the documents through the courts. It must describe the property to be seized and the owners as defendants. The investigator must enumerate the statutes and identify the jurisdiction and venue. He must make a statement of offense making the property a public nuisance and must note the attachment of the affidavit and name the ownership of the property. The investigator requests, based on the affidavit, that the property be declared a public nuisance and requests that the courts enter an order of abatement which provides the forfeiture of the defendant's property to his jurisdiction. The investigator also requests that the property be transferred to his department.

Seizure Affidavit

This affidavit mirrors any affidavit for arrest or search, chronologically depicting the events and showing probable cause for the complaint.

Motion for Temporary Restraining Order (TRO)

In this document the investigator refers to the civil action number and again describes the property. As the plaintiff in the action, the investigator refers to the statute regarding restraining orders and shows grounds for the action. He states the statutes showing public nuisance and TRO. In this document he restates his request to seize the property and to take temporary possession so that the property cannot be disposed of prior to court disposition.

Temporary Restraining Order

This document describes the terms of the restraining order. It gives the same information contained in the motion for TRO. It also orders the defendants to turn in the property to the investigator's agency, giving time limits. It also orders the defendants not to sell, transfer, encumber, damage, mortgage, or in any manner destroy the property.

Seizure Summons

In the summons the investigator is directing the defendant to file with the clerk of the court an answer to the summons within 20 days. It states in the document that if they fail to respond in writing within the 20 days, judgement for the plaintiff will occur.

Once the investigator gets all these documents prepared, he should show them to the district attorney and then take them to a circuit court judge. The judge will review and sign the documents. Then the investigator needs to serve the summons with a copy of the affidavit, the motion for TRO, and the TRO.

Court Preparation and Testimony

12

Introduction

The criminal investigator will be frequently called upon to testify in court. It is his investigation that got the case to the courtroom and his testimony will likely be weighed heavily by the jury. He will be representing his department and the district attorney's office and himself as an investigator. Remember that the investigator may have developed the best case there is, but if his testimony is not perceived as credible by the jury he will most definitely lose. The greatest evidence in the world is worthless if no one believes the investigator.

This chapter is designed to give the new investigator a look at what will be expected of him and to give seasoned investigators a refresher course.

Tips for Presenting Testimony

An investigator's behavior when testifying is very important. When an investigator is called to testify, the defense will attempt to discredit his testimony. The investigator should be prepared and listen carefully to the questions. Presented here are some suggested rules for the investigator. Not all of these suggested rules will apply to each investigator or to all cases, but nonetheless they are important.

- Show confidence when taking the oath in front of the judge. Say "I do" in a clear voice and be sincere. After all, the investigator swears to tell the truth. That is his job.
- Dress conservatively and wear clean, crisp clothing. A suit and tie are most appropriate. Do not make the mistake of wearing casual clothes

or a humorous tie. It takes away from the investigator's credibility. Do not wear sunglasses in court, even if they are prescription.

- Always have a professional demeanor both on and off the stand. When on the stand, sit in a comfortable position using good posture. Do not fidget or wiggle around in the chair. Do not chew gum or anything else. Avoid any mannerisms which the jury may interpret as signs of nervousness or falsity. Mannerisms such as covering your mouth with your hand, rubbing your nose, or avoiding eye contact give the perception of deception, do not do it. Keep it serious on and off the stand during the trial. Do not joke or make disparaging remarks in the hallway. The jury may be returning from their break and may hear these comments.

- Avoid memorizing any testimony. Do not talk in a monotone voice. Tell the story and tell it well. When preparing to testify, do not try to figure out what the defense is going to ask. Just study the reports and the facts of the case. The investigator is sworn to tell the truth. Do not attempt to determine whether an answer will help or hurt either side.

- Listen carefully to all the questions. Be sure to let the attorney ask the entire question before answering it. If the investigator does not understand the question, ask the attorney to repeat it. Answers should be thoughtful and deliberate, but, on the other hand, do not take too much time to answer as it may look like the investigator is trying to think up an answer.

- Avoid looking to the prosecutor's table for an answer when the defense asks a hard question. Just be honest. Never guess or assume. If the investigator does not know the answer to a question, he should say he does not know or cannot remember. It is not a sin to not know the answer to a question, but it is a sin to lie or a big mistake to guess. Truth stands the test of time, while lies are soon exposed. Judges, lawyers, and jurors remember who is credible and who is not. Once an investigator is known as a liar, he will always have problems in court. He might as well go out and find another job.

- Include the jury when testifying. Develop a relationship with that jury. Try to gain eye contact with every juror during testimony. These are the people who have to be convinced of the guilt of the suspect. If the investigator does not make some good impressions on the jury, he may lose his case.

- If an error is made during testimony, correct it immediately.

- When testifying, never give a sarcastic answer. The investigator does not want to come off as a wise guy. Be polite and respectful to the prosecutor and the defense lawyers. Remain polite, even under the most intensive cross-examination, to avoid appearing like a jerk.

- Avoid the use of technical language. The investigator wants the jury to understand what he is talking about.
- Always be confident on the stand. Speak clearly, positively, and confidently. If the investigator is not confident about his case, tell the prosecutor and he will act accordingly. Develop a reputation for being connected with competent investigations only. Always be attentive while on the stand. Speak clearly and distinctly.
- Do not volunteer answers. Only answer the questions asked. If the answer takes more than a yes or no, give the answer, but do not talk about other things.

Case History #33

In 1999 CID finally finished a 3-year investigation with a 2-year trial. A two year trial might seem unusual. It all happened because a witness volunteered an answer to a question that was not asked. If there was blame to be placed, it had to be with the prosecution for not preparing the witness.

The case involved a correctional captain who was charged with multiple counts of sexual assault by a person in a position of trust. This captain was alleged to have sexually assaulted at least five and maybe seven or eight inmates. Most of the assaults stemmed from captain using his authority and threats to gain sexual favors. The case did have some physical evidence and some admissions by the suspect (through pretext calls). There were also several inmate witnesses. In many cases where inmates have leveled charges against staff, a polygraph has been utilized as an investigative tool. While it cannot be used in court, it can help investigators in determining the truthfulness of witness statements.

At trial, one of the inmate victims, during her testimony, blurted out that she had passed the lie detector test. A mistrial was declared and the case had to be retried. It was difficult getting all of the witnesses together as many inmates had been released and had to be located. Several months later, the case appeared in court for the second time. Some of the witnesses could not be located, the lead CID investigator was retiring, and everything seemed to go wrong. This court appearance ended up with a hung jury. The DA had to decide if the case should be tried again. Expenses were mounting and witnesses kept disappearing.

The DA decided that the case was too important to let drop and that the case would be retried. This time, all witnesses were endorsed and CID actually found a couple more inmates who had been assaulted in the past and were out of prison before the case started. The investigator came back from retirement and CID was ready to go.

As it turned out, the suspect decided, through his attorney, to enter into a plea agreement that was accepted by the court.

- Never answer a question by starting out with "to be honest" or "to tell the truth," or "truthfully." The investigator has already sworn to tell the truth, under oath, and saying these things may imply to the jury that he is not telling the truth. Do not exaggerate.
- Be careful of using "Isn't it true…," "What your saying then is…," or "In fact…." The investigator should make sure that he fully understands the question and if not, be sure to tell the attorney. Defense attorneys often misquote the investigator's previous testimony when asking these types of questions. Listen carefully to all of their questions. Listen to all the questions the district attorney asks as well. He may ask a question he did not want to ask. Be sure to have him repeat the question if there is any doubt about what he wants. The jury probably did not understand the question if the investigator did not.
- When there is an objection raised while the investigator is testifying, he should stop talking until the judge has ruled on the objection. Do not try to squeeze something in under the wire. An investigator cannot object to a question on his own. If the prosecutor missed it, that is just too bad, the investigator should answer the question to the best of his ability.

In some jurisdictions, the investigator is almost always the advisory witness. This means that he will have to be at the prosecutor's table during the entire trial. He will need to maintain his confidence and demeanor during the entire trial. This is true on and off the stand, while sitting at the table, and out in the court hallways.

Sometimes the way a defense attorney asks an innocent question makes it sound like the investigator did something wrong. Do not overthink the answers. One question the investigator will frequently be asked is if he has discussed this case with the district attorney. Of course the investigator has discussed the case with the district attorney. The defense attorney may even imply that the district attorney told the investigator what to say in an effort to discredit him. Of course any attorney knows not to ask a question he does not know the answer to and it is times like these that sometimes offer opportunity. For example, the defense asks the investigator, "What did the district attorney tell you to say?" The investigator's response was, "He told me not to forget to mention when the defendant told me he was sorry for killing his cell mate."

Many of the investigators out there are considered experts in an area of law enforcement. When testifying as an expert witness, the defense may use many ploys to discredit the investigator's testimony. One of the most common ways is to ask the investigator if he has read a certain textbook on the subject. The attorney is trying to get the investigator to recognize the book as an authority on the subject matter so he can use it to challenge his testimony. The investigator can state that he has not read the entire book and does not know if he would agree with everything in it. If the attorney quotes from the book, the investigator should ask to read the quote himself and should study the context of the statement.

In almost every case the investigator will be asked to identify the suspect. In corrections there may be cases where the investigator has never seen the suspect. The district attorney will usually subpoena another witness to do the identification, but sometimes there is not enough time to find another witness.

Case History #34

The DA and the investigator were sitting at the prosecutor's table. The DA told the investigator that he would be used for the identification on the case being heard.

In this particular case, the investigator and the inmate had never met. The case was a simple drug possession where correctional staff had found the inmate with the drugs. The staff talked with the inmate before CID investigators were called. The inmate immediately asked for a lawyer which meant that the investigators could not talk to him.

This was a preliminary hearing and the investigator was going to hearsay all of the staff statements and get the case bound over for trial. The DA and the investigator looked at each other and knew that the same idea had occurred to both of them.

Whenever an inmate's criminal case is tried a "pen pack" is provided. A pen pack includes the inmates's sentencing information, other papers, and the inmate's photograph. It basically corroborates that the inmate is lawfully incarcerated. The investigator took a good look at the photograph.

During direct examination by the DA, the investigator identified the inmate. It was clarified that the identification was made from an official department of corrections photograph that the investigator had looked at prior to the court appearance. The identification was not disputed.

Trial Preparation

The investigator's testimony is vital to the prosecution. The investigator is the highlight of the trial. He is a witness and a professional and his testimony should be sharp and focused. The investigator's testimony is the thread that binds the physical evidence and the witnesses testimony. His testimony will be used to impeach the defense witnesses. The jury expects to be led by the investigator to a logical conclusion. If he fails to do this, he will lose the case.

When does the investigator's preparation for trial begin? It begins the day he starts his investigation and continues through the trial. The entire case depends on how the investigator develops his case, collects evidence, interviews suspects, interviews witnesses, writes his reports, and testifies in court.

Investigators must report all information pertaining to a case. The investigator must ensure that his reports contain all the elements of the crime and are very complete. The reports should be in a chronology that tells the story of the crime, what the evidence is, and where it was collected.

When the investigator is not prepared, the defense case goes up and the prosecution case goes down. The investigator needs to be better prepared that the prosecuting attorney. The prosecuting attorney covers the whole county and all the law enforcement agencies in the county and this case is not the only one he is working on. The investigator has to help guide the prosecutor to success. There are times when the investigator will not even have time for a pretrial conference with the prosecuting attorney.

Review the case a day or two before trial. Read, do not skim, over the reports. The investigator will always refresh his memory with facts he has forgotten.

The investigator should bring *all* his reports, witness statements, and physical evidence to the courtroom. Be sure to have a documented chain of custody for the evidence. The prosecuting and defense attorneys will have all the reports, but not the evidence. Make sure that they have all of the investigative reports and that they are complete. If it is not in the reports, it did not happen. If the defense has not received the reports, they do not exist.

Be sure that when testifying to the facts that they are the same as in the written reports. Do not add anything that is not in the reports. Investigative reports are very crucial as they may impeach defense witnesses.

Preparing for the trial also includes meeting with the district attorney. He should have already told the investigator his approach to the prosecution. As the lead investigator in the case, the investigator may have an idea or a different approach. Be sure to tell the district attorney; he may not use it, but tell him. Always keep him informed and help him whenever possible. The investigator spent a lot of time developing the case and no one should know it better than him.

Internal Affairs Investigations

13

Introduction

In any workplace there are rules and procedures that need to be followed in order to conduct business in an efficient manner and to insure the safety and well-being of the agency and its employees. In most cases these rules and procedures are enforced by supervisory staff. In government operations, the need to follow these rules and procedures becomes even more essential. Government operations often deal with legal issues as well as the normal operating rules and procedures. This opens the door to litigation from outside citizenries as well as employees. Government agencies have a higher expectation of professionalism from their employees. In most cases infractions are addressed by supervisory staff, but there are instances where it would give the impression of favoritism or bias if the investigation was conducted by one's supervisor. Herein comes the need to have a separate, yet within the department, investigative body to conduct investigations into infractions originating from workplace violations.

In any department of corrections it is essential to have an investigative force to conduct internal investigations. In the inmate population there are literally thousands of lawsuits and grievances filed every year. Each of these is usually preempted by some sort of complaint that has to be investigated. In addition, with thousands of employees, there are many complaints of misconduct every year. All of these allegations and complaints need to be addressed in some fashion. Most of these can be handled by supervisory staff within the facilities, but there are many that need to be investigated. This is where the internal affairs division comes into play. These investigations have to be conducted in a fair and impartial manner which necessitates that the internal affairs division be separate from normal departmental operations.

Investigators from the internal affairs division need to be separate from the criminal investigations division. The only time a criminal investigator should be involved in a staff investigation is when it becomes a criminal matter.

This chapter provides a basic understanding of sexual harassment complaints and examines the different types of internal affairs investigations. It will also discuss some investigative techniques that are unique to internal affairs. Some criminal investigations involving staff will also be reviewed. This chapter identifies some of the tools available to the investigator during an internal affairs investigation that are not available in a criminal investigation. Some guidelines are provided to help the investigator, but they are not intended as a real resource for investigations. The internal affairs department should insure that every investigator if fully trained in these investigations. Sexual harassment complaints are of utmost importance to internal affairs, and they cannot be overlooked or ignored.

Sexual Harassment

There has been an ongoing and valiant attempt by legislators to eliminate harassment and bias within workplaces throughout the United States. This type of behavior has been and remains a serious problem throughout the world.

> The vast majority of employers do not intentionally close their eyes to sexual harassment within their organizations, management personnel do not intentionally allow sexual harassment to occur within their workplaces, employees do not intentionally sexually harass other employees, and investigators do not intentionally mismanage sexual harassment investigations. Yet, the impact of how some employers, management personnel, employees, and investigators are currently dealing with this issue is creating expensive lawsuits and emotional hardships for everyone.
>
> **Anderson-Davis, Inc.**

Most state agencies have taken a no tolerance view of sexual harassment. They have educated their supervisors and investigators in how to deal with these situations. In addition, most corrections academies offer a significant amount of training to their new staff in dealing with sexual harassment and provide regular and ongoing in-service training for all staff. It is to the advantage of the employer and its management to recognize and stop all sexual harassment before it negatively affects employees and creates legal and financial liability.

'l'here are always two sides to every coin. There are individuals that receive this training, learn all the buzz words, and use this knowledge in a self-serving manner. Investigators run into many of these cases. The motives for these individuals are many. It may be for the intent of filing a lawsuit and getting a monetary reward, an unwillingness to perform their assigned duties, or some form of retaliation. It does not matter to the investigator what the motives are, he only needs to be aware of the possibilities when conducting an investigation. This chapter identifies some of these cases to bring an awareness to the investigators.

When obvious sexual harassment occurs in the workplace, both employers and employees tend to recognize it, but when subtle sexual harassment occurs it is harder to recognize. An investigator needs to be able to identify sexual harassment in its many forms.

Basic definitions of sexual harassment are:

1. Sexism is an attitude. It is an attitude of a person of one sex that he or she is superior to a person of the opposite sex (i.e., a man thinks that women are too emotional, or a woman thinks that men are chauvinistic).
2. Sex discrimination is a behavior. It occurs when employment decisions are based on an employee's sex or when an employee is treated differently because of his or her sex instead of his or her work experiences or qualifications.
3. Sex-based harassment is defined as a behavior that denigrates, ridicules, and/or is physically abusive of an employee because of his or her sex.
4. Sexual harassment is defined as unwelcome behavior of a sexual nature. There are two types of sexual harassment.
   a. Quid pro quo sexual harassment is when employment and/or employment decisions for an employee are implicitly based on that employee's acceptance or rejection of unwelcome sexual behavior.
   b. Hostile work environment sexual harassment is a work environment created by unwelcome sexual and/or sex-based behavior that is offensive, hostile, and/or intimidating and that adversely affects that employee's ability to do his or her job.
5. Subtle sexual harassment is a practical term, not a legal term, that describes unwelcome sexual or sex-based behavior that, if allowed to continue, could create illegal sexual harassment (i.e., unwelcome sexual comments, ogling, sexual jokes, etc.).

Many government agencies use the same definition of sexual harassment. Sexual harassment is any unwelcome sexual advances; requests for sexual favors, whether verbal or nonverbal; or physical conduct of a sexual nature when:

1. Submission to such conduct is made either explicitly or implicitly as a term or condition of an individual's employment.
2. Submission to or rejection of such conduct by an individual is used as the basis for employment decisions affecting such individual.
3. Such conduct has the purpose or effect of unreasonably interfering with an employee's work performance or creating an intimidating, hostile, or offensive work environment.

Such conduct stereotypes a gender into a degrading, less than desirable status within the workplace, creating an intimidating, hostile, or offensive work environment. Any deliberate, unwanted or unwelcome behavior of a sexual nature or sexual stereotyping, whether verbal, nonverbal, or physical, constitutes sexual harassment.

Investigating Sexual Harassment

There are some elements of a sexual harassment investigation that the investigator needs to be aware of before he begins internal affairs investigating.

In most crimes the investigator needs to develop probable cause before he can take the case to the district attorney. The investigator knows he has built a solid case, and if the witnesses and the district attorney do their job, he will get a conviction.

When investigating a sexual harassment complaint the investigator needs only to develop a preponderance of the evidence. The investigator will need 51% or the majority of the evidence to show it is more likely he or she did it rather than not.

Another really important fact to remember is that it is not necessarily what someone has done that matters in these investigations. The case is based on the perception of the recipient of the alleged sexual harassment. Remember also that in many cases, there will be litigation after the investigation has been completed. The investigator should not dismay if he has found no cause for action and yet the plaintiff wins his or her civil case. Just be sure to do a thorough job with the investigation. Remember also that most of these cases will become political.

Case History #35

A couple of years ago a female staff person filed a complaint. Her initial complaint was against one staff member who, she alleged, assaulted her during a search of her handbag. In short order, the complaint widened to virtually every member in her work area. She alleged sexual-biased harassment from everyone in the workplace. During the investigation it was found that the complainant and all the staff in the area frequently engaged in horseplay. This horseplay eventually escalated into a situation one evening. During this incident a security officer ordered this staff member to submit to a search of her purse. The staff member refused, which is in violation of regulations. It was also a search that did not need to be done and was more than likely done in retaliation for earlier comments made by both participants. The two struggled over the purse and the complainant wrenched her wrist. The complainant broadened her complaint to encompass a 2-year time frame. This investigation lasted entirely too long and became very convoluted. During the investigation the complainant's husband was interviewed. During this interview he told investigators that the main reason for his wife's complaint was that she wanted to file a lawsuit and gain some monetary reward. At that time he did not agree with her decision.

The investigation finally concluded with the following facts surfacing.

1. The initial complaint was considered to be a third degree assault, stemming from an argument between the complainant and the harasser.
   a. The complainant reported her wrist was broken. The attending physician reported that the injury was insignificant.
2. The complaints of sexual harassment were without merit.
3. The complaints of workplace harassment were inconclusive.

The results of the investigation included the harasser being convicted of third degree assault in a court of law. He negotiated a termination of employment. Although the complaints of harassment were without merit, the facility took significant steps to improve the working environment in her work area.

The complainant served notice on the department and filed a workplace harassment lawsuit. Her suit progressed for a couple of years. The end result was that she won her lawsuit.

Initial Reports

After an initial complaint is made, the investigator records the alleged harassment and begins his investigation.

Based on the initial report, determine what the controlling elements are:

- Was this a violation of department policy (on sexual harassment and employee misconduct)?
- Was this a violation of federal or state law?

The investigator should review department regulations and policies as they relate to sexual harassment. Be sure to include notices to all employees. Get copies of applicable state and federal laws and review them for the investigation. The investigator does not need to determine the scope of his authority or establish specific ground rules for his investigation because, as an investigator, he will have been assigned the case.

Be sure to obtain all the data available regarding the participants in an incident (i.e., employment history, past complaints, and investigations).

Interview the Complainant

During the in-depth interview several facts need to be ascertained. The recipient will identify several other witnesses and nonwitnesses that may or may not have any information. Be sure to contact all of these people. Do not limit the interview to preliminary facts. Establish *prima facie* evidence of sexual harassment during this interview. Obtain specific details in response to questions dealing with who, what, where, how often, who else, time, place, opportunity, history, contemporaneous events, and reports. Be sure to prepare a chronology of events and confirm specific sequences with the complainant (this will offer the opportunity to corroborate statements). During the interview attempt to:

- Identify the participants. Identify people directly involved in the interactions and others who may have seen or heard the interaction.
- Determine the relationship of the participants.
- Objectively identify the behavior. Objectively describe the behavior of each of the participants in the interaction.
- Determine if the behavior is unwelcome.
- Determine if the unwelcome behavior is sexual or sex based.

Case History #36

A few years ago there was a case involving a new employee. She had just finished the academy and was on her first assignment. She had received sexual harassment training and was familiar with the process.

At her first assignment there was an older male who would make what she perceived as sexual comments to others in her presence. These types of comments were specifically mentioned in her training. These comments began to bother her when he began to include her. Initially, she decided not to report these comments to her supervisor because she was a new employee and did not want to make any waves, but she also remembered in her training that she had an obligation to report these comments to her supervisor. Eventually, she made mention to a fellow employee that the comments bothered her. She was advised by her co-worker to report the incidents to their supervisor, which she did. Sexual harassment had become a problem at this particular facility and most reports were immediately turned over to the inspector general's office before any facility investigation was done. The investigator assigned to the case conducted his initial interview with the reporting staff person. The investigator identified several witnesses who had heard the same type of comments from the offending staff person. The comments were right out of the 1940s and 1950s mentality. The comments were not deemed welcome by the reporting staff person or others. However, no one had ever told this person that the comments were unwelcome. It was perceived that "he was just that way." The investigator finished all of the preliminary work on the case and set up an interview with the offending staff person. During the interview the investigator asked pointed, specific questions that identified the exact behavior questioned. To his surprise the staff member acknowledged the statements and questioned why anyone would be offended. As it turned out this person had slipped through the cracks. He was in his 60s and had been with the department for almost 30 years. He had never received any training in sexual or workplace harassment. He did not think he had done anything wrong. It was the way he had acted for 30 years. This man did not intend to offend anyone. He had acted like this for his entire adult life. It was simply the way he was brought up and the way he was. He never intended to offend anyone and since no one had ever complained, he was not aware that it offended anyone.

As it turned out the case was easily resolved. The offending staff person was given a corrective action and directed to attend training in sexual harassment. The offended staff person was quite satisfied with the outcome as well. It was considered one of the most quickly resolved cases that ended well for everyone.

When conducting sexual and workplace harassment investigations, it is not the intent of the offending person that is considered. It is the perception of the recipient that is considered. So even if a person does not mean to offend anyone, if someone was offended it is classified as harassment.

Review the Physical Scene

Check the time line. Is it the same date as the incident? Find out if there are obstructions blocking the view of potential witnesses. If it is not the same date, determine if the physical scene is the same today as it was on the day of the incident. Determine which employees were working the day of the incident. (Do not depend on the alleged victim to provide all witnesses, especially those who might not testify in the manner the alleged victim would like.) Find out if the alleged harasser has a habit of visiting the area or if this was an isolated incident. Find out if the alleged harasser had the opportunity to be in the area. Question staff working in the area to determine any additional facts that would be of value to the investigation.

Interview All Witnesses Given by the Recipient

If the investigator has done his homework with the recipient he will be able to corroborate or dispute the recipient's statement. Include fellow workers of the alleged harasser in the interviews. Be objective and look for the truth.

Do not let preconceived notions, particularly those expressed before the investigation, control or limit the scope of the investigation. Do not make moral judgements or let personal opinions regarding the alleged harasser or the alleged recipient control the investigator's fact finding efforts.

This may sound like a contradiction, but the investigator should limit his investigation to obtaining sufficient information for decision making. Do not gather all possible information. These types of investigations tend to go on and on. There may have been difficulty in this work area for years. This investigation is not going to cure all problems. An extended investigation will traumatize an organization, and responses to interview questions will become increasingly conditional and unreliable if an investigation extends beyond a third day in a large organization.

Evaluate the evidence collected. Identify any inconsistencies between the people interviewed about the alleged sexual harassment behavior, circumstances, location, dates, and times. Reinterview people only if necessary to clarify previous testimony and to determine the basis for inconsistencies.

Sexual harassment investigations must always remain "confidential." The investigator should keep the facts of the investigation confidential, even among fellow investigators.

In the summary of the investigation report, cross reference the evidence used to determine the merit of each allegation. The investigator may put in a series of points to consider. Do not write conclusions in the report. The investigation should be sterile and should not contain any personal observations, comments, or suggestions for resolution. Deliberation should be handled by the appointing authority. Just be sure to have all the facts.

Note that the investigator will be looking to answer many questions. He will want to know the alleged behavior, where and when it took place, was there physical evidence, were there witnesses, did the harasser have the means and opportunity to commit the alleged harassment, and many other questions. One thing he does not need is a motive. Motive is not necessary in a case such as this.

As in any investigation a check list of things to do that includes pre- and postinvestigation elements should be prepared.

Remember, no matter what the initial complaint is, be sure to investigate thoroughly. The investigator may have a more serious complaint that becomes a criminal matter.

Case History #37

This sexual harassment case was recently concluded. The harassment had allegedly been going on for a few years. It involved a security lieutenant and at least four alleged victims. The only reason the case came to light was because a conversation was overheard between two of the victims.

All four of the victims who were identified did not want to come forward for various reasons, but once a complaint is received, it has to be investigated. At the beginning of this case, the investigator did not notice the severity of the complaint. It appeared as though it was some sort of retaliatory effort on the part of some of the complainants. This was initially supported by the alleged harasser. This investigator, however, was very tenacious. He pursued the matter completely and to a logical conclusion.

In the end, this non-specific complaint by a disinterested party turned out to be a case of virtual sexual assault. It included all the elements described in publications about sexual harassment. It had quid pro quo, sexism, sex discrimination, sex-based harassment, sexual harassment, hostile work environment sexual harassment, subtle sexual harassment, and sexual assault. This case nearly became a rape investigation. The investigator identified all of the elements needed for determining merit to the sexual harassment complaint and the probable cause for a warrant for the arrest of our harasser for sexual assault in the third degree. The alleged offender was duly prosecuted with a conviction. His employment was terminated and the case was closed.

It is necessary for investigators to understand another element of the investigation—the aftermath. An investigator is concerned about finding the truth, but keep in mind what happens after the case is concluded. In many cases the offender, even after cleared of any wrongdoing, will be labeled and will have some sort of negative reputation. The victims in almost every case will experience difficulty in their careers. They can and will be labeled by their coworkers in many different ways. This is why the investigator needs to handle these cases quickly and efficiently. He needs to understand of the feelings of everyone involved. He needs to keep the investigation confidential.

Workplace Discrimination/Harassment

A typical workplace harassment definition would include "to irritate, torment, continually annoy or pester, creating an intimidating, hostile, or offensive environment, or interfering with staff's performance."

Workplace harassment regulations are usually contained within the sexual harassment sections of departmental rules and regulations. It stands to reason that workplace harassment investigations are handled in the same manner as sexual harassment cases and are equally important to the department or agency. There are many bonafide complaints surfacing every day. Sometimes these complaints are not investigated fully because they do not give the appearance of a complaint with merit. Make sure to investigate fully every complaint that comes across the investigator's desk.

There are also many workplace harassment complaints that are not valid. The investigator needs to be able to recognize these false complaints during his investigation.

When investigating any internal affairs case, be it sexual harassment, workplace discrimination/harassment, or any other case, there is a tool available in most government agencies. This tool is an internal investigation warning. It is similar to Miranda in that it is an advisement of rights. What is distinctive about it is that the warning directs the subject to give a truthful statement. The basis is that a staff member has to cooperate with investigators and give a truthful statement as a condition of employment. The statement, however, cannot be used against the subject in criminal charges. If the subject is advised of this internal warning and either lies or fails to cooperate with the investigators, he or she may be subject to administrative sanctions. One name given to this warning in some agencies is "Garrity."

Like any tool, Garrity should be used only when necessary, for example, if the case is likely to become a criminal case. In most instances the investigator would not want to give Garrity because nothing the suspect tells him will be usable in court. More so, anything the investigator learns as a result of that information cannot be used in court either.

Another example of when an investigator might not want to use Garrity is if the suspect is being cooperative initially. By giving Garrity the investigator might anger or scare the suspect into remaining silent (regardless of the consequences).

Whether working an internal affairs case or a criminal case, most investigators want to be sure the suspect has done what he is alleged to have done. Even though the investigator is not responsible for making the decisions, his report will be instrumental in any action that is taken. So investigate to the fullest and find as much truth as possible.

In sexual and workplace harassment cases there is always verbal and/or physical contact. There are seldom any witnesses to the alleged harassment and little corroboration. There is another tool at the investigator's disposal—the pretext phone call. It is so simple, and it works. Colorado law allows for the taping of telephone calls if one party of the call is aware it is being taped. If the victim is willing, get him or her to make a taped telephone call to the alleged harasser. During this call have the victim discuss some of the facts he or she has related to the investigator in the interview. Frequently, the alleged harasser will at least show knowledge of the incident in question.

Case History #38

A female correctional officer reluctantly came forward with information about some alleged harassment. She related that during the last year a security supervisor had made sexual advances toward her on many occasions.

She said he would frequently tell her that he wanted to have sex with her and offered to "let her" perform oral sex on him. She said on one occasion he took her in his state vehicle to a remote place and talked of wanting to make love to her. She said that he put his hand on her leg and ran it up between her legs. She said that when she protested violently he stopped and took her back to work. (Internal affairs cases are to be held confidential, but many times because of the chain of command that has to be maintained, people know and people talk.)

When the word got out that this security supervisor was being investigated for sexual harassment, there were four additional women that came forward with information. Their stories were all different, but had similarities. The investigator that was handling the case had only the word of these women. The supervisor had been with corrections for several years and was a highly respected, married individual. Through his investigation the investigator had a preponderance of evidence, but he was not satisfied. He convinced the initial complainant to make some pretext phone calls. The victim agreed and placed a few calls to the supervisor. During these taped conversations the supervisor not only corroborated the complaint, but tried to get the woman to meet with him. Case closed. The investigator felt much better about the case because like any good investigator he wanted to be sure he was right.

Staff Involvement in Drugs

In the prison setting the investigator will be involved in many cases involving staff and drugs. Most of the information on conducting drug investigations is contained in Chapter 2. Investigators should be aware of the different kinds of cases that involve staff and drugs.

Occasionally, investigators work cases involving staff that are alleged to have used illegal drugs or in some cases abused prescription drugs. Many of these cases arise out of contact with outside law enforcement agencies. A staff member will be caught in possession of small amounts of drugs or they may even be involved in a larger drug operation. In these cases the investigator's duty would only require obtaining police reports and writing an informational report to the inspector general and appointing authority.

When a staff member is believed to be using illegal drugs on duty, the investigator becomes more involved in the investigation. He arranges a urinalysis screen to be taken, interviews the staff member, and possibly follows up leads on the case. This type of case is handled like any other internal affairs case. It is possible, depending on the circumstances, that it would become a criminal case. There are other issues that may surface during the investigation. If, for example, the staff member refuses to provide a urine sample, the investigator is required to document the refusal in his report.

Possession of drugs could fall into two categories. One would be off-duty related and handled by local law enforcement with the aforementioned exceptions. The other would be possession on duty or on prison property and in most cases would be handed by internal affairs as a criminal case. If it is a criminal case, the investigator should copy his internal affairs section. This should be true of any criminal case involving staff. The internal affairs investigator merely puts an internal affairs number on the case and forwards it to the inspector general and the appointing authority for administrative action. Remember that whenever criminal charges are brought against a staff member there needs to be an internal investigation as well. This will insure that administrative action is taken.

Introduction of illegal drugs into prison is sometimes committed by staff members. In these cases it would most often constitute criminal charges. Not all contraband in a prison are drugs. There are many items, which vary from agency to agency, that are considered contraband. Recently, some prison systems have outlawed tobacco totally from their prisons. The rationale, in some cases, has been that they have been litigated over second-hand smoke causing cancer and other ailments. Because of this cigarettes have become another item of contraband. Staff seem to have a hard time adjusting to this. Since they may not feel tobacco is illegal, they have little problem in rationalizing the introduction of tobacco products. With new legislation it is now criminal to introduce tobacco. An unforseen problem is that some district attorneys are reluctant to prosecute these cases. Even with this reluctance, the investigator has other options. There is, of course, the administrative avenue which will be investigated by the internal affairs section. The other is bribery. A staff member may introduce tobacco and be paid for his violation of regulation and law. When this happens, he or she has committed bribery.

For details on conducting investigations of drug crimes, see Chapter 2.

Staff/Inmate Relationships

In the prison setting the investigator frequently investigates inappropriate relationships between inmates and staff. Usually these violations are predictable. Supervisory staff need to be aware of the way their staff interface with the inmate population. The signs will be obvious and the cure is simple. The problem is that everyone wants to get along and staff are encouraged to treat the inmate with respect. The old standby correctional adage "be firm but fair," "friendly but not friends" goes a long way in training staff. Some staff, however, have difficulty maintaining a constant professional demeanor. When it comes to inappropriate relationships, fear is sometimes the motivator. Some staff have a very real fear of the inmate population. Rather than work on this fear with their peer group or supervisor, they suppress this fear. What some-times happens is they overcompensate by being overly friendly with the inmates and are soon manipulated by them. Staff have said that the reason they were so close and personal with the inmates was because if there was a riot, they would be safe. This of course is not true. It is mob rule during a riot and no one is safe. Their friend would not be able to help them even if he wanted to.

It would be safe to assume that most of the sexual relationships that occur between staff and inmates are initiated by the manipulating inmate. The reasons are unclear, but there seems to be a propensity of staff with low self-esteem to become involved with the inmate. Others are motivated by a maternal instinct, while others are moved by the excitement. Regardless of the motives, this activity is totally unacceptable and dangerous to the entire facility.

The investigator should note that much information regarding relation-ships between staff and inmates comes from other inmates who may be jealous or have problems with the inmate. Many staff relationships move on to more serious offenses such as introduction of drugs or weapons.

Investigating Staff/Inmate Relationships

The Investigation

When investigating a case such as this the preliminary assessment is impor-tant. You need to find out where the original complaint came from. Was it an inmate? Was it a staff member? Was it a supervisor? This information in important to the investigation.

Surveillance

Sometimes the information that initiates this type of investigation reveals that the staff person and the inmate have an ongoing relationship. The information may be anonymous and only states that the offense is happening. The investigator may want to employ the use of surveillance. This can be tricky in the prison environment. Any surveillance is easily detected. The use of hidden cameras is most effective in cases like these. The trick is to install the equipment in a very covert manner. The investigator needs to find a time that he can enter the facility under cover of darkness and when there are no employees in the area he wants to install the camera. He will need to enlist the assistance of some person within the facility to negotiate his entry. Some of these violations take place off facility grounds. It may be a contract employee involved with an inmate under their supervision on an off-grounds crew assignment. Active surveillance can work in these cases. Surveillance is an excellent way to corroborate information given by inmates. Electronic surveillance gives the facts in living color. Remember that in video surveillance the investigator may not include audio unless one of the participants knows he or she is being recorded.

Interviews

The investigators should first interview the complaining witness. This gives him a basis to start his investigation. During this interview the investigator can make a personal assessment of the credibility of the complainant and obtain any supporting evidence the complainant may have. All of these interviews must take place away from the workplace or in a covert manner. When investigators show up at a facility, everyone knows they are there and will soon know who they talked to. Any of the suspects will have friends within the staff and inmate populations. The investigator will not be able to maintain confidentiality if he is not careful.

Corroboration

Sometimes the investigator is able to corroborate information after he conducts his interviews. Say, for example, that the complainant tells him that the staff member committed the offense on a certain day. He can check the work schedules and see if the staff person worked on that day. He can find out where the staff person worked that day and if he had access to that inmate. The complainant is often an inmate and sometimes there is no corroboration of the statements made. If that is the case, the investigator may decide to provide a polygraph (lie detector) examination to the inmate. It is not uncommon for an inmate to try and set up a staff member by fabricating a violation of some sort. This is one of the most common false reports made by inmates. If the inmate fails the polygraph and there is no other evidence, it may be time to end the investigation. The investigator might still develop enough information to file false reporting under the code of penal discipline and charge the inmate for trying to set up a staff member.

Phones and Mail

Quite often when there is a sexual relationship between inmates and staff there is frequent telephone and mail correspondence. Even though all staff know that mail and phones are monitored, they use them anyway. Some of these inmates and staff are pretty sharp and cover up their activity. In one case the inmate put the staff member's telephone number on his inmate phone system list under a false name. Thus, it was very easy to check the staff member's number against the inmate's phone list. Phone calls were listened to and the case was started. In another case the inmate wrote a fictitious name at the staff member's address. The same results were easily attained.

In most cases where there is a concerted effort to hide the relationship, the inmate will call the staff member at a different location. They will correspond through the mail by using a fictitious name and a post office box purchased by the staff member. While it is more difficult, the connection can still be made. The investigator merely listens to all calls made by the inmate until he finds conversations that are suspicious. He then listens for key words in the conversations. It is common for them to talk about what happened at work on a certain day, which is a good indicator that the investigator is listening to the right phone call. Another method is to have a trusted staff supervisor, who knows the suspect, listen to a tape of a call and possibly identify the voice as that of the suspect. It is not hard to cross reference the telephone number with that of a known friend or relative of the staff member.

When the staff member has purchased a post office box and the inmate writes there to a fictitious name, again, it is not too difficult to solve. First the investigator checks all the inmate's incoming and outgoing mail. It is not difficult to identify someone writing to him who has knowledge of corrections. It almost always is revealed in the letter. Once the investigator establishes which letters are suspicious, he can go further. He can check with the U.S. Postal Service and find out who purchased the box. In some cases the staff person has someone else purchase the box. The investigator then gets known handwriting samples of the staff member and checks them against the letters. If the investigator keeps looking, he will find the thread that binds the two together.

Case History #39

An inmate reported that an officer was having an affair with another inmate. The initial information was vague, but it did contain some dates of incidents. The complainant said that the officer was doing special favors for the inmate. He bought her presents and frequently had sex with her. The complainant said that the officer bought the inmate lots of makeup and jewelry that she was not allowed to have.

Facility staff searched the cell of the inmate alleged to be having the affair with the officer. They found many items of contraband, including lots of makeup. They found some unsigned love notes in the cell. The handwriting did not appear to match that of the officer.

An interview was attempted with the inmate, but she refused. An interview was set up with the officer. The officer gave every appearance of being truthful. He did not hesitate in his cooperation. He brought documentation where he was off duty on the days he allegedly had relations with the inmate. There was documentation that proved the makeup items were purchased by the inmate and covertly introduced into the facility through family members.

This short-lived investigation was terminated and the officer was cleared of any wrongdoing. All seemed well until another investigator received some information from yet another inmate confidential informant. This information included a post office box. Some letters were found in the suspect inmate's cell that included passages that indicated a staff member was writing to her. The box was checked through the U.S. Postal Service. It had been purchased by the officer. Money began to show up on the inmate's banking records in the form of money orders. These money orders were sent under a fictitious name, but they had been purchased by the officer It did not take long to close this case out, but the results were quite different.

The number of staff and inmate relationships cases investigated is astounding. Inmate relationship training is extensive during the academy and ongoing throughout a correctional officer's career. No one knows the reason why there are so many violations. It may be as simple as the fact that when you put men and women together, anywhere, there will be sexual relationships.

Case History #40

There was a case where an inmate had a serious problem with his case manager. He was not getting what he thought he deserved in the way of benefits. He began to make allegations against the staff member. He reported that his case manager did not do his job properly because he was always drunk on duty. He knew that this officer had a problem with drinking off duty. The case manager made the mistake of confiding in this inmate. The inmate knew too much about him and made some of his accusations seem real. The facility began to investigate the allegations. They even took a urine sample after one of the complaints. The inmate thought that even if he did not get the case manager fired, he could at least get a new case manager because of the fuss he started. As it turned out, the facility investigation did not reveal any wrongdoing by the staff member and the investigators never got the case.

His attempt to set up the staff member failed and this angered the inmate. He began to correspond with his wife. An alert mail room officer found a letter that was suspicious. This inmate received a letter from his wife that appeared to be an answer to a request. The letter read, in part, that since they could not get him (named the case manager) this way, they would get him another way. She wrote that she had run some checks on him and found out where he lived. She said that she had him under surveillance. She eluded to "him," saying he was bound to go to a liquor store one day and maybe they would find a bottle in his car at work. She further reported that she had run credit checks on him and was getting driving information on him.

The investigators had little information on the wife and began to search for information. During the search investigators were notified that another inmate had said that he knew this original inmate was trying to set up the case manager. He gave information that the wife was an insurance investigator. This helped in finding out more about the wife. She did in fact work for an insurance company as a secretary. She fancied herself as a private investigator.

From the letters between the two, it seemed they were going to great lengths to set up the case manager. It seemed that they were escalating into more serious things. The confidential informant said that he heard that the inmate was going to have someone go to the case manager's house and beat him up or even worse.

The case manager was advised of the situation and told to take precautions. The investigators did some loose surveillance on his home and put a local police watch on his home. They did not want to wait too long to stop this conspiracy. They did not have evidence to seek warrants at that time and from what they found the wife had not done a credit check and did not get driver's license information.

The wife was called into the office for an interview. During the interview she did admit that she was following the case manager. She claimed to have been a private investigator. She said that she was only following him to catch him driving drunk and to report him. She said that if she had seen him purchase liquor and go to work she would have called. She denied attempting to set up the officer and stated she was not part of a plan to harm the case manager. She said that she had not run credit or driver's license information. She agreed to take a polygraph examination.

In the end the inmate was convicted of related administrative charges and visits with his wife were terminated for a period of time . There was not enough evidence to bring any criminal charges, but the conspiracy was stopped.

These inmate/staff relationships never have a happy ending. In most cases the inmate has an agenda and receives little or no punishment for the relationship. Correctional staff need to remain professional.

The issue of sexual misconduct in the prisons and jails of the nation is on the increase. It is a problem shared by virtually every agency to some extent. The following article discusses the issue of sexual misconduct.

Officer in Trouble—Sexual Misconduct*

The problem.   There does not seem to be an ascertainable answer to a growing problem throughout the United States prison systems of inappropriate relationships between staff and inmates. Most correctional agencies have training in place that deals with inmate/staff relations. Unfortunately, this training has not been enough to curb these relationships to any great extent.

The problem of sexual misconduct in the workplace is shared equally in all professions. The 1990s morality seems to be lacking in self-control. Media report acts of sexual misconduct in virtually every arena, including our political leaders.

In corrections the problem of sexual misconduct is much more than an issue of morality. It most often enters the world of criminal acts. Even when consensual sex is involved there is a perception of criminality that cannot be ignored.

These seemingly minor infractions create serious breaches of security and sometimes end up in costly litigations. The number and type of relationships go beyond counting. There just seems to be some attraction, or unidentified need, that is the causation.

While many relationships between officers and inmates have the appearance of innocent social interaction, they often lead to romantic liaisons. This is where the major difficulty begins. These relationships grow into sexual encounters and even though the liaison is consensual it becomes a matter for administrative and criminal action.

Departments of corrections continue to address this issue actively. Inmate/staff relations have become such a serious problem that the basic training academies have dedicated several intense hours of training in this area. Additionally, there are in-service training hours also dedicated to personal relationships between inmates and staff. The administrative regulations, which are mandatory reading for officers, address these relationships, ethical standards and contain numerous rules regarding these relationships. The departments utilize many textbooks that outline in detail the makeup of the inmate population. Books such as *Inside the Criminal Mind** and *Games Criminals Play*** are two of these textbooks. In the book *Games Criminals Play*, two California correctional officers put together actual case histories and illustrate the lengths convicts will go to in trying to get an officer to do something that is against the rules. With all the training in place to help the correctional line staff in identifying the pitfalls and danger signals that can trap them in an inappropriate relationship with an inmate, one might expect fewer instances of such relationships. The fact is that sexual misconduct is on the rise and training alone will not begin to resolve this growing problem.

The effect.   The effect of sexual misconduct within the ranks of our departments of corrections is devastating. Not only do individual officers end up in the worst possible situation they can be in, but the morale of the entire department suffers.

Let us examine a typical sexual misconduct case and try to put yourself in the position as the officer involved in the misconduct.

For whatever reason, you begin to develop a friendship with an inmate. You may be having personal problems or you just do not seem to fit in to

---

* S.E. Samenow, *Inside the Criminal Mind*, Crown Publishing Group, New York, 1984.
** B. Allen and D. Bosta, *Games Criminals Play*, Rae John Publishers, Sacramento, 1997.

the group you work with. Because you feel like you are alienated from your peer group you begin to spend more time with inmates than you do with other staff.

The inmate seems to understand your problems and offers friendship and a listening ear. Skipping all the events and manipulation that occur, let us say that you become romantically involved. You know you are wrong, but maybe you feel that love conquers all and it does not matter. You have put yourself in a situation that is about to rock your world.

Because the situation has already gone too far you separate yourself further from other staff. There are rumors, but no one is talking to you about it.

The next thing you know there is an investigation into your actions. Staff are spreading all the rumors they hear among the troops. Inmates who were jealous of your relationship with the inmate are coming forward with information to the investigators.

You are suspended from duty. You have retained your pay status until the completion of the investigation, but you have to explain to friends and family why you are not going to work. You think you are in pretty good shape because you do not think they have any physical evidence and only the word of other inmates and suspicions from other staff members.

Officers who you thought were friends begin to avoid you. You cannot make any contact with your inmate lover and cannot talk to your family about your problem. You are alone and do not know what you are about to go through.

During your first interview with the investigator you realize you are between a rock and a hard place. If you refuse to cooperate with the investigation or are caught in a lie, you will be terminated from your job. It is now that you are amazed at the evidence they have against you. Where did they get my letters to the inmate? How on earth could they have DNA evidence? Why would this inmate, that I have poured out my soul to, given my body freely to and grew to love so deeply, have collected and preserved my most personal bodily fluids? These and many questions will be crossing your mind as the investigator quizzes you and lays out the evidence against you.

At this point you know that you will be very lucky if you only lose your job. If you are prosecuted, win or lose, your name will be in the newspapers. If you are convicted you will face a possible jail or prison sentence. Even if you enter into a plea agreement and will not have to serve any time you will be labeled a sex offender. As a sex offender you will have to enter treatment. You will have to register as a sex offender wherever you live within the United States. No one will know what your crime was and will most likely think of you as the worst of sexual predators.

Regardless of the outcome you will be jobless. If you are married you will have the best chance of heading for divorce court. If you have children you will be faced with some questions from your children that you may not want to answer.

Of course in fighting prosecution you will be faced with high dollar lawyer fees both during your trial and your impending divorce.

Once the smoke has cleared and the case is closed there is a high likelihood of costly litigation from the inmate. The inmate will assuredly claim that the department did not adequately protect him or her under the eighth amendment. Unfortunately, the inmate will have a high probability of winning the lawsuit. The department you took an oath to will have to live with the image you portrayed of their staff and pay a severe penalty both in reputation and dollar value.

Of course while you are having your entire life turned upside down and running the emotional roller coaster that never ends, the inmate that suckered you in is sitting in his or her cell, same as before, looking for the next unsuspecting officer. More often than not the plans are already in the making for a lawsuit that has the potential of many thousands of dollars to help them upon their release. Of course the story the inmate will tell to the civil courts will paint an ugly picture of the sexual encounter.

There is no end to the problems associated with merely failing to keep your libido under control. These officers did overstep their bounds, but with stronger guidance they may not have ruined their careers. Most of these officers have had the potential to continue a very productive career in corrections. Remember that sometimes good people do bad things.

Although there are no pat answers to this very serious question, and although there are rigorous training methods utilized to keep this from happening, we need to do more. There is always more that can be done when trying to protect our own most valuable resource. Simply put, we must never allow the convicts we are responsible for to use their craft in destroying our officers.

The cause.   Today we continue to look for the cause of officer misconduct, and we still realize that we may never root out the actual cause. It would be like trying to discover the cause for crime. Dr. Samenow probably gets closer to anyone in determining a cause. Simply put, Dr. Samenow reveals that criminals commit crimes because they choose to. Everything we do boils down to a choice, whether it be a poor choice or not, is irrelevant; the choice was made.

If you were to ask a group of administrators what the cause is for officer misconduct, you would get a multitude of answers. Some think that hiring practices must be examined. The truth is that most departments of corrections have a rigorous background investigation into each employee. These background investigations, obviously, have not weeded out every employee that will fail as a correctional officer.

Inside any bureaucracy, when there is a serious problem, the fault must be shared with everyone. In a problem such as this we cannot lay blame entirely on the affected staff member. We expend an enormous amount of time, energy, and money in preparing an officer for duty. There is an expectation that comes with this effort. Unfortunately, our expectations sometimes are not realized. Maybe we need to do more than expect an officer to always do the right thing. Maybe we should insure that our new officers do the right thing.

Let us examine the issue at hand. The issue is that officers often develop close relationships with inmates. These officers know from their training that it is not appropriate, but some get involved anyway. Why these officers stray from the norm is not hard to identify. Our problem is that we choose not to identify the cause.

It seems very simple. Not all officers fall into the mold of what their peers and supervisors see as the ideal correctional officer. These officers do not seem to fit in for a variety of reasons. They may not have honed social skills or may not fit the physical profile or may just lack experience in dealing with convicted felons. They may even have a personality that does not fit the mold. Other staff and supervisors, rather than attempting to create a good working environment for these new staff, seem to distance themselves. When they see behavior that does not fit their expectations they ignore the signs and further distance themselves from these staff. The problem is not only new staff. During the course of one's life there are many obstacles. We each deal with these obstacles in different ways. Some people are not able to discuss their personal problems well with other people and they began to withdraw from the "group."

These neglected staff begin to further distance themselves from other staff. They try to do their job, but are no longer a part of the team. While attempting to do what they think is expected of them, they find that the only people that will talk to them and listen to them are the inmates. After all everyone needs communication to exist. The convict is a good listener. He or she listens to identify what he or she perceives as weakness and then takes advantage of the weakness.

In Maslow's theory on the human hierarchy of needs, sex is coupled with other physiological needs that are the very basic needs. A need for security and social acceptance is next on Maslow's ladder. It may be that correctional officers that are not able to get the security and social acceptance they need to survive in the work setting are substituting sex and inappropriate relationships with inmates for the security they need to survive.

It does not take Maslow to make one realize just what a powerful physical drive sex is. A person in love is a person who does not have control of the heart or the body. When the urge strikes, we do not always have the willpower to resist the instant gratification it offers and do not always think of the repercussions.

The panacea.   Like dealing with an illness, it is sometimes necessary to try many remedies in search of a cure. This dilemma is no different, in that there is no one "set in stone" approach in dealing with the problem. We think we have restrictions in place that would create a deterrent to an officer, but it obviously is not enough. We do not have a deterrent for the convict though. Without both participants fearful of some punishment, one may always be able to manipulate the other into an infraction. This problem is serious enough, and its frequency should put us on notice that we need to do more. All departments should consider some serious alternatives in dealing with sexual misconduct in the work place.

Criminal action.   Since the act of having sex with an inmate is always in violation of department regulations and quite often is criminal, any department should actively and vigorously prosecute those offenders. You cannot condone such actions and must aggressively prosecute every violation. In addition to vigorous prosecution of current statutory law, departments should explore the inclusion of a statute that makes sexual contact between inmates and correctional staff a felony for both participants, thus creating a deterrent to both the officers and the convicts.

Training.   The training should not only continue, but each department must explore new and innovative training that deters inappropriate interactions between inmates and officers. This training should not only be for new staff during basic training, but should include the current staff and supervisory staff. This training should also reflect the danger signs, enabling peer groups and supervisors to recognize when a staff member is withdrawing from the group. The investigating arm of your department should also get involved in the training. They should provide classes that illustrate what has happened to other officers that have become involved in inappropriate relationships. They should solicit ex-staff members who have been terminated or worse to speak with staff on what happened to them as a result of their misdeeds.

Supervision.   Departments should learn to recognize the signs of potential problems and take steps to insure that staff are not put in a position where they would be likely to develop inappropriate relationships.

- Reduce the chances of staff being alone with inmates, particularly during late night hours when there is little traffic in the units. Assign counts and other cell house duties to teams rather than individuals.
- Watch for staff that seem to be withdrawing from other staff.
- Be mindful of staff requests for transfer coming on the heels of an inmate transfer.
- Insure that staff exposure to inmates during one-on-one encounters are kept to a minimum.
- Pay special attention to interaction between staff and look for staff that are having difficulty. Make efforts to identify these difficulties and take appropriate action when necessary.
- Utilize staffing patterns to minimize lone inmate/staff interactions.
- Never allow one-on-one movement of inmates regardless of security level.
- Rotate cell house staff on a regular basis. Discourage staff from being in cell houses they are not assigned to.

A vigorous attack on all levels may facilitate a reduction in instances of sexual misconduct. By treating each offense with effective prosecution we will send out a message of no tolerance. By increasing the training we might create a knowledge not only of the violations, but of what might happen to the officer, which may also become a deterrent. Finally, by effective supervision we might keep an otherwise valuable employee from making the mistake of their life.

A pro-active approach to this issue will not only keep our officers from failing in their duties, but will insure a good reputation for our departments and reduce the costly litigation associated with these offenses.

Conclusion.   In dealing with this highly volatile situation we cannot accept it as though "these things just happen," while dealing only with the cases as they present themselves. We must root out the causes and vigorously attack at the core of the problem. While continuing to aggressively prosecute each case we must always be vigilant in identifying the reasons these relationships occur. In identifying the reasons we must continue to find methods to keep our officers out of harm's way by intense training and effective supervision. We can no longer afford to merely pay lip service to the term "TEAM," but we have to "BE A TEAM" and help our brother and sister officers preserve their integrity. This can only be accomplished by instilling the work ethic and building the team with better training and supervision at all levels.

---

* Reprinted from Bell, W.R., Officer in trouble—sexual miscounduct, *The Chief of Police,* March/April, 2000.

Figure 13.1 Officers are frequently alone while making rounds in the prisons. This lone exposure to inmates can sometimes create inappropriate associations with inmates.

Figure 13.2 Male and female officers can sometimes fall prey to inmate manipulation, creating a dangerous atmosphere for the officer and the facility.

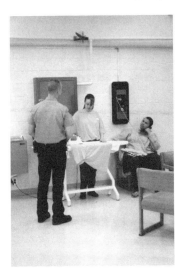

Figure 13.3 Officer conversing with an inmate ironing clothing at a women's prison in Colorado.

Figure 13.4 Lone officer in corridor converses with two inmates. (Note no surveillance cameras.)

Figure 13.5 Typical darkened cell block in a correctional facility. Officers are alone in this situation frequently.

All photos courtesy of the Colorado Department of Corrections.

What the Prosecutor Expects

14

Introduction

When departments of corrections initiate a program to curb prison crime and begin to utilize criminal investigators to investigate these crimes, it puts an extra burden on the district attorney's offices throughout any given state.

This has been the case in the 11th Judicial District in the state of Colorado. In this district the district attorney has assigned a deputy district attorney to cover nothing but the prison cases. There are ten prisons in this district that generate hundreds of criminal cases.

Norman Cooling is one of the deputy district attorneys for the 11th Judicial District. He is currently assigned to cover the prison cases for this area. In this capacity he has been instrumental in providing prosecution with the best results for the department of corrections and the state of Colorado. Cooling has been instrumental in creating an atmosphere of professionalism between local law enforcement and the department of corrections investigators. Cooling graduated from law school in 1984 from the Tulsa University College of Law in Oklahoma. During his college days he worked part time as a student law clerk for The Honorable Hez Bussey, the presiding judge of the Oklahoma Court of Criminal Appeals. Cooling worked in a private practice for only six months before accepting a position as a deputy district attorney in the 11th Judicial District in the state of Colorado. Cooling has been prosecuting felony crimes arising from the state prisons for the past 12 years.

Cooling has graciously offered to submit information for this chapter dealing with what a prosecutor is looking for in a corrections criminal investigation.* This chapter should prove valuable to any investigator.

* The remainder of this chapter was written by Norman Cooling, assistant district attorney for the 11th Judicial District in Fremont County in the state of Colorado.

What a Prosecutor Looks for in a Department of Corrections Investigation

When a report hits a prosecutor's desk, he or she will examine it to see how well or poorly it has been organized. The better the report has been organized, the more easily it will be understood, especially if it is a long or complicated report involving multiple witnesses or defendants. The investigator's job in this respect is to make the report easy to understand by the prosecutor. A dog-eared report missing a couple of referenced pages will not impress the prosecutor, even if the case is solid. Incomplete reports may cause a prosecutor to hesitate to file the case. Check with the prosecutor and, if possible, build a rapport with him or her to understand their filing policies and guidelines. These could vary from prosecutor to prosecutor even within the same office. For example, in the case of an inmate stabbing another inmate with no staff or inmate witnesses other than the two participants, lab results of blood testing and other physical evidence could be crucial. On the other hand, such evidence may be relatively unimportant if six staff members witnessed the entire stabbing. Thus, the investigator would want to delay sending the report to the district attorney in the first instance until he could include the lab results in his report. No such information would be initially needed in the later instance because the prosecutor could likely make his filing decision based on the eyewitness' accounts. If the need arises, communicate in the report that specific, additional evidence and reports will be forthcoming.

It is important to list the names and business addresses of every potential witness in the initial report. Many states have rules of criminal procedure that specifically require the district attorney to supply a written list of every potential witness's name and address to the defense attorney in advance of trial. If the investigator fails to disclose these names to the district attorney in his report, the prosecutor may miss that information also and may face sanctions for this failure. *Potential* witnesses are emphasized because even though the investigator does not believe that a certain witness will be called to testify, the prosecutor may disagree. Therefore, the better practice is to list every potential witness in the case report, even if the investigator believes the chances are remote that a particular witness will testify.

Document carefully the physical evidence that has been gathered. If possible, take 35-mm photographs of as much evidence as possible, especially from the crime scene if it has not been disturbed. Clear photographs could possibly save a case from being dismissed if the actual object of the photograph is destroyed or lost.

An investigator must note when and where a piece of evidence was seized and by whom. The initial person who seized the object as evidence should mark that evidence in a way where he can positively identify it several months or even years later in a court proceeding. Obviously, it should be marked discreetly so as not to hinder or impair the authenticity of the evidence. An example would be to mark photos on the back side with the person's initials and date taken or to attach with string a small blank index card with identifying information to a seized weapon.

This leads into the area of what is commonly called a "chain of custody." A chain of custody is simply documenting each and every person who took control of an exhibit from the time it was seized to the time it appears in court to be admitted into evidence. For example, this would include the officer who first seized the marijuana in an inmate bandit's cell, his supervisor who deposited it in his facility's locked evidence box, the investigator who unlocked the box and retrieved it, a second investigator who transported it to the state lab for scientific testing, and the lab tech who got it from the investigator and tested the dope. It is a good practice for each person who gained control of the dope to note it on the evidence in some manner. For example, if the dope is initially placed in a small, brown paper bag that has been securely fastened, each person should mark his initial on the bag and the date and time he took control of the bag. The prosecutor would not likely need everyone in the chain to testify if the last person in the chain, the lab tech, could state that he observed no tampering with the bag, which was securely fastened when he opened it to begin his tests. However, it is better to be thorough and to note all potential "links" in the chain in the case report.

Documenting an accurate chain of custody is critical when dealing with fungible evidence. Fungible evidence means evidence which lacks specific, identifiable characteristics. For example, marijuana is fungible; line up ten separate and similar quantities of marijuana on a table and it would be nearly impossible for the officer who seized a small quantity of dope from an inmate bandit to correctly identify it from the ten quantities on the table. On the other hand, a homemade knife taken from an inmate bandit would likely possess distinct characteristics that would make it more easily identifiable. It could have been made from a piece of hard, green plastic, $4\frac{5}{8}$ in. long, sharpened with a two-edged point, and wrapped with layers of dirty white adhesive tape to form a homemade handle. A chain of custody is not needed here if the officer who first seized it and put his identifying mark on it or on an attached evidence tag could identify it and testify that it appeared in substantially the same condition as it was when he first seized it.

Officer's Reports

Investigators may be involved in cases based on reading officer's reports of incidents that had happened weeks before they became involved. In these "cold" reports, the investigator must play the part of the district attorney. Examine the quality and quantity of the evidence that has been reported.

The investigator needs to scrutinize each officer's report. Did he include the basic "who, what, when, where, how, and why?" Examine whether and to what extent his report may be contradicted or different from other reports. Do the reports appear complete or are pages missing? It is vital that every officer who participated to the smallest extent write a legible report. Often one officer's report will refer to other officers who were present, but the investigator will find that those other officers wrote no reports. Each potential witness should write a report as soon as practicable. It will help him remember the incident if and when he is called to testify a year later. Additionally, it is an important tool to avoid an implication on cross-examination that he cannot be believed because he did not even write a report!

Commonly, the investigator will need to interview the officer who wrote an incomplete report. Often, officers have no idea that their report could be used to impeach them in a criminal trial. Many officers believe their reports are for use administratively, rather than criminally.

Cold Crime Scenes

If the investigator was not called out to a crime that just happened, he may still have a crime scene. He should still take photographs of the scene because it may change. The adage of "a picture is worth a thousand words" holds weight to a jury. The crime scene may be simply the inmate's cell and the location of the bed in relation to the window or it could depict the view the control room officer had as he looked down a hallway. If possible, use a video camera to document a scene. It is less subject to an argumentative, picky defense attorney than is an officer's report. Further, it will be most helpful to a witness's memory and testimony to be able to review such evidence in advance of trial. The importance of showing such evidence to a jury to make the scene become more real and thus persuasive cannot be understated.

Interviewing Inmates

It is vital to interview all inmates who may be witnesses. Inmates are generally strict believers in the inmate "Con Code," which is the unwritten understanding or code among convicts that inmates always stick together rather than turn against their own and assist officers and investigators. The dynamic present is that an inmate who points the finger of blame at another inmate will be labeled a "snitch" or a "rat" and will be subject to retaliation among his fellow inmates.

Therefore, it is vital to interview witness inmates regardless of what the investigator believes they might say. The object is to lock them into their "story" whether it is true or false. Thus, if they testify differently at trial, they can be impeached by the prosecutor with this prior inconsistent statement.

For example, the investigator interviews the inmate and he simply says he did not see the stabbing of inmate Smith by inmate Jones. His subsequent trial testimony that Jones was defending himself will be much less credible to the jury. Obviously, the best practice is to separate possible witnesses as soon as practical so they do not have the opportunity to get their story straight among themselves.

Depending upon the type of case, the experienced prison investigator will want to pin down an inmate witness with specific details. For example, in an alibi case, times and locations will be critical in the investigator's effort to disprove the alibi. While it will be common for inmates to not want to be interviewed, giving them the opportunity to give their story is important. The reason is that giving them the chance to make a statement while the incident is fresh in their minds circumvents that witness from testifying at trial that nobody from the prison interviewed him, which a defense attorney will use to be critical of an incomplete investigation. Additionally, by failing to interview an inmate witness, he could testify at trial that nobody interviewed him and then relate his story to the jury for the first time. Such a situation will make it difficult for the investigator and prosecutor to have adequate time to rebut or impeach the inmate's testimony.

Theft Investigations   15

Prison Thefts

According, in part, to the Colorado Revised Statutes, "A person commits theft when he knowingly obtains or exercises control over anything of value of another without authorization, or by threat or deception."

You might think that thefts within the prison are uncommon. After all, what are inmates going to steal. It is a fact that most people that are incarcerated in our prisons are in for some sort of theft, be it bank robbery, extortion, burglary, or shoplifting. It stands to reason that with all these thieves there would be some thefts occurring.

The prison criminal investigator is called upon to investigate many thefts. He investigates thefts committed by inmates and staff alike. Occasionally, he investigates a civilian who is involved in the theft of state property.

These investigations normally are handled in much the same manner as a street cop would handle them. There are some differences in that the prison investigator has some resources not available to the street investigator.

Discussed here are some of the types of theft that occur daily within the prison walls. These thefts are usually not reported to the Criminal Investigation Division (CID) for investigation. In addition, the CID would normally not investigate these thefts.

- Inmates steal food or commissary from the facility. This is a daily occurrence and is usually not reported. If an inmate is caught stealing items of little value, the case will normally be handled through administrative charges. The result can be loss of earned time, loss of privileges, and time spent in administrative segregation. The CID rarely gets involved in misdemeanor charges.

249

- Inmates steal personal items from each other on a daily basis. They steal food, tobacco products, canteen items, clothing, radios, televisions, and anything of value. They, in turn, exchange these items for other things of value or other favors. These cases are rarely, if ever, reported to staff. When the offending inmate is caught, he may be punished by the victim or the victim's friends. This usually comes in the form of some sort of assault and sometimes leads to a homicide. In other cases the offended inmate may retaliate by committing his own theft.
- Inmates sometimes take items that have no value, but may be used in the manufacture of weapons. Pieces of metal, parts of metal doors, sandpaper (to sharpen their homemade knife), and anything else they may deem necessary. These thefts normally go unnoticed.
- Inmates steal information regularly. Information is power. Most inmates can read upside down better and faster than most people can read regularly. Anything that is laying around with information on it is mentally recorded and passed on. Information on other inmates is always a valuable tool to use in extorting favors later. Any information on staff or on the operation of a facility is also valuable information. This also is a theft that usually goes unnoticed.

There are continuous thefts and frauds being committed by inmates throughout the prison systems in the United States. This chapter examines some of these crimes and gives some examples of how a prison investigation may differ in some ways from a street investigation.

Theft by Deception

Trick

A "trick" is the name an inmate refers to someone being used to obtain money. This name is used in the same manner prostitutes refer to their customers. Inmates develop tricks by either advertising in lonely hearts magazines or by answering these advertisements. They establish contact initially by writing a letter and usually end up having telephone contact with them later.

The common thread in these cases is that the inmates give false information to these tricks in order to exact money from them. This method is widely used among inmates of both sexes.

Drugs

After establishing a relationship with these tricks, inmates sometimes solicit them to bring in drugs. They use the methods outlined in Chapter 2.

Money

While establishing a relationship with these tricks, inmates minimize their crime. They portray themselves as victims who have made a mistake and want to change their lives. They will go to any lengths to get money out of their tricks.

- They need money or the really bad inmates will kill them.
- They are getting out of prison soon and need money to pay restitution.
- They need money to pay their attorney who will file a motion that will get them out of prison.
- They need money for the canteen, makeup, a television, a radio, or a stereo.
- They broke the meanest inmate's radio and have to pay to replace it.
- They need an operation and the prison will not let them have it unless they pay for it.
- They need dental work.
- In one case a female inmate claimed to have a trailer full of antiques, motorcycles, tools, and other things valued at over $100,000. She lost her appeal and would not be getting out of prison. Since he (the trick) was so nice to her she wanted to give him all those things. All he had to do was send $500 to have the trailer brought to his house.
- She wants to marry the trick and needs money to get a wedding dress.

These are but a few examples of the hundreds of ways inmates dupe their tricks into sending money. They use the promise of sex and a good life. They beg for the help to become a better person. They promise not to ever commit a crime again. They have found the Lord. Whatever works to convince their trick that they are worthy. Most of these inmates run a string of tricks. Their targets vary:

- Senior citizens
- Overweight
- Insecure
- Not comfortable with opposite sex
- Low self-esteem
- Think it is exciting to be with an inmate
- Think they can rehabilitate the inmate (maternal instinct)

Case History #41

An inmate had one of her tricks for about 2 years. (A trick is a term that convicts give to anyone from whom they are fraudulently obtaining funds.) The trick began to question the inmate about the thousands of dollars he had sent for her court appearances and other things. The inmate knew that she was about to lose him and decided to use him one more time.

A CID investigator got an anonymous call regarding this inmate bilking some old man. The call probably originated from another inmate. The investigator started monitoring telephone calls and the mail. He began to pick up on some conversations with this trick.

The inmate told the trick that she had lost her court battle. She was crying and carrying on. She said that she would have to stay in prison for many more years. She complained that her attorney must have run off with their money. She said she was desperate and wanted to pay him back for all of his help. She said she had a trailer filled with tools, antiques, clothing, furnishings, and a new Harley Davidson motorcycle with only 200 miles on it. She said that she did not need any of these things and wanted to give them to him as repayment. She said that there was over $100,000 in property in the trailer and it was all his. She said that she had to pay some storage fees and had hired a trucker to deliver these things to his house. She told him it would cost $500 to have the trailer delivered to him.

But now the trick was suspicious about what was happening. He asked where the trailer was, who was bringing it, and how he could believe her. She convinced him that she had three-way calling capabilities on her phone and said she would call her lawyer and he could talk to him. She pretended to make a three-way call and a male voice came on the phone. This male voice answered the trick's questions and seemed to put him at ease. The trick said he would send the money.

The money arrived in the form of the usual money order. The money was put on her books, but there was a hold put on it because of the amount. The investigator had already contacted inmate banking and let them know what was going on.

A few days after the money order arrived the trick called and asked if she got it. She told him she did and had sent it to the storage place. She said that the truck driver said that the fees were higher than expected and he needed another $200. The trick balked at this and questioned why it would cost more money. She tried to explain and then offered for the trick to talk to the truck driver. She pretended to make another three-way call and another male voice got on the phone. The phony truck driver answered all of the questions and the trick agreed to send the $200.

The investigator found out during his investigation that the inmate was using different voices to sound like these different people. She was scamming the trick all the way. She had already taken this guy for thousands of dollars and wanted to get him one more time.

Most of these cases go unreported because the trick feels stupid and is too embarrassed to come forward. They do not think that the department of corrections would do anything about it anyway. They usually chalk it up to stupidity and go on with their lives.

Investigating Theft by Deception in the Prison

To investigate this crime the investigator needs to establish the elements of the crime. To do this he will have to monitor mail and telephone conversations.

1. Gather the information the inmate gives to the trick. Attempt to verify what the inmate is saying through known facts and records.
    a. Verify court dates.
    b. Verify what the money on is spent on.
    c. Verify the crime the inmate is in prison for.
    d. Verify the physical description the inmate gave to the trick.
    e. If the inmate said the money was needed to buy a television, see if the inmate bought one or already had one.
    Whatever story is told to the trick, make sure the inmate is deceiving the trick with the information. Once the investigator finds that the inmate is lying to the trick and trying to get money under false pretenses, he may begin his case. Be sure to copy letters and tape telephone conversations that could be evidence in the case.
2. Track the money. Money can be sent to inmates in the form of money orders only. They are easily traceable. Make sure that your trick is the one who purchased the money order and that the inmate did receive it.
    • Get copies of money orders.
    • Get copies of inmate banking statements.
3. Contact the trick. The investigator needs to be very careful in how he approaches the trick. After all the trick is a victim and does not know it yet. He or she will be embarrassed and may not want to talk about it. The investigator will have to use his best interview techniques.
    • Make the trick feel like he or she is not at fault.
    • Assure the trick that inmates do this all the time and he or she is not the only one.
    • Maximize the ability of convicts to con people.
    • Let the trick know that the investigator will help him or her in any way possible. Be sure to tell the trick that the investigator will do everything he can to recoup his or her money.
    • Find out if the trick wants to prosecute.
    • Find out if the trick is willing to testify.
    • If the trick has additional evidence, i.e., letters and photographs, ask him or her to send them to the investigator for evidence.
    • Note that the investigator will not be able to prosecute without the trick signing a complaint.
4. Interview the inmate. The investigator will be armed with indisputable facts that will make his interview easier. It does not matter if the

investigator gets a confession or not, what he wants is to get the inmate locked into a statement.

These cases are not limited to female inmates tricking men. Male inmates do the same with women tricks. They both use the same tactics with the same results.

Case History #42

A few months ago an investigator received a call from a man who said that he felt he was being set up and used by an inmate. He claimed that he had sent money to a female inmate and something was not right. He gave the name, address, and identification number of the inmate. The inmate's name was Francis. The address was a men's correctional facility. During the brief investigation it was learned that the inmate had sent a picture of his girlfriend to the trick and was bilking money out of him under the pretense that the two of them would become romantically involved upon her (his) impending release. The red-faced complainant refused to sign a complaint because of the embarrassment he felt.

These cases most often go unreported. On rare occasions a trick will complain. Sometimes when the call comes in it becomes too late to gather any evidence. Letters are destroyed, phone tapes are erased, and all that is left are the banking transactions. Those alone will not fulfill the elements of the crime. The complaint will only serve as notice, not evidence. In those instances the investigator needs to set up a sting operation for the next time, perhaps using some pretext phone calls.

The best way to deal with these cases is to be proactive in the approach. The investigator's job is to detect crime. Sometimes he has to seek it out, particularly when it is a crime like this.

Proactive Approach

- Have the mail rooms contact the investigator when inmates begin to get money orders from new people, especially out of state money orders.
- Check the publications for lonely hearts. See if inmates have written ads. Ask facilities to monitor those inmates.
- Once you have a possible target, start to monitor the telephones and mail. Look for deceptions in those conversations.
- Begin the investigation.

On rare occasions investigators have tried to use their own method of deception, but they have little experience at being tricksters. It is time consuming and given the caseload, it is difficult to do. Nonetheless, the following is an example of what an investigator can do.

An inmate had placed an ad for female companionship. The inmate happened to be known to have solicited females to bring in drugs in the past. There had been evidence that he had also received cash from several females. Apparently his tricks had run dry and he was looking for another one. Investigators began to correspond with him on a temporary basis. In the second letter to this fictitious female the inmate offered her an opportunity to make large sums of money by bringing in drugs. This was not a theft case, but a drug case.

Supplemental Security Income Social Security Theft

Inmates are not eligible for social security benefits. Cases involving social security theft are hard to detect. Inmates apply for social security benefits prior to entering prison. They provide an address and get on the rolls and start receiving their checks before incarceration. After entering prison they continue to collect their benefits illegally. The checks are sent to the application address and the inmate has someone forge his signature, cash the checks, and send him the money. In some cases the checks are made out for deposit only to his account. Sometimes people mail the check to the inmate for him to sign and return. Since this is a federal case and not in the investigator's jurisdiction, there are only a few things to do:

1. Seize the check and give the inmate a receipt.
2. Interview the inmate and get a statement from him.
3. Gather documentation of the inmate's incarceration.
   a. Mittimus, a warrant of commitment to prison
   b. Inmate profile
   c. Other paperwork showing he is an inmate
4. Contact the local social security office and take the check and documentation to them.

The investigator should also notify the prison mail room and case management offices to keep an eye out for these violations.

Case History #43

An inmate had applied for social security income (SSI) benefits through the address of his mother. He was awarded the benefits and began to receive checks at his mother's home. His mother would cash the checks and send some of the money to the inmate. Since convicts are **not** eligible for SSI benefits, the investigator obtained documentation and the SSI check and took them to the Social Security Administration (SSA). They were very polite and said they would take care of the problem. For the next 6 months the checks kept coming. The investigator notified SSA and asked if they wanted him to pick up the checks. They declined and said they would take care of it. The following month the inmate died from a chronic disease. He died, but the checks kept coming. The investigator contacted the SSA and notified them, but he wondered how long those checks would keep coming.

Regardless of any problem the investigator might incur, he should always report the crime. The investigator should not violate his own integrity because the situation or an individual frustrated or angered him.

Motor Vehicle Theft

There are very few auto thefts committed by inmates. Normally, an auto theft would be committed by an escaping inmate. When this happens there are only two alternatives the inmate has: either he keeps the car or he abandons the car.

If the inmate keeps the car he will undoubtedly stop somewhere and steal some fresh license plates. This happens in public places. An airport long-term parking lot is one of the best places to steal a plate as the owner will not know it is stolen until he returns. People do not always notice when their plates are taken.

Motor vehicle thefts are also committed by inmates in situations other than escapes. Inmates have their fingers on the pulse of crime in every venue. Although an inmate may not physically take the vehicle, he may be directly involved in schemes to deprive people of their cars.

Case History #44

There was a case where an investigator was acting in an undercover capacity as a hit man. The credibility of the investigator was being tested by the inmate he was investigating. During this testing of the waters, the inmate solicited the investigator for titles and vehicle identification numbers (VIN) plates for three 2000 Chevrolet Corvettes. Working with the state, the investigator was able to get quality titles and had a lead on getting factory VIN plates for these cars. The inmate bandit began to contact his people on the streets to set up the theft of three Corvettes. He was utilizing a parolee and another ex-convict who worked at a dealership to set up the deal. The bandit contacted the prison investigator and related that he did not have the money to purchase the titles, but asked if a new 2000 Dodge Viper would be taken in lieu of the cash. All was agreed upon, and it appeared that the bandit was serious about the transaction. Unfortunately, the inmate bandit could not foresee that his co-conspirators would not hold up their end of the bargain. This case never saw the inside of a courtroom.

This case was an example of inmates involved in motor vehicle thefts from inside the prison. Good intelligence brought the initial criminal activity to the eyes of the prison investigator. This case would have come to a successful conclusion if it were not for the inmate bandit having friends that could not produce (or would not produce).

Prison investigators should be aware that motor vehicle theft is possible from behind the walls of the prison. A good investigator will not turn a blind eye to any information concerning vehicles or any other thing of value.

Continuous monitoring of inmate mail, telephones, and activities often creates information and leads that will help the investigator curb prison crime.

Burglary

The crime of burglary is committed by incarcerated inmates. Not only are inmates involved in burglaries as conspirators, they actually commit the crimes themselves. These burglaries, however infrequent, do happen. Although some burglaries are crimes committed during an escape, there are some which are stand-alone crimes that are committed by incarcerated inmates.

In order to commit a burglary an inmate has to have access to the community. There are many programs that allow inmates into the community to perform some sort of labor or other community service. Minimum security inmates are frequently allowed to attend school or work within the community in other functions.

Not all of these programs have adequate security practices and some are vulnerable to the seasoned burglar.

All burglary investigations are the same, whether investigated by a prison investigator or a street cop. The differences come in the prevention tactics and postcrime activity. Under most circumstances a prison investigator would not even become aware of a local burglary unless an inmate was suspected of committing the crime. Here are a few tips for the prison investigator:

- Establish a rapport with the local police and sheriff's departments and try to get a list of all burglaries committed in the community.
- Keep apprised of the locations, dates, and times of all inmate assignments that are outside of the prison.
- Compare burglaries with outside crew assignments. If there is a burglary that coincides with an inmate work crew, get a list of stolen merchandise and conduct some searches of inmates assigned to the crews.
- Whenever possible go to the scene of recent burglaries and look for signs of inmate participation (i.e., inmate notched footprints or other prison-marked prints).

- Interview inmates assigned to outside crews in the area of burglaries. Inmates may not have a problem giving information about crimes committed by civilians.
- Conduct or cause to conduct surveillance work at inmate worksites.
- If local law enforcement has fingerprints of suspects and an inmate crew was in the area, offer fingerprint comparisons for all inmates on that crew.
- If local law enforcement has a witness to the crime, offer photographs of inmates assigned to crews for photo lineups.

If the prison investigator suspects inmate involvement,

- Take photographs and impressions of any suspected inmate footprints in addition to all evidence collection procedures.
- Take all shoes of inmates on outside crews and compare with prints found at the crime scene.
- Search all inmates and their cells for stolen merchandise.
- Interview all inmates on the crews in the area. Inmates will do whatever is necessary to remain on outside crews and tend to give more information that usual to keep their outside work assignments.

Counterfeiting

The FBI's *Uniform Crime Reporting Handbook** defines counterfeiting/forgery as the altering, copying, or imitation of something, without authority or right, with the intent to deceive or defraud by passing the copy or thing altered or imitated as that which is original or genuine; or the selling, buying, or possession of an altered, copied, or imitated thing with the intent to deceive or defraud.

Many state departments of correction have print shops to supply contract work throughout the state. These print shops are responsible for the production of many official state documents. These print shops also provide training and employment for inmates to assist in their successful reintegration into society. The utilization of inmates is always a risk.

As an investigator it is good practice to check on the security practices in any print shop where inmates are assigned. If there are any obvious problems, it would benefit the facility and the investigator's agency to make suggestions for improvement. The investigator will find in most cases that the print shop lacks inventory control and inmate observation. Sometimes funds are not

---

* The Federal Bureau of Investigation, *Uniform Crime Reporting Handbook,*

available to correct security problems, causing some frustration for the investigative unit.

The investigator can utilize key staff to gather intelligence on all inmates that work in the print shops. Some of the methods are listed below:

- Have telephone calls of inmates working in the print shop monitored on a regular basis.
- Request mail rooms to monitor incoming and outgoing mail of print shop inmates on a frequent basis.
- Suggest a rotation of inmates assigned to print shops.
- Conduct random searches of print shop inmates and their cells.
- Request frequent searches of trash containers in the print shop, looking for paper inventory and items printed that were not part of a recent contract.
- Request that security staff do random walk-throughs of print shops on an unscheduled basis (just for show).

Case History #45

A prison investigator was working a confidential informant in an unrelated drug case. One of the bandits in the case approached the informant and asked if he knew someone who wanted to purchase some driver's licenses that were being made in the print shop of one of the state prisons. The bandit wanted $40 per copy. These licenses were the type that were valid without a photo because they were issued for lost or misplaced driver's licenses.

The investigation continued while the bandit was introduced, via telephone, to the investigator who was acting in an undercover capacity. The investigator purchased two driver's licenses. These were delivered to the investigator though the U.S. mail. The money for the licenses was sent to the inmate through the mail prior to delivery. The bandit engaged the investigator in conversation and related that he could reproduce U.S. Postal money orders. The inmate wanted a $300 blank money order to use as a master. He stated that he could make a plate and produce hundreds of counterfeit money orders. The investigator was offered 100 of the counterfeit money orders for supplying the one real $300 money order. Although the logistics of introducing the money order were difficult, they were worked out and soon the bandit had the money order. After receiving the money order, the bandit ceased communication with the investigator. The informant was being put off by the bandit as well.

It was determined that the investigator no longer had control of the situation and there was some concern that the inmate would be able to produce and distribute money orders prior to the bust. The investigator decided to raid the print shop, with simultaneous searches of all inmates and their living quarters. During the subsequent raid the money order was recovered and it appeared that no plates had been made. Some 300 counterfeit driver's licenses were also recovered in the print shop at the work station of the bandit inmate. The investigation revealed that 2 years prior to this investigation the print shop had a contract with the state to produce these driver's licenses. The inmates had stolen the plates for these licenses and began to reproduce them in a scam to make money. The case ended with the prosecution of three inmates on various charges stemming from this investigation.

Investigators should never think that there is any theft crime that cannot be committed by the resourceful inmate. Between 70 and 80% of all inmates are convicted for some kind of theft charge, ranging from armed robbery to larceny. With all the innovations in the world in the last 20 years, "anything man can think, man can do." In the world of the inmate they have 24 hours a day, 7 days a week to think of ways to separate people from their valuables.

The following is a short list of theft crimes known to have been committed by inmates incarcerated in state correctional facilities throughout the United States:

- Internal Revenue Service fraud
- Credit card theft
- Check fraud
- Check kiting
- Embezzlement
- False pretenses, swindles, and confidence games
- Computer fraud
- Bribery

The correctional criminal investigator has many options not available to the street investigator: phone monitoring, mail monitoring, surveillance cameras, and a multitude of correctional staff. The correctional investigator must remember to utilize his outside contacts and the resources available. These outside resources not only conribute to a solid case, but they also solidify relationships between the prison and the community.

Figure 15.1 Crime scene photograph of a business place burglarized by an escaped convict.

Figure 15.2 Inmate burglars entered this office to obtain keys to vehicles stored at this location. They were unable to match keys to a vehicle and left on foot. Escape teams and a K-9 unit apprehended the escapees hours later.

Figure 15.3 Evidence collected from a theft of electrical supplies from a prison-operated business. Culprits in this case were staff members and inmates.

Figure 15.4 Computer parts stolen from a computer shop ended up in department computers. This case involved staff members and inmates.

All photos courtesy of the Colorado Department of Corrections.

Proactive Approaches to Conducting Prison Investigations

16

Prison Investigation

Like any good law enforcement agency, the prison investigators cannot just respond to crime as it happens and be an effective crime fighting tool. Investigators must be proactive in their approach to crime fighting and become innovative in their attack on prison crime. These prison investigators are up against the subculture that exists behind the walls of prisons. Inmates are seasoned criminals who are dedicated to crime and experienced in the art of criminal activity. Prison investigators need to develop an understanding of their advisories and utilize all the resources available to them. They must seek out this criminal activity and vigorously prosecute each and every felonious act.

In years past, convicts had the misconception that they were in prison and there was not much anyone could do to them for the crimes they committed within the prison walls. In some ways they were correct. There was no criminal investigation team to thwart their efforts and hold them accountable for their acts. Now there is a new cop on the beat and these new crime fighters must seek out ways to continue the attack on crime. This chapter demonstrates just a few of the methods prison investigators can do to proactively fight crime.

Outside Work Crews

At lower security level prisons the inmates frequently are assigned to jobs outside the walls of the prison. Some of these assignments include working in the community. Some of these community assignments are supervised by civilian volunteers rather than correctional officers. On occasion these inmates involve themselves in criminal activity. Rather than react to this criminal activity, the investigator should plan and prepare.

- **Training**—All civilian personnel supervising outside crews should obtain training. If that training is not acceptable to the supervisors, they should be immediately excluded from participating. The training should include, but not be limited to, how to manage inmates, what rules have to be followed, what to look out for, and what to do in case of an incident. Any time civilian supervisors are utilized, a background check should be completed on each supervisor. Stress the importance of training for these individuals. Understand that a civilian sometimes does not realize the importance of some rules. They sometimes feel that if they can do certain things, so can the inmate?
- **Surveillance**—All outside crew locations should be covertly observed from time to time. This should be done by the facility that has placed these inmates into the community. It would be a good idea for investigators to assist occasionally.
- **Monitoring**—The outside crew locations are perfect for introducing drugs and other criminal activity. The sending facility should be aware of this and frequently monitor the mail and telephones of these inmates for criminal activity. They should also be aware of who these inmates associate with inside the prison. It is likely that an outside crew member will bring contraband into the prison for someone else, rather than being the "brains" behind the operation. This is because most prisons carefully select inmates for outside crews that have not been involved in criminal activity in the prison before. These inmates become targets for the experienced convict.
- **Major incidents**—Although a major incident is unlikely at an outside crew site, it can happen. It is advisable to have an investigator attached to SORT or SWAT as an advisor or observer. Maps of the crew site, including floor plans of buildings and structures, are advisable to have on hand. Actual scenario planning should be part of the SORT training. Your facility emergency response teams and department escape teams should be involved in this training.
- **K-9 units**—If the investigation unit has a K-9 unit and the dogs have the capability to detect illegal drugs, the investigator should conduct random drug searches of every off-grounds worksite.

Keep in mind that most of these off-grounds worksites go unchallenged. Most staff and investigators do not even know where all these sites are located. Sharing of information is all important in the correctional setting. If no one knows what the other is doing or more importantly knows where the convicts are, there is no way to expect assistance. For example, if the majority of the staff knew where the crews were working they would most likely look at that area when they are driving by, whether they are on or off duty.

Staff Training

Investigators find that when they create their investigative unit they encounter a significant amount of resistance from staff members. Most of this comes from the perception that investigators are head hunters and are looking to put staff in a bind should they make a mistake. The creation of this unit is not designed to have investigators sneaking around trying to catch staff making mistakes. It is primarily designed to protect the public, staff, and other inmates from the criminal element within the inmate population. Inform the staff of these objectives.

- Create training that specifically deals with what it is investigators do. This training should include how the investigators work with staff to curb criminal activity.
- Create training in drug identification. This should include known methods of drug introduction and concealment. Line staff can probably tell investigators a thing or two about concealment.
- Create training in crime scene management. This training is essential if the investigator does not want his crime scene destroyed prior to his arrival.
- Create training that will show line staff how easy it is to get involved in a situation that could cause them a problem. This training may well be presented by the internal affairs section as a means to create an understanding. They need to know that the investigator will not only be discovering bad acts by staff, but will be clearing the majority of them from being wrongfully accused. Inmates go to great lengths to set up staff members. It is a pretty good feather in their cap to destroy a staff member's career. What inmates do not expect is to get disciplined for attempting the setup. This is what investigators do. This training should provide guidance and identify the assistance staff can expect from the investigation unit.
- Create training that will better enable investigators to use line staff in their investigations. In addition the investigator should solicit the assistance of line staff whenever it is feasible. This, of course, must be approved by their appointing authority.
- Create training to show staff how to protect themselves from civil litigation and criminal actions. They need to know what there rights

are and how and when to exercise their rights. This training develops a trust that is needed to gain cooperation between the investigative unit and the rest of the line staff. This training will not inhibit the investigator's ability to prosecute wrongdoers and will be appreciated by all.

In addition to creating effective training, the investigator must also in his daily actions continue to develop trust. This can be accomplished by making frequent visits to facilities in his jurisdiction. During these visits the investigator should check in with the wardens and managers. Discuss any problems and offer assistance. The investigator should also develop friendships with the line staff under their supervision.

It is estimated that about 70% of a prison investigator's caseload involves drugs. There are several drug deterrence programs currently in use.

- Frequent K-9 searches of visiting areas, prison units, and prison grounds.
- Random drug screening
- Drug deterrence programs
- Implementation of an intelligence unit
- Staff training on drug identification
- Frequent shakedowns of inmates and living units

Action Planning

Departments of corrections are aware of the growing gang problem within the prisons and have created groups of gang coordinators that work with local and state law enforcement in identifying gang members and tracking their movements and behavior. This information is shared with the criminal investigators.

Investigators should continue to develop relationships with outside law enforcement agencies, sharing intelligence and actively working to assist the communities and solicit assistance from them.

Mapping was commonly used in the past to identify high-crime and high-accident locations. It was simply a map of a city with different colored pins depicting different crimes, accidents, or other information placed at the location of the incident. In recent months police departments are returning to this process to assist them in specialized areas of law enforcement. This concept can readily be used by the prison investigator to identify specific areas of a prison most affected by criminal activity. The prison investigator can utilize this method to determine if these crimes are random or are the acts of organized criminal activity. The prison investigator has specific information on each of the inmates housed in a prison and can easily identify many different interpretations based on this information.

When prison investigators learn to utilize intelligence information available to them, they can better prepare for criminal activity.

Monitoring inmate banking is another way to determine if there is an increase in criminal activity. Investigators should become active in reviewing banking activity of the inmates to determine new trends.

Utilizing the available inmate phone system is one of the best tools available to the prison investigator. Investigators, rather than only monitoring inmates under investigation, should routinely work with staff that do random monitoring of telephone calls. These monitoring officers should be schooled on identifying coded conversations.

Investigators should be in frequent contact with mail room personnel. There is information received daily by these mail room officers that could be transmitted to investigations if there were a closer relationship with the investigators.

Investigators should become very familiar with their district attorneys, finding out what they expect in a criminal case and how they would like presentations to be made. It is sometimes a good idea to get these prosecutors involved in the criminal cases as they develop. This gives them an idea of how the investigator works and offers them a chance to give their input into the case. This gives ownership to the district attorney and ownership breeds proprietorship. There is nothing like watching a prosecutor work on a case he has helped develop.

When a crime pattern emerges, get involved with security personnel to assist in the location of monitoring and additional security cameras. Stay involved with security people. Get them involved in investigations. They are the most valuable resource the prison investigator has. They know more about what goes on behind prison walls than anyone. Remember that they are cops also and everyone is on the same team. Act as a team and do not settle for responding to criminal activity as it happens. Do not settle on working cases confined inside the walls of the prisons. Attack crime at every level. Get out into the community and work every case that touches the prison system. Get creative in the approach to crime fighting and remain on the cutting edge. Be proactive.

Homicide and Other Inmate Deaths   17

Introduction

The prison investigator knows that there are four basic inmate deaths that occur in the prison setting. These deaths are caused by natural causes, accident, suicide, and homicide. The major difference between investigating an inmate death vs. investigating a citizen death in the community is that in prison all deaths must be initially approached as homicides.

Because of the dynamics of the inmate and the prison culture, it is important to remember that "nothing is as it seems." Virtually every inmate death requires a purposeful and enthusiastic investigation, regardless of the reported cause of death.

The investigator will find that, because of the inmate mentality, the significance of physical evidence becomes more essential in a prison homicide investigation than in any other prison investigation and most street homicide investigations. This assumption is based on and initially stems from the credibility of inmate victims, inmate witnesses, and inmate suspects.

Death by Natural Causes

The prison investigator will find that death by natural causes will be the most common death investigation he will examine.

Given the latest sentencing laws throughout the nation, inmates are confined for longer periods of time. Convicted felons are now serving more of their sentences than ever before, causing overcrowding of prisons and an aging inmate population. These aging inmates, like any aging population, begin to die of a variety of diseases and other natural causes.

Although many of these deaths occur under the supervision and care of a medical doctor, the criminal investigator is and should be called to initiate a limited investigation. This investigation, like any other death investigation, should be concluded with an autopsy conducted by the local coroner. The coroner, if he has sufficient documentation, may elect to circumvent the autopsy and as the chief law enforcement officer for the county, he has that right.

The investigator, of course, must draw a conclusion based on probable cause that the death was of natural causes. Much of the information needed will come from officer witness accounts, medical information, and the attending physician's statement and records. A complete report should be attached to all medical reports for the coroner and departmental records. It is important that these records be maintained, as there seems to be a propensity for litigation against state prison facilities, regardless of the cause of death, and a demand for factual documentation by the department.

Whenever a death investigation is conducted, regardless of cause, the investigator must insure that the victim is positively identified. This is usually done by insuring that fingerprints of the deceased are taken and compared with FBI records. For immediate identification, the attending physician and on-duty staff can be consulted for confirmation of the identity. It may seem like an unnecessary step, but it is very important. The prison population is increasing at an alarming rate. With this population explosion it is not beyond reality for an inmate to take the identity of another inmate. Should this be done at the death of another inmate with a lesser sentence, the results are obvious.

Be prepared to receive disinformation from the inmate population when investigating a death by natural causes. There is nothing more satisfying to some inmates than to disrupt any criminal investigation with bogus information. Although there is nothing that can change the facts of a case, the investigator may end up wasting a lot of valuable time following up obviously bogus information.

Case History #46

On one occasion an investigator was called to a prison license plate factory on a report of an accidental death. The crime scene, as frequently occurs, was not sufficiently protected and witnesses were not sequestered, making it difficult to take charge of the scene. The coroner had already been notified and was on the scene. Prior to conducting any interviews, the scene was searched and photographed. The general scenario given to the investigator was that the inmate had fallen to the ground, hit his head, and was rendered unconscious. The inmate never regained consciousness and was pronounced dead at the hospital.

Staff witnesses reported that no one, except medical personnel, went near the body and that the scene had been protected. Evidence of blood leaving the area where the inmate had fallen was in trace amounts. This trail led from an area about 100 ft from where the body was found to where medical personnel had picked up and removed the body. A piece of metal, that appeared to have blood on it, was also found in the first area. This crime scene was beginning to look like more than an accident. One puzzling fact was that there was very minimal blood on the floor, which might rule out the inmate being hit on the head with a piece of steel. There was no evidence of blood spatter anywhere in the shop. Because of the positioning of staff in the shop, it was unlikely that the inmate was assaulted somewhere else and brought to the shop.

The investigation continued, involving 40 interviews and collection of evidence and physical inspections of all inmates in the shop at the time of the incident. Remember that nothing is as it appears in the prison investigation. As it turned out, the substance on the possible weapon was not blood. The blood trail was caused by an inmate walking through the blood of the victim to another area of the shop. A few days later and with the autopsy report in hand, it was determined that the inmate had fallen to the floor, but only after he had suffered a major heart attack. He was more than likely dead before he hit the ground. His medical history evidenced serious heart problems throughout his incarceration. The cause of death was natural causes.

Death by Suicide

Suicide, attempted suicide, pseudo-suicide, and homicides veiled as suicides are the second most frequent death investigations encountered by the prison investigator. It is important to remember that when responding to a reported suicide, the investigator should treat the incident and the crime scene as a homicide.

Case History #47

This is not a case history, but a repeated historical fact that occurs in many prisons throughout the United States. Given the mentality of the convict, it is more than likely true. Some suicides are actually accidents, meaning that in an effort to gain attention some people will try to make it look like they committed suicide, but in reality they will survive the alleged attempt. In the prison setting, sometimes they will need to conspire with a fellow convict to have him call for help after the attempt is made, so the responding officers will save them before they complete the act. In many cases, for whatever reason, these convicts pretend to hang themselves. The suicide deceiver will have the inmate in the next cell agree to call officers as soon as he begins the pseudo-hanging. What actually happens is that the deceiver will give the signal and start the hanging. Here is where things go wrong. The inmate begins to hang himself, expecting a call for help from his neighbor. The neighbor makes no such call for help. The inmate can no longer yell or stop the hanging and soon passes out. By the time officers find him during the next count, it is too late and the inmate is dead. The official cause of death, because he is alone in his cell, will more than likely be suicide.

At the scene of a suicide the investigator should treat the entire investigation as a homicide until he has indisputable evidence that it was, in fact, a suicide. This would include the investigation in total and the coroner's findings. The seasoned investigator knows that crime scenes are often staged by inmates. In addition, witness accounts of events leading up to the suicide may conflict with known facts and cause confusion. These altered crime scenes may come in a variety of ways for a variety of reasons, and the inmate accounts need to be reviewed, as illustrated below:

- An actual suicide is altered to look like a homicide. This may be done just to frustrate authorities, to implicate an enemy in a homicide, or for some monetary gain (i.e., insurance fraud).
- A homicide scene is staged to depict a suicide. These altered scenes are very frequent in homicides to prevent detection of the crime or to hide the perpetrators of the crime.
- A suicide is altered to look like an accidental death.
- An accidental death is staged to look like a suicide.
- Insure that any trauma to the body of the suicide victim is fresh and can be attributed to the cause of death. In some cases the investigator will find that the inmate has suffered trauma from some other incident, prior to the suicide. This trauma may not have anything to do with the alleged suicide.
- Be aware that during interviews some inmates may give disinformation to confuse the investigation.

Suicides in the prison are not often accompanied by a note. Sometimes a phone call or a letter is sent to a loved one, but the communication rarely states the suicide intent. Although some of these attempts are merely calls for help that go too far, the majority seem to be real attempts and are successful. Motive is rarely obvious in the prison suicide. Some inmates cannot live the prison life, some have family problems, some will soon be released from prison and do not want to go back into society, some have medical issues they do not want to face, and some have just given up on life. The prison suicide can take many forms and even the best security officers will not see it coming or will be unable to stop the attempt. These convicts have

24 hours a day, 7 days a week to determine a method and time to get the job done.

Case History #48

An inmate, who had once been found before he could complete his suicide, tried it again. During his prior attempt he had slashed his wrists, but alert officers saw blood on the floor and interceded, saving his life. The inmate manipulated the mental health staff into believing he no longer wanted to end his life. He was placed back in the general population. He developed a pattern of going to bed early and getting up late. Security officers did not think there was anything wrong when he apparently slept through breakfast one morning. It was not until several hours later that an officer observed the inmate was not breathing and entered his cell. The inmate had once again slashed his wrist during the prior evening, only this time he had taped a large plastic bag over his arm and hung it off the bed on the wall side, hiding it from staff. The bag quickly filled with blood, but did not pour out onto the floor as before. There was no note, no letter, and no phone call. The inmate just went silently to wherever he was heading.

The prison investigator must conduct every death investigation as if it may be a criminal act. Using the best investigative techniques and being thorough during the investigation is always necessary.

Accidental Deaths

Prisons are made of steel and stone and are built to keep the bad guys in, not to be a safe place to live. There are mandates and needs to keep inmates busy. This entails many work and educational programs that help the inmate keep busy and build toward a successful reintegration into society. Many of these programs are industrial or manufacturing in nature. There are license plate factories, furniture factories, metal shops, wild horse programs, and many other programs that could be the scene of an accident.

Prison investigators need to be careful when investigating any accidental death. Remember that many death scenes become altered or staged by inmates that may or may not be involved in the death.

Be sure to secure the accident scene in the same manner as a crime scene. Insure that witnesses are sequestered and the scene is processed much like a homicide scene. Treat this case like any other. Do not take anything for granted or accept any information that is not corroborated. One thing that the prison investigator must not forget is the need to investigate all safety procedures and Occupational Safety and Health Administration (OSHA) requirements in an accident case. The investigator needs to establish what caused the accident as well as what caused the death.

When investigating an accident within a prison, the investigator should use established investigative techniques. Like any investigation there are elements that are necessary to come to a logical conclusion. Review the following suggested guidelines when investigating an accidental inmate death. Remember that these are merely suggested methods and not necessarily in any particular order of need.

- Treat each accident scene as if it is a crime scene. Include photographs, measurements, sketches, and evidence collection.
- Check the crime scene to insure that it is consistent with statements and evidence.
- Sequestering witnesses is usually in the best interest of the investigator.
- Interview staff in addition to getting written reports from them.
- Review any security camera footage that may be available.
- Interview all inmates present. Remember not to draw any conclusions on initial inmate statements as the need to separate disinformation from fact is important. Gauge the facts of the case against inmate statements. (This does not mean disregard any statement.)
- Check with the victim's case manager and review chronological entries, looking for any custody issues with fellow workers at the scene of the accident.
- As in any inmate death, notify and work closely with the coroner. Make sure to include an autopsy and be sure to get a copy of the coroner's report.
- Insure that positive identification of the victim is made through prints, photos, and personal knowledge.
- Conduct a search of the victim's cell and property for any evidence or clues.
- Determine the cause of the accident and the cause of death (i.e., was it horseplay, were safety rules ignored, is there a need for additional safety rules, was it victim error, etc.).

If the criminal investigator treats the accident scene like any other crime scene, he will be able to determine the cause of death and the cause of the accident and will be prepared to submit a complete report that will withstand any scrutiny imposed.

Homicides

Homicides and other inmate death investigations in the prisons are as difficult as any prison investigation. The inmate populations throughout the country are a group of very dangerous and violent people and they live by a different code of conduct than the average citizen. Inmate suspects, victims, and witnesses share a common distrust and anger toward the establishment. They rarely give a factual account of events as they have seen them. Crime scenes are almost always staged or altered in some way. Alteration of a crime scene is not always done by a suspect or a co-conspirator. Crime scenes are often altered and evidence is destroyed or stolen by any inmate that may happen into the scene. In addition to this, the investigator receives disinformation from every corner of the prison. The prison investigator also finds that in a prison murder the motive is not always apparent. When the motive is realized, it might surprise the investigator that the motive was a nonmotive. In any event, with the elements of noncooperation, crime scene staging, and lack of apparent motive the prison investigation needs to depend greatly on physical evidence.

Crime Scene

Street cops know only too well that protecting a crime scene is very important. It becomes even more important and more difficult in prison. Once a crime scene has been discovered, the scene must be secured and access must be controlled. Anyone who traverses the scene may alter it and impair the evidence that could contribute to the solution of the crime. It is usually during the first crucial minutes following a violent crime that evidence is lost. In the prison, as on the streets, medical personnel or persons who discover the crime may destroy or alter evidence in their efforts to help. The first officers on the scene may not be experienced and as always spectators arrive. In the prison, as on the streets, the "brass" or administrative staff are compelled to make a showing and observe the scene. In the prison atmosphere, hundreds of inmates having initial access to the scene are in a position to destroy the crime scene and each of them is a potential suspect in the case.

Evidence Collection

Much in the same manner as the street detective, the prison investigator has the crime scene secured with limited access. He utilizes resources available to collect and preserve evidence. The prison investigator must be particularly prudent in his search for evidence because he may not have another chance at solving the crime. For further details on crime scene management and evidence collection, refer to Chapter 9.

DNA Evidence

The forensic use of DNA in human identification moved from the laboratory to the courtroom in 1984. This genetic fingerprinting has proved valuable to the criminal justice system and citizens alike. Since 1984 there have been tens of thousands of crime victims and their families who have seen their assailants brought to justice. There have been tens of thousands of falsely accused suspects exonerated. There are also hundreds of thousands of children who will grow up knowing who their biological parents are. All of this has been possible with the help of DNA testing. For the prison investigator it would be safe to assume that identification of suspects and victims in criminal cases is the primary reason for using DNA evidence.

Prison homicides, because of the unreliability of the inmate population, depend greatly on physical evidence. The use of DNA testing in prison homicides and other serious crimes has greatly enhanced the criminal investigators' ability to identify the perpetrators.

Some of the DNA identification applications include but are not limited to:

- Sexual assaults
- Homicide and other violent crimes
- Exculpate wrongly accused suspects
- Identify serial crimes
- Identify human remains
- Sex offender tracking
- Parentage testing

DNA is found in almost every cell in the human body. The most common sources of DNA for testing come from blood, semen, tissue, bone (marrow), hair root, saliva, urine, and tooth pulp. The value in obtaining a positive identification of a person through collection of any of these sources is obvious to the investigator.

The prison investigator must be aware of not only these sources, but when to collect samples and how to preserve them for testing.

Blood—Blood evidence is always collected when present at a crime scene. DNA from dried blood can be extracted from glass, metal, hard plastics, or lightweight cloth rather easily. Extracting from denim, vinyl, carpet, automobile seats, and other dense and heavily colored fibers can be done, but it requires additional steps.

Semen—Semen is most often collected in sexual assault cases and cases involving correctional staff being suspected of having relations with an inmate. As in any prison case, never discount any possibilities.

Tissue—Like blood evidence, tissue can be retained in a weapon, under the fingernails of the victim, or scattered about a crime scene. DNA testing can identify suspects and victims.

Hair roots—One to five hair roots contain sufficient tissue for analysis. In the past, shed, or telogen, hairs were difficult to analyze because they contain only trace amounts of DNA. Fortunately, there are newer methods of testing, making the prior assumption obsolete.

Saliva—DNA can be typed from saliva deposited on envelope flaps or stamps. It can also be taken from cigarette butts found at crime scenes and even from cups, bottles, telephone mouth pieces, bite marks, and penile swabs.

Urine—Urine has not and is not a common method of identification. Most healthy individuals do not shed nucleated cells into their urine. There has only been limited success in the use of urine to obtain DNA identification. Urine should continue to be used to determine drugs in the bloodstream.

To preserve DNA evidence for testing,

- Air dry (no heat) all stains and swabs.
- Store frozen in paper bags, not plastic.
- Store frozen tissue preferably without preservatives (formalin or embalming fluid).
- Refrigerate liquid blood up to a few weeks (longer term, freeze for DNA testing).

Motive

Murders in prison will sometimes be spurred by what is considered traditional motivations. However, behind these walls are many nontraditional, even nonmotive, motives. Traditionally, murders are committed during an act of rage, commission of another felony, for financial gain, for revenge, or during mutual combat.

In 1992 the statistical abstract of the United States for murder motives, based on police investigations, charted the following motives for murder:

- Narcotics   7.1%
- Arguments   37.7%
- Robbery   10.1%
- Other felonies   6%
- Other motives   22.5%
- Unknown   16.5%

When scanning police homicide investigative reports, the investigator will also find jealousy, racial motives, serial killers, and political killings among the lists of motives. Investigators may find a vampiric motive as well (catasexual urge motivation).

Self-defense and other justifiable homicides are also motives. In a 1999 homicide case, evidence indicated the possibility of a self-defense killing. The case became entangled in a maze of cover-ups and false statements, making the use of physical evidence and creative interrogations very important.

Case History #49

At about 10:30 p.m., investigators were called to a correctional facility on a report of an assault. Prison investigators arrived at the scene to find that the victim had been taken to a hospital and his condition was serious. Prison officials had secured the crime scene and made a list of all inmates who may have been in the area.

The crime scene was an area where inmates lifted weights and used universal weight equipment. It was loosely supervised and at the time of the assault there were no staff members present. There was a sign-in sheet for inmates in the weight area. However, it was maintained by inmates and there were outside entrances allowing free access by any inmate. It was learned that the incident took place at 7:30 p.m. that evening, allowing 3 hours for inmates to get their stories together. In addition, there were no suspects in the case and most inmates had not been interviewed by anyone.

Staff at the prison indicated that initially the incident was thought to be an accident. It was reported by inmates that the victim fell and injured his head. The crime scene showed little in the way of physical evidence. There was one small area of blood where the head of the victim had struck the cement floor of the weight area. Based on statements of staff members, a few pieces of weight equipment were taken into evidence, but they appeared to be void of trace evidence.

Prison investigators conducted interviews of staff and reviewed staff reports. Inmates were interviewed throughout the night and into the early morning of the next day. As a result of these interviews, a possible suspect was identified. Investigators decided to leave the suspect in general population and not confront him until all the evidence was collected. Searches were, however, conducted of the personal property and cells of key participants in the weight room. The victim had ultimately died in the hospital of injuries sustained in the assault. During the autopsy it was discovered that there were four distinct marks on his forehead that were consistent with knuckles. All testimony to date included the suspect punching the victim in the forehead and him falling to the cement floor, hitting the back of his head. Investigators and the coroner had taken many photographs and measurements from the forehead of the victim. At this time no one knew that there were experts in a field that worked with knuckle prints. One such expert was found in California who could examine the knuckle prints, photos, and measurements and say with absolute certainty that a given set of knuckles were not the ones causing the injury. The expert could not say positively that the knuckles were the same knuckles, but could say that they were consistent with the injury and could have been the ones. Investigators now had some physical evidence and eight eyewitness statements to work with in solving this crime.

The suspect was brought in for his interview. The skillful investigator gave the suspect every opportunity to claim self-defense or to explain away his actions in some other fashion. The suspect elected to engage in an elaborate alibi, including several inmate and staff witnesses who could put him somewhere else at the time of the crime. It took only a few hours to disprove the alibi given by the suspect. The case was filed at the 11th Judicial District Court. Prior to trial, after he and his attorney reviewed the evidence against him, the suspect entered into a plea agreement which added an additional 10 years in prison for manslaughter.

In the prison atmosphere investigators find many motives during a murder investigation. They also find that murders can be initiated by a mere look in the direction of the killer by another inmate. This look may be perceived as a threat with only one way to deal with it— murder. Inmates believing that another inmate is a snitch is a common motive in prison. There is never a need to prove an allegation against another inmate to become a target of a murder. Gang slayings are commonplace inside the prisons. Inmates kill during turf wars over drugs, homosexual favors, hate crimes, and other racially motivated reasons.

The bottom line is that no motive is needed to commit a homicide in prison.

Case History #50

At about 1:30 p.m. officers observed an inmate being carried from the exercise yard. The inmate was suffering from multiple stab wounds. He was given immediate first aid by prison medical staff and an ambulance was called to the scene for further treatment at a local hospital. Criminal investigators were notified and responded to the prison and to the hospital where the inmate was being transported. Investigators were notified that injuries to the inmate were life threatening.

Investigators responding to the prison quickly learned that much of the crime scene was left unsecured and there were too many inmates in the yard at the time of the stabbing for officers to identify. The facility housed over 1000 inmates and it was estimated that over 300 inmates were in the yard at the time of the stabbing. With a contaminated crime scene and no staff witnesses to the stabbing, investigators knew they needed a break.

Arriving at the hospital, one of the investigators learned that the inmate had already died. The tentative cause of death was cardiac arrest after multiple stab wounds. The attack, it was learned, was particularly violent with three major wounds. In the left upper arm was a puncture wound and a large laceration which very nearly cut the arm from the body. There was a large stab wound to the left back and the right chest regions. It was later found that the chest wound was the exit wound from the stab to the back. The investigator at the hospital took photographs of the victim and gathered medical information. Emergency medical technicians, doctors, and correctional transportation staff were interviewed as well.

The facility was locked down and investigators began to compile a list of inmates known to have been in the yard or near the victim when he was found. All the staff on duty were interviewed.

A break finally came from the hospital where one of the transporting staff reported that during the transport of the inmate he identified his assailant. The staff member asked the medical technicians if the inmate was going to make it. He was advised that the inmate's injuries were life threatening and that he may not make it. The inmate told the officer that he was not going to make it and then told him who had stabbed him. He soon lost consciousness and never regained it. This statement had most of the elements of a deathbed statement that could be utilized in court, but moreover, it gave investigators a starting point for their investigation.

Investigators at the prison were given this information immediately. The suspect inmate was identified and taken into custody by investigators. During an interview he exercised his rights and made no statements. His living quarters were searched and several items were taken into evidence, including items of clothing belonging to the suspect which had blood on them. There was a fresh cut on the suspect's hand and a jacket he had been seen wearing prior to the killing was taken into evidence. This evidence proved to be of great value to the investigation.

Hundreds of inmates and staff were interviewed over the next several days. Through skillful interview techniques, investigators were able to identify two additional suspects in this case. As it turned out there were nine inmates that gave information consistent with other facts in the case and implicated the suspects. Investigators, knowing that inmate statements alone would not be enough to insure a conviction in the case, continued their investigation.

The suspect was identified as a gang member. He was associated with the Aryan brotherhood and was an active member. The suspect, all of his friends, and other members of the Aryan brotherhood were monitored. All mail and telephone communications were subject to monitoring. Through this effort, the suspect was heard making several incriminating remarks to family and friends. Letters he wrote to other inmates and associates also incriminated him. His handwriting was compared to known samples with a positive match and voice recognition was made through case managers.

It was learned who had fashioned the weapon used in the homicide, but the weapon was never recovered. The homemade knife was fashioned out of $\frac{1}{2}$ in. steel from the metal shop. The knife maker was identified, but never charged for lack of evidence.

The motive for this killing was established through inmate interviews and staff recollections of events leading up to the incident. The victim and the suspect were housed in the segregation unit for a period of time. The victim, a black inmate, and the suspect, a white Aryan brotherhood associate, became involved in heated arguments while they were housed in this unit. The victim made statements that he was going to have sex with the suspect's mother when he got out of prison, which angered the suspect. The suspect made statements that he was going to kill the victim when he got out of segregation. The suspect got out of segregation prior to the victim. He and several inmates conspired to get the murder weapon. He did not need a sanction from the brotherhood as this was a personally motivated hit. The victim was not well liked within the inmate population. Although there were only three inmates involved in the actual murder, many inmates knew of the planned killing and did not come forward. The cousin of the victim was present at the stabbing, but did nothing to intervene. It was possible that his cousin was actually used to lure the victim into the yard so the crime could be committed.

Other inmates played a part in the introduction of the knife to the yard and many inmates may have been involved in creating diversions or otherwise getting the attention of security officers in the yard. There were more than the normal amount of inmates in the yard on the day of the murder, which should have been an indication of potential trouble. This homicide had little in the way of motive and without some initial breaks in the case it may have been more difficult to solve. It is obvious that physical evidence played a big part in the case and that persistence by the investigators in getting additional information was paramount.

There were no confessions extracted from any of the suspects that were charged, but all three were convicted of second degree murder in this case, receiving lengthy sentences. No other inmates were ever charged in the case.

Prison Murder Weapons

Most prison homicides are violent. In prison homicides, most of the weapons utilized are fashioned out of any item that can be found within a prison. This is easily illustrated by compiling a short list of weapons used in reported homicides and assaults:

1. Homemade knives (fashioned from any conceivable item)
2. Plastic bags
3. Rope
4. Shoelaces
5. Padlock in a sock

6. Homemade spears
7. Free weights
8. Steel cables
9. Rocks
10. Feet and fists
11. Torn sheets and bedding
12. Razor blades
13. Broom and mop handles
14. Tree limbs
15. Volatile liquids
16. Acids and other toxic items

These are but a few items utilized by inmates in assaults and homicides. These and others give hundreds of variations of weaponry.

There seem to be only a few methods of murder within the prison walls. Stabbings, beatings, and strangulations seem to top the list. The prison investigator, as always, must be aware that no two prison murders are alike and typical scenarios do not always emerge. Take, for example, a stabbing. In many cases a stabbing is done by a lone assailant, but this is not always true. On the other hand, strangulations normally are typically committed by multiple perpetrators. This, of course, is also not always true. Some strangulations are preceded by a beating, but not always. A good prison investigator will always remember that nothing is as it seems when it comes to prison investigations.

Assaults tend to take a twist to the bizarre. This could indicate that these assaults were meant to serve as a warning rather than an actual murder attempt. The following case history is an example of bizarre behavior.

Case History #51

An inmate had been receiving verbal and physical threats from another inmate who was attempting to gain control over the first inmate. This is commonly referred to as bulldogging. The investigation revealed that this continual badgering went on for several months. Since he considered himself a convict and would not resort to telling prison staff about his problems and since he was a loner, doing his own time, the inmate receiving the threats and attacks decided to take matters into his own hands. Early one morning the prior victim became the aggressor. When investigators arrived at the prison, they found a victim that had been assaulted with boiling oil and a homemade battle-ax.

Based on investigators reports, physical evidence, and a confession by the inmate, here is an account of what happened in the days leading to the assault and the morning of the assault.

The inmate realized that all the other inmates in his pod knew that he was being bulldogged by this other inmate. He further realized that he would be marked as a snitch if he went to staff. He was relatively certain that he could not beat this inmate in a fair fight. He also knew that he had over 20 years to do in prison and if he did not do something he would become a victim for the rest of the time he was in prison. He thought seriously about what he was going to do. He knew it had to get the attention of every inmate in the prison and send a message not to mess with him. He knew he had to look crazy in order to overcome. He knew that if he looked crazy, even if his plan failed, he would be left alone.

On the morning of the assault the bulldogging inmate was known to play dominoes with his friends. It was at a location close to the victim's cell in the center of the pod. He carefully took all the hair gel that he had in his possession and put it into his coffee pot. He slowly brought the concoction to a boil while he tore apart his bulletin board. He used the wooden sides of the board as a two-piece handle. He took several large lids from cans taken from the food service area. He did not need to sharpen these lids, but had to poke holes in them with his pen in order to attach them to the handles. Thread and pieces of bedding were used to tie the handle and blades to the battle-ax. Once the hair gel came to a boil, he quickly poured it into a container that he could easily carry with his battle-ax.

The inmate came quickly from his cell and directly to where the bulldogging inmate played dominoes with his friends. He immediately threw the boiling solution of hair gel at the face of the domino-playing bandit. Unfortunately, the bulldogging inmate looked up as he ran up and started to retreat from his seat, causing the boiling liquid to fall short of its target, onto his neck and chest. The attacker quickly went to his battle-ax, slicing several times at his target. He only made a few swipes with limited success before the bulldogging inmate took the battle-ax from him and began to turn the tables on the attacker. The inmate immediately retreated to an area where staff would certainly see the assault and picked up an ironing board to use as a shield while he waited for staff to arrive and disarm the now attacking bulldogging inmate. Staff responded, disarming and subduing the two combatants.

The inmate confessed to the attack and planned to plead guilty to the assault charges. In his confession he revealed that although he did not intend to kill the bulldogging inmate, he would not have minded if it worked out that way. He said that he did intend to blind him with the boiling oil or otherwise maim him. He said that would have put out a signal not to mess with him. At trial, he will be able to tell the court of his experience with the other inmate. Since no inmates will be in the courtroom to hear, they will only know that he plead guilty. He will not be labeled a snitch. The inmate is happy with the outcome and is not concerned about the additional time he will receive. He knows that all the inmates at that prison think he is crazy and probably will not be bothering him. If they do, they may be attacked with boiling oil and a battle-ax.

Rule of Thumb for Time of Death

If You Find	Minutes since Death	
	Least	Most
1. Absence of vital signs (pulse, respiration, etc.)	0	0
2. Dilation of pupils	0	5
3. Clotted blood (cases of wounds)	4	10
4. Pallor (pale, white skin)	0	20
5. Mucous membrane dryness	0	30
6. Incontinence (bowel and/or bladder evacuation)	5	35

If You Find	Hours since Death	
	Least	Most
1. Tendon reflexes present	0	2
2. Clouding of cornea (pupil of eye), eyes open	$\frac{1}{2}$	2
3. Cadaveric spasm (death grip, electrocution; head injuries)	0	3
4. Dried blood (wounds), estimate by drying pool from periphery inward	$\frac{1}{2}$	4
5. Livor mortis, mild (pink coloration of lower portions of body)	$\frac{1}{2}$	4
6. Tympanic abdomen (resonant)	$\frac{1}{2}$	5
7. Rigor mortis, onset (stiffening of muscles) Subtract 1 hour for each 10°F average temperature above or below 70°		
Jaw muscles	2	6
Neck and fingers	3	7
Wrists	4	8
Elbows	5	9
Shoulders and knees	6	10
Hips	7	11
Abdomen (complete rigor mortis)	8	12
8. Livor mortis, livid (do not confuse with lividity of asphyxiation)	8	12
9. Blanching of livor (finger pressure on livor areas)	8	12

Figure 17.1 On January 8, 1992 this inmate was found underneath his bed. The crime scene had been sanitized. The motive was that three inmates had stolen items from the victim. The suspects were concerned that the victim would tell officers about the theft and decided to kill him. They only faced minor administrative sanctions if convicted of the theft.

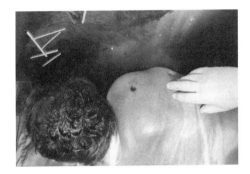

Figure 17.2 Victim suffered a blow to the back of the head and a bruise to the right rear shoulder. Notice the lividity where blood has settled to the back.

Figure 17.3 A pair of socks was used to strangle the victim.

Figure 17.4 The hands of the victim were bagged by investigators to protect any trace evidence. As in most prison beating/strangulation homicides, there were three suspects who were ultimately convicted of murder.

Figure 17.5 On June 19, 1999, while working out on the weight pile, two friends began to horseplay. The victim told the suspect he was going to take the weights he was using and the suspect hit him once in the forehead. He was knocked to the cement floor, hitting the back of his head. He later died of closed head injuries.

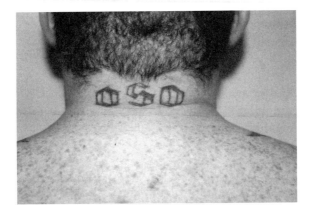

Figure 17.6 The suspect, unknown to one witness, was identified by a prison tattoo on the back of his neck.

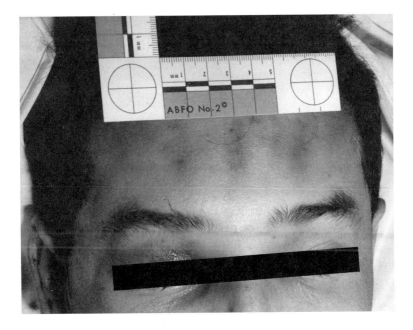

Figure 17.7 The victim has three bruises to the forehead that appeared to be from knuckles.

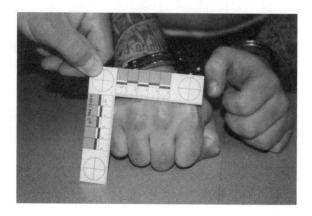

Figure 17.8 Measurements taken from the hands of the suspect were matched to the marks of the victims head. These proved to be consistent with the marks to the forehead of the victim which aided in the prosecution. The suspect had been allowed to remain in the general population for a few days before he was questioned. He had manufactured an elaborate alibi that was easily broken by investigators, insuring his conviction.

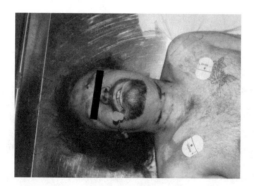

Figure 17.9 On August 25, 1996 this inmate was found beaten and strangled. The crime was committed by three inmates, with two others assisting in cleaning of the crime scene. The inmates originally hung him on a coat hook in an attempt to make it look like a suicide. The coat hook broke and the victim was placed in his bunk to make it appear that he was sleeping. The motive for this killing was that the inmates heard that the victim was a snitch.

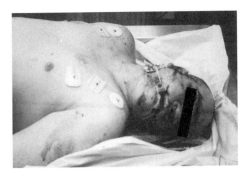

Figure 17.10 On September 24, 1998 the victim attacked two inmates with a homemade knife. The knife was fashioned out of a toothbrush handle sharpened to a point. The victim had tied the toothbrush to his wrist so he would not lose the knife during the assault.

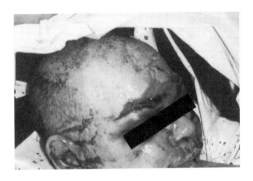

Figure 17.11 The suspects lost their bid for a self-defense plea when witness accounts by staff members and forensic evidence showed that the victim was beaten and kicked after he was unconscious. In addition the suspects gave a "high five" to each other after they had killed the victim. The motive was never fully established. However, it was suspected that the victim was labeled a snitch.

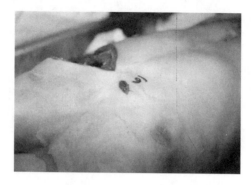

Figure 17.12 During a stay in segregation, this victim had harsh words with another inmate. They could not get at each other, but continued the verbal assaults. The suspect got out of segregation early and purchased a large homemade knife fashioned out of band steel. He enlisted the aid of others to locate the victim when the victim was released from segregation.

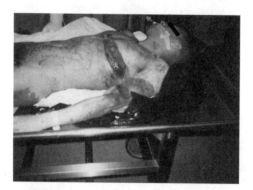

Figure 17.13 The victim's left arm was nearly severed from the torso during the assault.

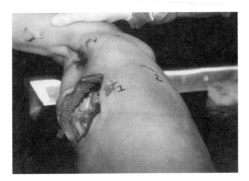

Figure 17.14 Several puncture wounds and a large laceration to the left chest cut the heart of the victim. He made a deathbed identification of the suspect. Many inmates aided in the destruction of evidence that was never recovered. The suspect was, however, convicted.

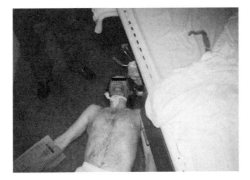

Figure 17.15 On October 27, 1997 this inmate was found sitting on the floor of his cell with an ace bandage tied around his neck and attached to the upper bunk. Because of possible trauma to his face the case was initially treated as a suspicious death.

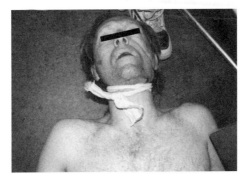

Figure 17.16 Autopsy results and forensic evidence concluded the inmate had committed suicide.

Figure 17.17 In this case the inmate was found several feet from his wheelchair. There was some trauma to his hand and head.

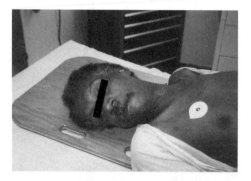

Figure 17.18 An autopsy revealed that he died of natural causes and the injuries were postmortem.

All photos courtesy of the Colorado Department of Corrections.

Appendix

Prison Investigator Survey

This information is the result of a survey that was sent to the State Department of Corrections office in all 50 states. The following explains the chart, which contains the results:

A State responding.
B Does your state use prison investigators?
C If yes, does the prison investigator have full police powers?
D Does the prison investigator work with outside law enforcement agencies?
E Does the prison investigator prepare criminal cases for the district attorney's office?
F Will the prison investigator testify as an advisory witness?
G Does the prison investigator prepare affidavits and warrants?
H How often does the prison investigator qualify with weapons?
I Does the prison investigator investigate Internal Affair's (I/A) cases?
J Does the prison investigator investigate traffic accidents that occur on state property?
K Does the prison investigator investigate prison staff on criminal matters?
L Does the prison investigator process crime scenes?

A	B	C	D	E	F	G	H	I	J	K	L
AK	No	–	–	–	–	–	–	–	–	–	–
AL	Yes	Yes	Yes	Yes	Yes	Yes	1	Yes	No	Yes	Most
AZ	Yes	Yes	Yes	Yes	Yes	Yes	1	Yes	Yes	Yes	Most
CA	Yes	Yes	Yes	Yes	Yes	Yes	4	Yes	Yes	Yes	Most
CO	Yes	Yes	Yes	Yes	Yes	Yes	4	Yes	Yes	Yes	Most
CT	No	–	–	–	–	–	–	–	–	–	–
DE	Yes	Yes	Yes	Most	Yes	Some	Semi	Yes	No	Yes	Some
FL	Yes	No	Yes	Yes	–	No	1	Yes	No	Yes	Yes
GA	Yes	Yes	Yes	Yes	Yes	Yes	1	Yes	Fatal	Yes	Yes
HA	Yes	Yes	Yes	Yes	Yes	Yes	2	Yes	No	Yes	Most
IA	Yes	No	Some	Some	Yes	Some	1	Yes	Some	Yes	Some
ID	No	–	–	–	–	–	–	–	–	–	–
IN	Yes	No	Yes	Yes	Yes	Yes	N/A	Yes	Yes	Some	Yes
KY	No	–	–	–	–	–	–	–	–	–	–
LA	Yes	Some	Yes	Yes	Yes	Some	Yes	Yes	No	Yes	Some
MA	Yes	No	Yes	Yes	Yes	Some	1	Yes	No	Yes	Most
ME	Yes	No	Yes	Yes	Yes	Yes	2	Yes	No	Yes	Most
MI	No	–	–	–	–	–	–	–	–	–	–
MN	Yes	No	Yes	Some	Yes	Yes	4	Yes	No	No	Most
MO	Yes	No	Yes	Yes	Yes	No	N/A	Yes	No	No	Yes
MS	Yes	Yes	Yes	Yes	Yes	Yes	2	Yes	Yes	Yes	Yes
NC	No	–	–	–	–	–	–	–	–	–	–
ND	No	–	–	–	–	–	–	–	–	–	–
NE	No	–	–	–	–	–	–	–	–	–	–
NV	Yes	Yes	Yes	Yes	No	Yes	4	Yes	No	No	No
NY	Yes	Yes	Yes	Yes	Yes	Yes	2	Yes	No	Some	Yes
OH	No	–	–	–	–	–	–	–	–	–	–
SD	Yes	No	Yes	No	Some	No	N/A	Yes	No	Some	Some
TN	Yes	No	Yes	Yes	Yes	Yes	1	Yes	No	Some	Yes
TX	Yes	Yes	Yes	Yes	Yes	Yes	4	Yes	No	Yes	Yes
WA	No	–	–	–	–	–	–	–	–	–	–
WI	Yes	No	Yes	No	Some	No	1	Yes	Yes	No	Yes
WY	No	–	–	–	–	–	–	–	–	–	–

Index